THE STARTLING JUNGLE

STEPHEN LACEY

The Startling Jungle

*Colour and Scent
in the Romantic Garden*

Introduction by Allen Lacy

DAVID R. GODINE, PUBLISHER
Boston

First U.S. edition published in 1990 by
David R. Godine, Publisher, Inc.
Horticultural Hall
300 Massachusetts Avenue
Boston, Massachusetts 02115

First published in Great Britain by Viking, 1986

Library of Congress Cataloging in Publication Data
Lacey, Stephen, 1957–
The startling jungle: colour and scent in the romantic garden /
Stephen Lacey.—1st U.S. ed.
p. cm.
"First published in the UK in 1986 by Viking"—T.p. verso.
Includes bibliographical references.
ISBN 0-87923-712-0
1. Color in gardening. 2. Gardens, Fragrant. 3. Gardens—Design.
I. Title. II. Title: Romantic garden.
SB454.3.C64L33 1990 88-46166
635.9'68—dc20 CIP

First U.S. Edition
PRINTED IN THE UNITED STATES OF AMERICA

*Grateful acknowledgement is made to the following
for permission to reprint previously published material:*

Collins Publishers: excerpt from Harold Nicolson's Estate,
lines from "The Garden" by Vita Sackville-West (Michael
Joseph, 1946); Eric Glass Ltd on behalf of the author's Estate:
excerpt from *Down the Garden Path* by Beverly Nichols
(Jonathan Cape, 1932).

To my mother and father, who gave me their garden

Contents

*Both the title and the chapter titles of this book are quotations
from Vita Sackville-West's poem 'The Garden'.*

List of Plates

5. Orange *Mimulus aurantiacus* with silver *Teucrium rosmarinifolium* and plum-coloured sedum (*Valerie Finnis*). The mourning widow, *Geranium phaeum* (*Valerie Finnis*). The honey-yellow torches of *Eremerus bungei* (*Valerie Finnis*). Venidio-arctotis, *Artemisia pontica* and lavender, backed by *Salvia sclarea turkestanica* and *Rosa glauca* (*Valerie Finnis*).

6. *Lavandula stoechas* hovering among *Sisyrinchium striatum* and catmint at Yoxford (*Michael Warren*). A copper beech provides the foil for this *Rosa hugonis* (*Valerie Finnis*). A play on verticals with *Ajuga pyramidalis* and *Iris pseudacorus* 'Variegata' (*Valerie Finnis*). Ceanothus behind irises and white and lilac comfreys (*Valerie Finnis*).

7. A pastel scene in Beth Chatto's garden in Essex comprising cardoons, bronze fennel, centaureas and apricot foxgloves (*Michael Warren*). A rustic setting for this rambling rose (*Iris Hardwick Library*). The drumsticks of *Arum italicum* next to glaucous *Euphorbia wulfenii* (*Valerie Finnis*).

8. *Rosa longicuspis* in the late Margery Fish's garden (*Valerie Finnis*). Violas 'Jackanapes' and 'Irish Molly' with woolly *Ballota pseudodictamnus* in the foreground (*Valerie Finnis*). Bronze-leaved *Crocosmia* 'Solfatare' (*Valerie Finnis*). *Clematis* 'Henryi' wandering through a variegated ivy (*Michael Warren*).

9. The laburnum walkway at Haseley Court underplanted with orange wallflowers (*Valerie Finnis*). The gallica rose 'Tuscany Superb' (*Michael Warren*). *Clematis viticella* 'Royal Velours' in the branches of a golden catalpa at Burford House (*Michael Warren*).

10. The bourbon rose 'Madame Isaac Pereire' (*Michael Warren*). *Lychnis flos-jovis*, stachys, catmint and white irises teamed with a purple smoke bush (*Harry Smith Horticultural Photographic Collection*). A jumble of old roses with variegated *Iris foetidissima* in front (*Valerie Finnis*). The alba rose 'Koenigin von Danemarck' (*Michael Warren*).

11. *Liatris spicata, Allium sphaerocephalum,* clary and lavender in
the Purple Border at Sissinghurst (*Michael Warren*).
Polemonium foliosissimum, Dicentra formosa, D. spectabilis and
a lilac viola (*Valerie Finnis*).
An old-world mixed border at Hidcote Manor,
Gloucestershire (*Harry Smith Horticultural Photographic
Collection*).
Astrantia major, an invaluable plant for pastel groups (*Valerie
Finnis*).

12. An edging of *Geranium* 'Johnson's Blue' and *G. endressii*
with catmint (*Harry Smith Horticultural Photographic Collection*).
Lychnis coronaria 'Alba' with *Malva* 'Primley Blue' behind,
and *Corydalis ochroleuca* and spotted-leaved pulmonaria in
front (*Valerie Finnis*).
The alba rose 'Félicité Parmentier' (*Michael Warren*).

13. Scarlet zauschneria with silver *Helichrysum petiolatum* and
artemisia and a variegated yucca (*Valerie Finnis*).
Lychnis chalcedonica with a pale blue delphinium (*Valerie
Finnis*).
Perovskia atriplicifolia silhouetted against fiery kniphofias
(*Valerie Finnis*).
An untamed rose, away from the bustle of the border
(*Valerie Finnis*).

14. *Euphorbia palustris* departs in a burst of lemon (*Valerie Finnis*).
An autumn scene in the Scotts' garden at Boughton House
(*Valerie Finnis*).
Euphorbia cyparissias peering out of *Berberis thunbergii*
'Atropurpurea Nana' (*Valerie Finnis*).
A tangle of *Clematis tangutica* and *Eccremocarpus scaber* (*Valerie
Finnis*).

15. A bronze view of the Savill Garden, Windsor (*Valerie
Finnis*).
Salix wehrhahnii knee-deep in the fallen leaves of *Prunus
sargentii* (*Valerie Finnis*).
Galtonia candicans in front of *Fothergilla monticola* (*Valerie
Finnis*).
Acer 'Osakazuki' makes a stunning autumn feature (*Valerie
Finnis*).

16. Echoes of spring with colchicums, cyclamen and *Hosta undulata* (*Harry Smith Horticultural Photographic Collection*). *Helleborus foetidus* half-buried in snow (*Valerie Finnis*). A solitary witch-hazel *Hamamelis mollis* (*Valerie Finnis*). The frosted stems of *Salix alba* 'Britzensis' (*Valerie Finnis*).

"Follow my steps, oh gardener, down these woods.
Luxuriate in this my startling jungle."
—Vita Sackville-West, *The Garden*

Introduction

I met Stephen Lacey in October 1987, at a horticultural conference in Toronto where several hundred North American gardeners assembled to attend lectures by speakers from Canada, Great Britain, and the United States. (Before going any further, I should say that we are of no kin, and it is my conviction that he spells his last name wrong.) It was a weekend that few who were present will easily forget, for powerful forces had combined to break into the usually peaceful scene found when people who love gardening assemble to share their common passion. Mr. Lacey's scheduled arrival in Canada that Friday was delayed a full day because of the tragic hurricane that laid waste to much of southeastern England, felling vast numbers of trees in parks and celebrated gardens. The following Monday, the American stock market suffered its own devastating storm. Despite these noteworthy distractions, everyone in the Toronto audience came away recognizing that Stephen Lacey's was a great new voice in British garden writing. Here was an infectious enthusiasm for often uncommon but highly worthwhile plants. Here also was the wit and humor that not a few British horticultural writers display in person, but often exclude from their writing. Here was a very wide knowledge of perennials. Here, above all, was remarkably frank and unabashed sensuality, of the kind that shines forth in almost every sentence of THE STARTLING JUNGLE — surely the only book about gardening ever written that begins in a steaming bathroom, where, as he puts it, "imagination can run riot."

Mr. Lacey, it is good to report, has a very powerful imagination indeed, but he does not allow it to run riot as do some people who write on gardening in such a way as to make plants sound far better in prose than they look sprouting from the earth. Obviously a man frequently smitten by superior perennials, bulbs, and woody plants, he conveys his enthusiasm without hyperbole — but with very thoughtful and vivid description. It is of some importance, I think, that he studied Modern Languages at Oxford, rather than being trained in horticulture along more traditional lines. The result is that he approaches gardening as an amateur, in the best sense of the word, and he brings to the task of writing about it a broad intellectual, cultural, and aesthetic background. He thus joins a noble band of writers on gardening whose first academic interests lay in other subjects. One thinks, in an American setting, of Elizabeth Lawrence, who majored in English literature at Barnard College in the 1920s, and whose deep understanding of the subject frequently showed in her writing about gardens and plants.

I do not want to patronize Stephen Lacey by saying that his knowledge of plants is vast "for one so young." His knowledge of plants is vast, period. After hearing him speak in Toronto, I decided to send him seeds of three fairly uncommon plants I was sure he would like but probably didn't know yet. They were *Onopordon acanthium*, *Gaura lindheimeri*, and *Nicotiana sylvestris*. Flying home from Toronto, I read THE STARTLING JUN-GLE with great pleasure and the wry recognition that he knew all about them. But Stephen Lacey *is* young, and at the start of a career that should make him one of the great garden writers of the twenty-first century, with a wide following on both sides of the Atlantic.

Since we met in Toronto, Mr. Lacey has come to the States twice on speaking engagements before large audiences. Those who have heard him invariably felt frustrated that THE STAR-TLING JUNGLE was not available in the United States. I have heard several stories of gardeners here who have implored friends traveling to Great Britain to bring them back a copy. As for my own copy, which Mr. Lacey gave me in Canada two years ago, it is one of very few books I won't lend. There is now cause for widespread delight that one of the most refreshing and passionate books on gardening in the past two decades will find the many American readers it deserves.

—*Allen Lacy*

Preface

I would be surprised to discover that I was the only person whose most exciting gardening moments are spent in the bath. Most keen gardeners are incurable romantics and every opportunity of drifting away into a world inhabited by stout Himalayan poppies, fat lewisias and giant marrows is greedily snatched. And where better for a prolonged and uninterrupted daydream than the bathroom? Within those tiled walls, with catalogues, seed lists and reference books at your elbow and warm soapy water rippling against your chest, imagination can run riot. Gardens become fragments of paradise. Exotic shrubs, exploding with flower and fruit, burst from every dark corner; velvet roses and sweet-scented jasmine cascade down every wall and pillar in clouds of spray; while great rivers of bulbs surge through orchard and shrubbery, cutting deep channels between trees laden with blossom.

Most memorable garden pictures, whether they are elaborate compositions or simple plant associations, have been conceived in such daydreams. They have a vague beginning, usually as a blend of colours or a mixture of scents, and slowly they take shape, evolving into wild and wonderful images which often seem absurdly ambitious, daring and frivolous in design. Romantic gardeners' notebooks are crammed with messages such as 'Build pagoda on site of old coal bunker,' or 'Turn terrace into Persian carpet'. Whenever we have an idle moment, at the breakfast table, in a bus queue or on a railway station platform, these precious notes are taken out and carefully considered, and eventually a way is found to translate the images from the realms of fantasy to the realms of reality.

Sometimes an idea has to be modified for one reason or another. A pagoda is all very well but it will probably be too expensive to construct and, truth be told, might look rather incongruous in the corner of a suburban garden. What we really want is an object which is attractive and which will conjure up the fragrant riches of the east; and, of course, that bunker does have to go. Or does it? Why not just remove its roof, its wooden door and window-frames, knock it about with a sledge-hammer and leave the rest to *Rosa longicuspis* which, given a well-manured start, will soon ramble through the apertures and conceal the brickwork in a tangle of growth? In midsummer it will be smothered in deliciously scented, creamy yellow flowers, as sumptuous an oriental feast as we could hope for.

But often an idea can be reproduced exactly. What about that Persian carpet? We picture a tightly woven pattern of reds and pinks with an occasional highlight of burnt orange or old gold. We want the stonework completely hidden so that from the drawing-room window it looks as if the contents of the house have spilled out into the garden. Let us turn to the summer-flowering helianthemums. We have an enormous choice of colours from the deep red, double-flowered 'Mrs Earle', the clear pink 'Wisley Pink' and the single red 'Red Orient' to the gold of 'Ben Nevis', the chrome yellow of 'Praecox' and the coppery orange of 'Ben Mhor'. They can be planted in pockets between the stones and will soon link arms to make a dense covering. They are more or less uniform in height but any variations will look like folds in the carpet and when they are out of flower, the different greens and greys of their foliage will make their own tapestry. All are easily raised from cuttings so we need only buy one plant of each.

Naturally, an image will not always survive the process of translation and the finished product will often fall far short of the original idea. But those occasions when we do succeed give us so much pleasure that the many failures are forgotten. Do you recall Beverley Nichols's excitement in *Down the Garden Path* when he managed to simulate an avalanche down his rockery by massing bulbs of the frosty blue chionodoxa? 'Delights . . . were endless in the lengthening twilights of spring, as I bent down, and looked up at the nodding spray of blossom, descending just as I had planned, a rivulet here, and cascade there and a grand torrent in the middle over the central rock, all outlined against the deep, quiet skies of

April. For my avalanche was an avalanche that really succeeded, that swept into my memory for ever.'

Composing such garden pictures is probably the most satisfying and the most rewarding aspect of gardening. It is also the most challenging, since it requires a fusion of two sets of skills, creative and practical. Few of us possess both in equal measure which is why our attempts at artistic gardening are largely such hit or miss affairs. Either we misplace shapes and colours or we misjudge the times certain plants are in flower and the size to which they grow. I suspect the great majority of us commit both sorts of error. Autumn is certainly heralded in my garden by the lifting of numbers of plants which I have failed to integrate properly into my various schemes. The wheelbarrow is filled with clumps of yellow daylilies which finished flowering a week before the pale blue agapanthus with which they were supposed to associate, with carmine tradescantia which was not after all subdued by a gentle backcloth of pale pink geraniums, or with mounds of dejected diascia which scarcely produced a single flower in their shady position behind fountains of silver dorycnium.

Fortunately, we do not have to rely entirely on a process of trial and error. If we did, those autumn operations would be monumental. On the practical side, there are many ways of improving our chances of success. Apart from observing closely the behaviour of plants in our own garden, we can visit botanical gardens and gardens open on the National Gardens Scheme and take note of methods of cultivation, the ultimate height and width of individual plants and the conditions in which they flourish. We can refer to an enormous library of gardening books, which covers every subject from the combating of aphid attack to the raising of prize-winning parsnips, from the pruning of Chinese wisteria to the propagation of carnations and pinks. We can watch the experts on television digging small ponds, making peat gardens and planting window-boxes and hanging baskets. Advice is available in all forms and on all subjects.

In comparison, creative advice is scarce. Of course, we can collect plenty of ideas from our garden visiting. Nearly everybody's garden has some aspect of design worth noting. There are also a number of books which deal with garden design, telling us how to devise an overall plan or how to site trees and paths. But the shortage of material is apparent when we start to think about the composition of particular plant groups, once the backbone of design is completed. We have our hedges and our paths, our lawns and our flowerbeds; wĕ have placed our trees and planned our focal points and our conceits; we have set aside an area for growing vegetables and fruit, a plot for the greenhouse and a place for the washing-line. The remaining task is to design schemes for each area of bare soil and to draw up lists of shrubs, perennials and bulbs. Where do we begin?

Classical gardeners will always start with shapes. They will see each area as an architectural problem which needs an architectural solution. An upright form at the back perhaps, slightly to the right, with a couple of large rounded shrubs in front and groups of smaller plants in the foreground; including on the left a short upright form to echo and balance the shape at the back. Maybe they want a contrast of broad leaves against narrow leaves or spikes of flowers against flat umbels; maybe they want a groundwork of small-leaved plants, above which the two vertical shapes will rise like church spires from a winter mist. Eventually, as they are making their list of plants they might spare a thought for colour and scent.

The romantic gardener's approach is entirely the reverse. Our starting-point is that hazy bathroom vision and our intention is to capture it by means of a careful selection of colours. Shapes and forms are still important considerations but they are definitely secondary ones. Each area of soil is pictured as a colour scheme and only when the colours have been decided will we begin to think about anything else.

The very best gardens are undoubtedly those which have had the benefit of both the classical and the romantic influence, for then the pitfalls of each approach – that the classical garden tends to be rigid and unexciting and the romantic garden tends to be wild and shapeless – are avoided. Sissinghurst is a prime example. It was made by Vita Sackville-West and Harold Nicolson. Vita was the romantic, the poet, the plantswoman; Harold was the classicist, the scholar, the politician. Together they fashioned the epitome of the perfect garden in which a strict linear framework is softened by exuberant and informal planting. It was not always an easy partnership for the classical and romantic temperaments do not give in to each other without a struggle, as this extract from Harold Nicolson's diary demonstrates: 'In the afternoon I moon about with Vita trying to convince her that planning is an element in gardening ... The tragedy of the romantic temperament is that it dislikes form so much that it ignores the effect of masses. She wants to put in stuff which "will give a lovely red colour in autumn". I wish to put in stuff which will furnish shape to the perspective. In the end we part, not as friends.'

Very few of us have the steadying influence of a classical partner to temper our activities (I am assuming that you, like me, have a romantic temperament), so we must make a special effort, at some stage in the design process, to stand back, assume the guise of a classical critic and look for flaws in our schemes. Have they got substance? Are there clear architectural lines? Do the different shapes make a coherent whole? Or are they just vague and disorderly images which will look untidy at flowering time and positively chaotic afterwards?

Providing we do remember to scrutinize our compositions for structural elements some time before we start planting, our pre-occupation with more poetic matters should not lead us far astray. Indeed, we have some justification for treating colour as the main aspect of design. The fact is that the eye appreciates colour before it appreciates shape. Look around the room in which you are now sitting and notice how your attention is immediately drawn to the brightest colours and not to the most striking shapes. The only time that we notice shapes straightaway is when the range of colours is limited. Hence it is extremely dangerous for any garden designer to consider colour only as an afterthought because its careless use can seriously interfere with the intended picture. There are examples of such occurrences in every Chelsea Flower Show, where designers have clearly laboured painstakingly over the architectural aspects of their plans and then unwittingly des-troyed their creations by the reckless use of colour. All the architectural movement advances in one direction while the bright colours (usually azaleas) compel the eye to follow a different course.

Although colour is the most important element in the romantic gardener's designs, most of us have little understanding of its nature or potential. Even if we think we have a clear impression of a particular scheme in our mind, its impact on the ground is often quite different, as colours react unexpectedly with their neigh-bours or are affected by changing light. Some of us have dif-ficulty matching colours, producing harmonious pictures or handling strong hues. Others know what mood they wish to convey but are unsure which colours will properly convey it.

All these difficulties can eventually be overcome by experiment but we can save ourselves a lot of time and trouble if we are prepared to devote just a few moments to an investigation of the colour laws and a study of the principles of colour combination. If we understand the relationships between colours, we will be better able to appreciate how a harmony and a contrast is produced and what its likely impact will be, and we will be able to solve our problems systematically. Of course, there are no firm rules for the making of colour schemes – and there is certainly no guarantee of success – but there are clear principles which, if followed, will considerably improve our chances of capturing the exact image or conjuring up the exact mood which engulfed us in our bath tub.

Scent is no less potent a substance and is never far from the romantic gardener's thoughts. Because it is not visual, it is generally distributed quite carelessly through the garden and rarely becomes an integral part of a scheme, but its presence is always keenly felt and it has as dramatic an impact on our senses as colour, often more so. It is because of this that the romantic seeks to sprinkle it everywhere. Unfortunately, we know far less about scent than about colour and because it is such an unpredictable substance, we are unable to manage it with quite the same confidence. Nevertheless, we are occasionally tempted to pursue scented themes in our borders, perhaps inspired by the perfumes of old roses infused with the fruity fragrance of philadelphus or the pungent odour of rosemary seasoned with lavender and thyme, and I shall therefore endeavour to provide us with sufficient information and ideas to enable us to increase our chances of success in this area too. For the most part, however, it will remain an undercurrent in the text as it does in the garden, sometimes stopping us dead in our tracks, sometimes teasing and amusing us, and sometimes acting in conspiracy with colour to transport us to distant countries more fabulous and exciting than our own.

A preoccupation with colour and scent is not the only trait which distinguishes the romantic from the classical garden. The role played by plants in each garden is also entirely different. In the classical garden plants are just another ingredient in the design, no more and no less important than paths and walls, but in the romantic garden they are the very basis of and reason for the design. Romantic gardeners have a deep passion for plants for their own sake and the design of our gardens has to be flexible enough to cope with an ever-changing and ever-increasing plant population. We are unable to pass any nursery by without investigating its content and making a purchase and are the slaves of any plant catalogue which falls through the letter-box. Our gardens thus tend to comprise a very broad and diverse collection of plants, each chosen on its own merits, rather than according to the strict requirements of a preconceived plan. It is our passion for scheming and the care with which each plant is sited that saves the garden from becoming a complete hotchpotch of disconnected images.

What sort of garden does result from this obsession with colour, this love of scent and this mania for plants? Well, I hope that by the time you have reached the end of this book you will see and be sufficiently stimulated to abandon all thoughts of a quiet and orderly life and disappear straight to the bathroom to concoct your own unashamedly romantic projects.

THE STARTLING JUNGLE

The Cloak of Harlequin

I am sure you can picture a garden in which no thought has been given to the arrangement of colour. It is like a little battle-field on which every plant must fend for itself. Blue lobelias and golden marigolds writhe in agony as they are impaled on the spikes of scarlet salvias; carmine roses bury their vicious thorns into multi-coloured rivals; and soft pink clematis clings desperately to the drainpipe to avoid searing burns from the red hot pokers below.

It is not difficult to create such a blood-curdling spectacle. All you have to do is to distribute the most garish shrubs and peren-nials about the garden in a haphazard fashion and leave no seed packet unopened which promises a riot of colour to its fortunate purchaser. The result will certainly be explosive, and indeed there are many occasions when such a bombardment of the senses is effective and memorable, giving visitors a thrilling surprise as they round a corner of dull shrubbery or enter a small enclosed court-yard off a grey city street; but it is not likely to be very beautiful. It offers the eye no element of unity or harmony; only continual discord and distraction from which it wearies quickly. Neither does it provide the sort of restful setting in which you will want to sip your cocktails on a summer evening or sling your hammock on Sunday afternoons. Nor is it the sort of garden in which to linger and explore. Once you have recovered from the initial impact, you will find that it is strangely monotonous. There are no changes in temperature or mood which occur in well-planned gardens whenever one colour scheme melts into another or one tone becomes dominant and another is suppressed; and, as it struggles for attention among its peers, no colour is allowed to demonstrate its full potential or show its true character.

Most of us want a garden which gives a deeper and more enduring pleasure. As plantsmen, we want to see every plant growing well in a position where it can parade its own qualities of shape, colour and texture, complemented not molested by its neighbours. And as designers we want to see each ingredient contributing to an overall scheme, full of variety and interest but at the same time harmonious and coherent. To achieve this we have to use colour rather more carefully.

Those gardeners who are naturally artistic find the task of making an attractive garden much easier than the rest of us. They can readily visualize the effects of combining particular colours and usually know at an early stage what moods they would like to convey and how to set about producing them. The rest of us have to rely on experiment, testing one colour against another and waiting to see whether schemes intended as peaceful and evocative associations actually match up to our expectations at their flowering times. It is a lengthy and often frustrating process and, although it eventually produces good results, many of us are too impatient to last the course. So we look around for ways of simplifying matters and improving our chances of success, and usually finish up by adopting one of three rough-and-ready systems. The first is to separate those colours which contain traces of yellow from those which contain traces of blue. Apart from the reddish purples, all flower colours fall happily into one of these categories. We are effectively dividing the spectrum into two groups of related colours and providing we ensure that at no time do members of one group come into contact with members of the other group, it is virtually impossible to make a jarring combination.

The second path to success is to eliminate altogether those colours which cause us problems. I recently visited a garden in Sussex in which there was a total absence of red flowers, and the reason was that the owner, although fond of red, found it a disruptive influence in her borders and had discovered no way of controlling its mischievous nature. I know of people who feel the same about yellow and about white, and no less a gardener than Margery Fish would warn people against the introduction of orange into the garden. The omission of one colour still leaves us with the task of managing the rest of the spectrum but at least the

2

main troublemaker has gone and the other strong colours have less competition.

The most cautious gardeners adopt an even more drastic approach. They limit the number of colours in each colour scheme to one or two, and are thus assured of a gentle picture. In fact a restricted colour range has its own special problems since it throws great emphasis on to shapes and textures but it certainly provides a ready solution to problems of colour.

The trouble with all these approaches is that although they do go a long way towards banishing crude and ugly colour combinations and encouraging attractive ones, they do so by limiting the number of possible associations. Consequently they shut the door on many of the most beautiful effects. To divide the yellows from the blues is to forbid most of the more exciting colour contrasts; to omit one colour is to prevent the creation of a whole series of images; and to restrict a garden or a border to one or two colours usually results in pictures which are lacking in visual stimulation. If, like me, you see part of the attraction of gardening as being the continual challenge it offers us to push forward the frontiers, both in terms of the range of plants we grow and the ways in which we use them, it is unlikely that you will be content with any of these restrictive practices for long.

The only way to be sure of avoiding unpleasant effects and at the same time to give ourselves complete artistic freedom is to study the subject of colour properly before we even begin to take up our trowels. This will involve some exploration in an area normally left uncharted by the romantic gardener, namely that of science, and I cannot promise you a safe passage, but I hope that at the end of it we will have acquired enough knowledge of the characters of individual colours and the ways in which they interact to be able to pursue any wild project we choose with some confidence that the colours we employ will be contributing to rather than detracting from the mood we are trying to convey.

Let us begin our exploration at the beginning with a reminder of what colour is and how it arises. You probably recall an occasion during one of those stupendously dreary physics lessons at school when your teacher produced a glass prism from the recesses of his desk in a desperate attempt to recapture the class's attention. He placed it in front of a narrow beam of light and you observed that whereas the light seemed to be white before it struck the prism, it was transformed into a clear rainbow upon contact. The purpose

3

of the experiment was to show that light is composed of various coloured wavelengths. As long as these wavelengths are travelling at the same speed as each other and in the same direction, they will appear to be white but when an obstacle is placed in their path, they are broken and dispersed and their true colours are revealed.

The wavelengths are either absorbed or reflected by the objects they hit, and it is the coloured molecules on the object's surface, which are called pigments, which determine which wavelengths are devoured and which are rejected. A glass prism rejects all of them but an object such as a pillarbox rejects all except the red wavelengths, which it absorbs; as a result it looks red. The same process occurs in plants, but there the matter is complicated by the presence of sugars and acids. They make the pigments ebb and flow inside the plants and, as they react to light and temperature, bring about changes in colour. There are two main groups of plant pigments, the carotenoids which are responsible for the reds, yellows and oranges and the anthocyanins which produce the blues, bluish reds and purples, and under their umbrella shelter a large number of pigments, many with familiar-sounding names like pelargonidin and delphinidin.

The activity of the pigments is obviously governed by the degree and quality of light they receive. Plants which dazzle you with their brilliance in sunlight never manage to do the same in shade, and even when they are given an open situation, they undergo continual change as the sun rises and sinks in the sky, and disappears behind clouds. In the early morning everything is tinged with pale yellow, and in the evening with blue and purple. It is only at midday when the light is at its whitest that objects can show their true pure colours. As the illumination increases and decreases in strength, colours succeed each other in importance. A drift of red poppies which immediately catches your eye at lunchtime becomes virtually invisible by early evening, at which time a patch of white lupins which you hardly noticed before will be shining like torches.

We might bear this in mind when planting areas of the garden which are only seen or visited at certain times of the day. A front garden, for example, which you look out upon in the evening from the comfort of your armchair could be planted in white and grey and luminous pale yellow for the longest period of visibility. You will find that many night-scented plants bear flowers in these colours, so if you left open a window you would be engulfed in fragrance as well, all without having to move a muscle.

The harder the sunlight, the stronger the colours need to be to make an impression. In hot countries where the light is at its most intense, the most startling colours can be defused and harmonized successfully, whereas the same combinations employed at home would be crude and vulgar. Draping a Hampshire rectory in magenta bougainvillea and yellow allamanda would not only be a feat of horticulture but a virulent attack on the optic nerve. Conversely, a *mélange* of pastel colours, which is so enchanting in an English border because of the soft quality of our light, would be quite lifeless in front of a Beverly Hills mansion.

The brightest colours benefit from being grouped in the sunniest positions. Blazing oranges and scarlets seem quite dull when cast in shadow, but in any open border on a hot summer's day they become ferocious and electrifying, the fiery core of the entire garden. Similarly, the cool luminous colours which show up best in poor light appreciate positions in shade. Blue hydrangeas, forget-me-nots, omphalodes and cynoglossum which are grown in the sun have none of the glowing intensity of those grown in the shade, and the same applies to white phlox, cimicifugas, geraniums and anemones; they produce just as many flowers out of direct sunlight so you have nothing to lose.

Apart from the quality of the illumination, the apparent colour of an object depends on the way the light is received and reflected. Leaves which have a rough or matt surface absorb more light than those with a smooth or glossy surface and thus appear deeper in colour, as do flowers which have a velvet as opposed to a satin texture. A bed of irises or violas always seems luxurious because the different reflections from their petals, deep and velvety on the inside and light and silvery on the outside, produce a range of quite distinct tones.

An infinite number of colour effects can result from the collision of different types of light with different forms and different combinations of pigment, and the human eye is so sensitive that it can detect several million variations. The task of making sense of all these and organizing them into some sort of logical sequence has occupied scientists for centuries. As long ago as 1600 Sir Isaac Newton invented a primitive colour wheel and it is this device, in ever more sophisticated guise, which has remained the conventional method of demonstrating the relationships between colours.

The colour wheel is really just a rainbow which has been forged into a circle and colours are arranged around its circumference according to their positions in the spectrum.

The primary colours, red, yellow and blue (these are the colours which will, if blended in different ways, produce all other colours) occupy equidistant places around the wheel. The secondary colours, green, orange and violet (these arise when pairs of primaries are mixed in equal proportion) are found equidistant between their respective parents; and the tertiary colours, red-orange, yellow-orange, yellow-green, blue-green, blue-violet, and red-violet slot in between them. All will be made clear if you turn to the illustration of the colour wheel (plate 1).

The value of the colour wheel to the gardener is that it groups related colours together and indicates which colours are likely to harmonize with each other and which are likely to contrast. A colour will have more in common with its neighbours on the wheel than with those on the opposite side. But we must be aware that the wheel only shows the position of the pure colours or hues. It ignores the pale colours, the tints, such as pink, cream and lavender, and the deep colours, the shades, such as navy blue, brown (this is really dark orange) and maroon, which occur when the pure colours are mixed with white or grey respectively. These lurk behind their parent hues and, to a greater or lesser extent, share their parents' characters.

You will notice that the hues on one side of the wheel seem to be much livelier and more welcoming than those on the other side. The dividing line can be traced roughly from the yellow-greens to the red-violets. If we want a garden scheme to be bright and cheerful we will look to the warm side of the spectrum, to the reds, yellows and oranges; if we want it to be crisp and refreshing we will draw our colours from the cool blues, violets and greens. The only colours which do not fit happily into these warm and cool categories are those which fall in the band between red and purple. Magenta and mauve are prime offenders, and are of course common colours in the garden. They seem neither cheerful nor chilling and, as a consequence, usually have to be treated separately, omitted from schemes intended to convey a strong feeling of temperature and isolated among white flowers and silver foliage. Interestingly these are also the most unpopular colours.

If you wish to introduce a note of contrast into your warm or cool schemes without dissipating any heat or melting the ice, then you must look not to the hues on the other side of the wheel themselves but to their shades and tints. Variants of a hue do not give precisely the same temperature reading as their parent, and so we can usually find a contrasting colour which matches the mood of a scheme tolerably well. In general, pale versions of warm colours are cooler than deep ones, and deep versions of cool colours are warmer than pale ones. Thus pale yellow is cooler than gold, and pink is cooler than red; navy blue is warmer than clear blue and deep purple is warmer than violet.

Black and white, although absent from the colour wheel, also register on the thermometer. Black is closely related to the reds and oranges, and white to the blues and violets. They have an especially useful role in schemes because they bring light and shade to colour groups without disrupting the temperature reading. Since the majority of warm colours are bright and lively and the majority of cool colours are heavy and shadowy, by introducing black and white into the scheme we are providing touches of relief and yet maintaining the tropical or arctic theme. I know that there are hardly any genuinely black plants available to us but dark purple serves just as well, as you will have seen if you have visited Crathes Castle in Scotland, where dusky purple smoke bushes billow over smouldering orange, scarlet and yellow plantings of roses, helianthemums, poppies and geums. In schemes of shadowy purples and violets, blues and lilacs, ice-cool and hostile, we can lighten the impact by laying a crystal carpet of silver foliage and admitting ghostly plumes of snow-white flowers.

One interesting characteristic of the warm colours is that they give the impression of advancing towards the eye, whereas the cool colours give the impression of retreating. This has something to do with the fact that the eye becomes far-sighted when it focuses on reds and oranges and near-sighted when it focuses on blues and purples. Whatever the reason, it can certainly be exploited in the garden. A long narrow garden will appear to be significantly shorter if bright scarlets and oranges are massed at the far end; and a short garden will seem longer if its boundaries drift away in misty shades of blue, violet and mauve. There is a portrait by Gainsborough in the Tate Gallery which exploits this effect to convey the subject's portly figure. His bright orange-scarlet waistcoat seems to erupt out of the deep blue folds of his velvet coat, as if no clothes would ever manage to contain his ample stomach.

It is as well to remember this optical illusion when we are associating large groups of strong colours, taken from both sides of the spectrum. Warm colours placed in front of cool colours are much happier than when placed behind them. If you follow this guideline, you will find it much easier to pull off some of the more dramatic contrasts. Try some flame-coloured crocosmia in front of some tall amethyst agapanthus or some golden-yellow achillea in front of intense violet delphiniums.

The precise temperature and mood of a colour is most clearly felt when the colour is seen in isolation. In the garden this usually means devoting quite a large area to it, to ensure that the eye is not distracted by neighbouring colours. But the impact on your senses will then be powerful, especially if you come upon this monocolour area after being intoxicated by schemes of mixed colouring. The effect is rather like listening to a piece of music in which, momentarily, one instrument emerges from the orchestra to play alone. Suddenly we are concentrating on one sound instead of a multitude of sounds and we are entirely at its mercy. It soothes us or disturbs us, makes us merry or melancholy. Skilful handling of one colour is the surest way to arouse a deep emotional response, and by acquainting ourselves with the idiosyncrasies of individual colours we will be able to predict that response more or less accurately.

Monocolour schemes have become extremely popular with the modern gardener. Not only do they have a strong character and make an immediate impact (and save you the trouble of devising harmonies and contrasts) but they are particularly well suited to the matchbox-sized gardens with which many of us have to contend, where more intricate compositions would look fussy and confused. The secret of a successful monocolour scheme is not to be too rigid in your approach. You must be prepared not only to admit the full range of shades and tints related to your chosen hue but also the occasional note of contrast. This will ensure that the scheme never becomes monotonous or insipid. The red borders at Hidcote, in Gloucestershire, for example, admit violet delphiniums, yellow corydalis and orange panther lilies, and these colours serve to highlight and relieve the scarlets and crimsons.

If you are not prepared to depart from your chosen slice of the spectrum then you must give your plants a background which is sufficiently different in character to act as a foil and set them off to their best advantage. A yellow border might thus require a backdrop of glaucous blue, a white border a backdrop of blackest green, and a pink border a backdrop of deepest purple. You must also remember that the narrower the range of colours, the greater will be the emphasis thrown on to form and texture, so more thought has to be given to the arrangement of foliage and the distribution of shapes.

However, most of your garden groups will consist of a blend of colours, either a restrained fusion of a few related tones or a rich mosaic of hues, tints and shades, and in mixed company individual colours cannot preserve their personalities intact, but are each affected by their neighbours. I expect you remember as a child holding a buttercup under somebody's chin to see if there was a yellow reflection (I recall staking people out with croquet hoops to conduct the experiment). Of course there always was. Well, it is this effect which is occurring all the time between adjacent colours, as each echoes, reinforces or modifies the other. Some hues are more susceptible than others. White, for example, always assumes a tinge of the strong colours beside it; the interiors of the sentry boxes outside St James's Palace are quite pink when occupied by guards in scarlet tunics.

This interaction does much to harmonize the colours around us, and explains why a kaleidoscope of colours, composed of thousands of different coloured dots, never seems discordant. Meadows full of crimson, yellow, violet, white, scarlet and rose-pink flowers, which display no evidence of divine colour-scheming, are invariably attractive; it is only when we use concentrated blocks of bright colour that individual interactions come to be important considerations. For the effect of combining certain colours is not at all pleasant. Placed side by side, some intense colours create an optical rivalry, each attempting to outshine the other, and if you wish to create a harmonious colour scheme such partnerships must be avoided.

The most violent partners are hues which lie diagonally opposite each other on the colour wheel. Yellow and violet, red and green, and orange and blue are examples. These are called complementary pairs. So intense is the rivalry between the partners that the eye often experiences a flickering sensation which can be extremely irritating. Clearly such associations will make for the most stimulating contrasts but the effects will only be attractive if the two colours are of different intensities. Strong blue and apricot, lemon yellow and deep violet, and scarlet and dark green are among the most striking of combinations.

But although complementary partners in their most intense forms should not be sited next to each other, they do benefit from being in close proximity. The eye likes to find relief after being saturated by an expanse of strong colour and if you provide relief near by in the form of that colour which is in complete contrast to it, in other words its complementary partner, the eye will be so anxious to absorb it that it will exaggerate its quality, making it appear even more intense. Thus a stretch of golden yellows will seem as brilliant as the midday sun if you turn to it from a deep pool of strong violet, and a sea of gentian blues will be as dazzling as the Caribbean if you come upon it from a furnace of volcanic orange.

Gauging the impact a colour will have on its neighbours is obviously the essential skill in composing a scheme. A hue will either put its companions at ease or on the alert. Since romantic gardeners will want to pursue many different images in their gardens, some thrilling and some restful, we have to learn to manage both sides of a colour's character. We encourage a colour's aggressive instincts whenever we think the garden needs a moment of sudden drama, when the senses need a sharp jolt. We encourage its passive instincts whenever we want to create a gentle and harmonious picture. Because most of us enjoy peace and quiet more than war and turmoil we tend to concentrate rather more on harmonies than on contrasts, thus establishing a relaxing environment against which we can play the occasional violent image. Before examining the most fruitful methods of making contrasting schemes let us therefore investigate the ways of arriving at harmonious ones.

The essence of a harmony is that there should be unity among the ingredients, and there are several ways of achieving this. Firstly and most simply we can assemble a number of variants of one hue. Cream, sulphur, primrose, lemon and gold will combine to make a tranquil and delicate harmony; the colours are so closely related that the eye will travel smoothly across the scheme, scarcely noticing the points at which one shade changes into another. Such a picture can be seen in many orchards in April as they become flooded with a dozen different varieties of daffodil, a great ocean of yellows sparkling in the spring sunshine. Either the individual colours can be muddled and diffused or, more effectively, kept separate and allowed to melt into their neighbours – the paler shades in the foreground, perhaps, the intermediate shades in the centre, and the deeper shades in the distance.

The second method of arriving at a harmony is to associate colours which are close to each other on the colour wheel and which have a similar temperature. We can assemble hues, tints and shades to make such a scheme. Let us take lemon, primrose, apricot, orange, mahogany, brown and gold as an example. Here too the eye can readily perceive common elements linking the group – we can see the yellow factor in the orange and the orange factor in the yellow – and the group therefore seems natural and spontaneous. High summer is the most likely time that you will see this combination in the garden, as the varieties of helenium, gaillardia, coreopsis and chrysanthemum take the stage and the gardener, inspired by blazing sun and tropical heat, decides to play with fire and compose the most exotic and gorgeous groups.

Both these methods rely on selecting colours which are naturally harmonious, but a harmony can be produced using colours which have nothing in common. This can be done, most simply, by selecting colours which are similarly reduced in intensity or tone. Red and blue will not harmonize in their most resplendent forms but pink and pale blue are a perfectly contented couple, as are deep red and deep blue (though rather dull). Bluebells beneath cherry blossom or pink tulips in front of powder-blue ceanothus are schemes popular in many late spring gardens.

Stronger colours must be harmonized by introducing a middle value into the scheme. Let us take pure red and royal blue as an example of a contrasting pair. You might find the association of, say, *Monarda didyma* 'Cambridge Scarlet' with a bright agapanthus like 'Bressingham Blue' too abrupt for your border, but if you place another colour between them, with which they each have something in common, you will have removed the element of contrast. In this case we could choose the violet-purple *Salvia* × *superba*, which contains hints of both red and blue.

Where there is no obvious middle value, you must look for a neutral tone. Grey is often an ideal choice since it is the colour upon which the eye most easily comes to rest. For example, a large mound of *Artemisia* 'Powis Castle' would successfully unite colours as hostile as the pink shrubby potentilla 'Princess' and the ferocious orange-flame variety 'Red Ace' (not that I would encourage you to grow either). The greater the contrast between the two colours to be united, the larger the area of neutral tone will need to be.

Green is the most important bridging colour because it is the most plentiful hue in the garden. It is restful to the eye and it does not attempt to compete with other colours, except perhaps red. But not all variants are non-aggressive. Grass green, the lime green of tobacco flowers and euphorbia bracts, and the golden green of many conifers are too lively to be satisfactory intermediaries and they clash horribly with the pinks and violets.

Because there is unity between the ingredients of a harmonious scheme does not mean that harmonies are necessarily soft and static. In fact they can be the richest and most dramatic of images. If the colours in your scheme are arranged according to their positions in the spectrum – pale blue, blue, violet-blue, violet, purple, for example, or apricot, orange, vermilion, scarlet, red, crimson – where each colour is taking over naturally from the one before, the eye will be greatly stimulated for it will perceive a sense of movement. This is most deeply felt when you are led towards yellow through red and orange, which is effectively a journey towards light, and towards violet through green and blue, which becomes a progression into darkness. These sensations are exploited a good deal in painting and were first utilized in the garden in the late nineteenth century by Gertrude Jekyll who enjoyed creating the most dynamic colour groups.

So it is quite possible to make an attractive garden, full of visual interest, by confining yourself to harmonious schemes. The mood and flavour of each scheme would change smoothly and delicately into the next to bring about a series of colour impressions, each with its own special character. Why then should we bother orchestrating contrasts? The reason is simply that they give us the opportunity of extending our repertoire and lifting the curtain on a further selection of images and effects. A note of contrast can bring a spark of life to an otherwise dormant colour group and it can make a scheme more subtle and more sophisticated. But above all it is a more challenging sphere for the colour-crazed gardener and as such irresistible territory.

A contrast is produced whenever you associate colours which have little or nothing in common with each other and make no attempt to disguise their differences. Such combinations are always arresting but not always pleasant. Before launching ourselves into the various methods of devising successful contrasts, let me therefore outline three general principles which help you to decide which colours are likely to make the best partners. The first is that you should, at the outset, identify the natural qualities of the colours to be associated and, whenever possible, respect them. We know, for example, that yellow is by nature a colour of light and blue is by nature a colour of shadow. If we wish to combine them in a scheme, we will usually do better to encourage these respective qualities rather than attempt to reverse their roles. Thus pale yellow and dark blue will probably be a more successful team than pale blue and deep gold, for each colour will retain its identity. Similarly, apricot and purple, light green and dark blue and primrose and deep red will be more comfortable partners than brown and lavender, olive and pale blue or gold and pink.

Secondly, contrasts are generally easier to manage when the colours to be combined are of different intensities. Bright blue and scarlet, for example, are likely to make a stormy pair, but if we vary one or both of the hues we can engineer the perfect marriage. Bright blue and pink, or scarlet and indigo, can be quite contented couples: so, occasionally, can pale blue and rich red, though this contravenes the principle in the previous paragraph, as you will see in plate 13, a pleasing group of silvery blue delphiniums beside radiant red lychnis.

Thirdly, opposing hues can often be united by introducing a range of shades and tints. Pure yellow and pure violet fight savagely but if you surround them with lemon yellow, primrose and gold, purple, slate violet and lavender you will restore peace. You could make such a scheme in early summer with violas, geraniums and aquilegias, lilacs and yellow species roses.

With these points in mind we can set about devising contrasting schemes. The simplest associations are based on just two colours, and we know that the closer the colours are to a complementary relationship, the more exciting the results will be. As well as allowing each colour to cover an equal amount of ground, you can vary the effect by letting one colour have the upper hand. Fountains of flame-orange crocosmia in an ocean of blue agapanthus is quite a different picture from an island of agapanthus in a swirling river of molten lava. Which you decide to compose will depend upon the impact you wish to make and the needs of the overall garden plan, but it is usually preferable to allow lighter colours to dominate darker ones and weaker colours to dominate stronger ones. With this rule of thumb you will generally avoid intimidating a colour by surrounding it with more muscular companions but of course, like all these guidelines, it is a rule to be twisted into knots.

Often we wish to build a scheme around three colours which are naturally inharmonious, and there are two satisfactory methods of achieving this. Firstly, we can devise what is called a split-complementary group, a frightening term which just means that we select one hue and associate it with the two colours which flank its complementary partner. Thus red would be combined with yellow-green and blue-green. Try the blood-crimson viola 'Arkwright's Ruby' between hummocks of lime-green *Alchemilla mollis* and a sprawling mound of Jackman's Blue rue, or a clump of damson *Cosmos atrosanguineus* between the small-leaved bamboo, *Arundinaria viridistriata* and a stretch of exotic-looking, glaucous blue *Melianthus major*.

Secondly, and most fruitfully, we can form a 'triad' scheme. Imagine an equilateral triangle revolving inside the colour wheel, its three corners pointing to successive teams of equidistant hues. Such teams always make attractive colour groups, providing all three colours are not used at full strength. Apart from the obvious examples of red, yellow and blue, and orange, violet and green, there are all the intermediate colours to play with, and if we take note of all the shades and tints, the possibilities are endless. An example of a grey-green, pale orange-yellow and plum scheme springs to mind, comprising grey-leafed sage, *Salvia officinalis*, the viola 'Sutton's Apricot' and a buttress of that sumptuous hybrid tea rose 'Papa Meilland'.

We have looked at various ways of softening the impact of a contrast but there are occasions when we want the most potent effect possible. This might be at the end of a long border to bring the planting scheme to an abrupt full-stop, in a place where attention needs to be diverted from an unsightly object, or simply in a spot which needs a sharp uplift. Apart from using complementary pairs or triads with all the colours at their most intense, there is one method which guarantees a startling result. This is called the 'zing' effect, and it involves selecting one brilliant colour and surrounding it with a gentle harmony of greys or delicate variants of its complementary and near-complementary partners. Imagine a patch of dazzling golden-yellow encircled by misty purples and violets, greys and powdery blues or an area of vivid scarlet among deep greens and grey-greens. This latter combination is often evident in woodland gardens, where the intense red of rhodo-dendrons is set against the dark foliage of neighbouring shrubs and the murky brown of the woody shadows. The bright colour leaps out at you like a jungle cat, and if all goes according to plan the impact will send you spinning.

Schemes based on strong contrasts have to be used sparingly. They stimulate the eye rather than relax it, and if they are scattered all over the garden, the overall picture will be restless and in-coherent. But there ought to be thrilling images somewhere in the garden to bring variety and adventure to the scene and cock a snook at the harmonies and quiet contrasts that prevail. So every now and then you should think about enlivening a group with gusto; such audacity does the naturally cautious gardener no end of good.

These then are the principles on which we can construct our colour schemes. They are not firm rules, but simply guidelines based on the way we all respond to certain colours and certain colour combinations. You can either follow them closely or use them as a point of departure from which you can experiment for yourself, but however you use them they do indicate the most fertile areas of colour combination, and if you concentrate your creative activities in these areas, you are likely to reap a rich harvest.

Having acquainted ourselves with the theory of colour asso-ciation, we must now look at the practical constraints and influ-ences which will affect our scheming and to a large extent help us to decide which colours to use in which parts of the garden. For the fact is that the gardener does not have as free a hand in the composition of a picture as the painter. To begin with, the gar-dener's canvas is already partly filled by existing structures and natural features before he even takes up his brushes, so he is under an immediate obligation to choose schemes which harmonize with their surroundings.

There is no point labouring painstakingly over a delicate group of silver, pink and violet flowers if the scheme is to be backed by a wall of new yellow brick, for example, or over a confection of crimson, purple and damask white which is to be arranged beside a gate painted pillarbox red. Indeed the environment often sug-gests a particular treatment. A honey-coloured sandstone wall might indicate a scheme of cream and lemon yellow, claret and maroon; distant woodland a scheme in copper and orange, lime and deep green; and a view of whitewashed suburban houses a scheme in mauve and pink, lavender and blue.

The distribution of light and shade has also been largely decided for you. The sun moves on a set course across the sky and the positions of buildings, walls and trees determine where shadows will fall. Colour schemes have to be arranged to make the best use of these conditions, and although the gardener can suggest further interplay of light and shade by juxtaposing glossy leaves and matt leaves or using golden and golden-variegated foliage to convey an impression of dappled sunlight, he has to acknowledge the existence of a masterplan.

To a lesser extent you will be influenced by plants which are already in residence and which you would like to retain. An aged wisteria against the house, for example, or a stand of junipers and white lilacs or an internal hedge of copper beech are all strong features which will have to be integrated into your planting plans, and so put further limitations on your artistic freedom.

Secondly, the gardener's palette is restricted to the colours being displayed by plants and these are constantly changing not only season by season but day by day. Certain colours are always abundant and others are always in short supply; certain colours dominate the garden at certain times and then disappear entirely, being replaced by others which were scarcely in evidence before. So instead of focusing attention on one picture gardeners must juggle with a series of transient pictures which are by nature fragile and unpredictable. To achieve precise colour associations we have to bring together plants which we are confident will perform at the same time as each other. This requires a broad repertoire of plant material and a good memory for their colours, for we will have to visualize schemes and plant them using material that is not in flower. In order to keep our palette as well-stocked as possible we should not confine ourselves to flower colours; the colours of foliage, trunks and stems also make valuable contributions and in some months will play a more important role than flowers.

Having decided which parts of the garden to give to which areas of the spectrum, therefore, the next stage is to choose a season during which each border will make its main contribution. This is a particularly important decision for those who wish to create breathtaking tableaux on the grand scale for everything in the border will be contributing to one lavish spectacle – a living rainbow for July and August perhaps, or a kaleidoscope of pastel shades for May and June – and there will be little of interest during the rest of the year. Those who prefer to have a series of images in each border which will keep them gently entertained during every season have more flexibility in adding and replacing ingredients and can keep altering the size and content of each season's pictures. Nevertheless they too must make some concentrated seasonal groups.

You will find that sometimes your chosen colour scheme will dictate your season or vice versa. It would be very difficult to arrange a scheme consisting of a quantity of blue for high summer, for example, or an orange and red scheme for midwinter. Spring cries out for schemes that are crisp and bright whereas autumn is a season for tawny shades and fiery incidents.

Lastly, and most importantly, the habits and cultural requirements of the plants themselves will determine where certain colour groups are sited. It might sound wonderful to transmogrify a gloomy strip of earth beneath your north wall with a carpet of glistening silver foliage but once you start considering the matter carefully, you will discover that there are hardly any silver-leafed plants that would tolerate such a position, since the majority require blazing sunlight and sharp drainage. Similarly, a sweep of golden foliage to complement the scarlet and orange flowers in your south-facing border would be sensational, but if you planted any of the real golden aristocrats you would find that they soon took on unhappy expressions, for their leaves are scorched by hot sun.

The desire to grow certain favourite sun-loving or shade-loving plants will often mean that the entire border will have to take its colour cue from them. For example, we could not possibly do without the Mediterranean aromas of cistus so at least one of our sunniest borders must be able to accommodate their greyish gummy foliage and their pink and white, maroon-blotched flowers, for they would not thrive anywhere else. A shady wall must be found for that remarkable yellow-flowered honeysuckle, _Lonicera_ × _tellmanniana_, so the other plants near by must be compatible with its strong colouring.

Choosing plants for a scheme is the essential and most exciting aspect of the whole process. No plant should ever be included simply because it is the right colour or shape or size for the group or flowers at the right time; you have to want to grow it for its own sake. Once you start admitting pedestrian plants through the garden gates and selecting them with a less than critical eye, you have embarked on the same road as the Victorian carpet-bedders, making coloured patterns out of plants which are essentially dreary and uninspiring. A garden is made or marred by the plants grown in it.

All these factors have to be considered before a colour scheme is carried through, but the gardener still has great freedom in his choice and use of colours and can move in many directions. It may be that you will want to pursue the types of scheme for which Gertrude Jekyll provides models, concentrating on the softest harmonies and subtlest contrasts and using mainly clear, pure colours, massed in large groups and arranged in thin drifts. Or you may wish to create dreamier pictures, perhaps composed entirely of pastel shades, in which each tone is mingled and interwoven with its neighbours so that there are no blocks of individual colours. Or perhaps you will want to orchestrate a series of swashbuckling effects about the garden based on potent contrasts.

Ideas for colour schemes can be gathered from many sources, not only other people's gardens, though these are rich with pickings, but also from magazine covers, glossy advertisements, shop windows and natural landscapes. The two most fruitful areas are, of course, painting and fashion. You will come away from any art gallery full of ideas. A scheme based on a Rembrandt palette of golds, warm browns and heavy reds perhaps, or an art nouveau scheme of violets and yellows. The Impressionists will furnish you with the most exciting images because their paintings are concerned almost exclusively with the impact of pure colours. To see the effect of great sweeps of bright colour applied to the garden in the Impressionist manner, you should visit Monet's garden at Giverny, just north of Paris, a romantic garden *par excellence*.

The world of fashion revolves around the use of colour. Ideas can be taken from contemporary designs in clothing and interior decoration or you can look back in history. Imagine a Victorian scheme of clarets, maroons, deep greens and blacks or one of those 1930s schemes of mustard yellow and grey or brown and violet-blue. You could make a masculine scheme of buff, brown and old gold or a feminine scheme of shell pink, rose, pale blue and lilac.

The possibilities for scheming are endless and the contemplation of them occupies much of the romantic gardener's waking and

Intoxication of the Air

If colour is the substance with which the romantic gardener spins his magic web, scent is his means of ensuring that his prey is powerless to escape. For scent drugs the senses and stirs the emotions even more surely than colour and once under its spell, all strength evaporates. It has the power to unlock childhood memories, to recall forgotten incidents and places, to bring a smile to your face or send a shiver down your spine; it can make your heart beat faster, your eyelids feel heavy, and can even cause you to lose your voice. The effects can be exhilarating, refreshing, comforting, distasteful or nauseating and the gardener who seeks to anticipate the likely impact of his plants and schemes needs to manage this potent substance as thoughtfully as he manages colour.

Because we are generally preoccupied with visual impressions as we design our gardens, scent tends to be one of the last ingredients to be considered. We decide on a mood and colour scheme and then select and position the appropriate plants according to their size, shape and texture, taking into account their individual personalities and cultural requirements as we do so. Once we have drawn up a preliminary plan, we scrutinize it for defects in architectural form and substance. It is at this second stage that we usually remember scent and, panic-stricken, scurry back through our lists of plants to reassure ourselves that our nose will not be disappointed by the finished product. But scent really deserves more attention than this for its inclusion can transform the character of the scheme, giving it an extra dimension with which to stimulate the senses and activate the imagination.

sleeping hours. Our aim is to create a garden which is fu
images, some gentle and harmonious, others wild and thril,
some dynamic, others static, some strange and exotic, otl
familiar and homely, some dramatic, others discreet, some v
and overwhelming, others minute and intriguing. There will
no moment in the year when there is not something to attract ou
attention and inspire us, and each season will have its own specia
flavour. Every plant that we add forms part of a great web of
colour, but it is a strange sort of web because although we spin it,
we are as vulnerable to its silken grip as are visitors to our gardens
and find ourselves entirely at the mercy of the colours we sought
to control.

In the majority of garden schemes scent must remain sub-ordinate to colour, for the visual impact is paramount. This is why I have sprinkled the sweetest perfumes quite carelessly through the remaining chapters, listing scented plants with their odourless colleagues according to their leaf or flower colour, instead of giving them a chapter to themselves. But within the colour parameters that we choose, we ought, whenever possible and desirable, to seek out our scented ingredients at the outset and stir them into the group. For if we think about scent early enough, it is often possible to develop and pursue a secondary theme which lurks beneath the colourful surface of a scheme, not apparent at a dis-tance but quite intoxicating at close range.

Unfortunately certain parts of the spectrum are poorly endowed with scent so it is not always easy to find fragrant material for every colour group. We face the greatest difficulties when de-signing schemes involving the stronger hues, for plants rarely pos-sess both intense colouring and rich fragrance. Plants have a finite amount of energy, I suppose, and must decide in which direction to channel it in order to obtain the maximum benefit. If their pollinators are attracted to them by smell, there is little point in adopting gaudy dress, and if they are attracted by sight then the effort of distilling a fine perfume is wasted. (This turns out to be fanciful thinking. The reason is far more boring it seems, and is all to do with heavy pigment impeding the movement of oils.) Nurserymen who concentrate on producing ever more colourful blooms, invariably find that they lose fragrance in the process (although this does not seem to worry them in the least. I could hardly detect a whiff of scent in the field of modern sweet peas on trial at Wisley recently, though the size and brilliance of the flowers were noticeably superior to the old-fashioned varieties).

It is not surprising, therefore, to find that plants with white flowers comprise the most scented colour group and plants with orange and scarlet flowers the least scented. The positions of the other colours on this scale of fragrance are, in order of potency, as follows: pale pink, mauve, pale yellow, pure yellow, purple, blue. The scale is a useful starting-point for those who wish to make a garden devoted to scent, directing us towards the most fruitful segments of the colour wheel, and gives some indication of which colour schemes are going to be the most troublesome to furnish with scent. Luckily there is a quantity of fragrant material among the most harmonious colours, the pastel creams, pinks and yellows, which can generally be slotted into the most fearsome and dazzling groups without unduly disturbing the visual impact, so providing we are willing to be a little flexible in our designs, a craving for fragrance can usually be satisfied.

But colour is not the only factor that influences our choice of scented plant. The nature and intensity of the fragrance itself ultimately determines its place and use in the garden, and to investigate this properly we need to take off our painter's smock for a moment and don the starched laboratory coat of the perfumer.

There is little practical purpose in the gardener classifying and analysing scents in the same detail as we analyse colour for our appreciation of scent is not yet so sophisticated that we can precisely identify different fragrances and comprehend fully how they harmonize and contrast with each other. There is no readily accessible scale or chart (the equivalent of the colour wheel) to assist us in plotting the position of a given scent and so discovering its relationship with other scents, and our memory for scent is poor and our vocabulary for describing it hopelessly deficient. Thus we do not have the means of developing it into a precise art. Nevertheless, we remain acutely sensitive to it, are able to detect very small quantities in the air, and react strongly and in many different ways to its various forms, so we cannot treat it with indifference.

I propose, therefore, that we undertake a very amateurish examination of the subject, avoiding the complexities of chemistry and the thrills and spills of atomic research, but delving sufficiently deeply to acquire a simple understanding of the nature and impact of the ten flower scent groups. We can then apply the facts we uncover to the design of our gardens. I should point out immediately that some flower scents are difficult to classify and often seem to belong to more than one group. This is because every scent consists of a mixture of compounds all swimming together and occasionally several distinct fragrances can be detected. You and I might disagree about which fragrance is the more pronounced and put the flowers under different headings but we would probably agree about the character and impact of the scent so our dispute would have no practical consequence. Fortunately most flowers have one dominant fragrance which is instantly recognizable.

The scents of the Indoloid Group are rarely encountered in

gardens, which is a great blessing for they are quite revolting. The plants that adopt these smells seek to attract flies and bluebottles and often disguise themselves as rotting meat by developing pink and purple blotches on their flabby, fleshy flowers. Their smell also resembles that of an advanced stage of putrefaction, either of carrion or fish. The only member of the group we are likely to grow and which can prove offensive is the bog arum, *Lysichitum americanum*, whose bright yellow spathes are a feature of many pondsides and ditches in early spring (curiously, the white-flowered species, *L. camtschatcense*, gives off a very sweet scent). Most indoloid scents belong to tropical plants.

The Aminoid Group comprises those scents which are also rather stale and sickly but which possess a sweetness that renders them more tolerable. The smell is still of decay, but is rather the decay of a unicorn than a cart-horse. Plants with such scents are common, particularly in our hedgerows, and include hawthorn, elder, mountain ash, sweet chestnut, pyracantha, cotoneaster and pear blossom. The flowers are mainly cream. The sensitive gardener will keep all these plants well away from the house.

In the Heavy Group the unpleasantly scented compounds are so completely submerged in sweetness that they are scarcely detected, except when the fragrance is at its most concentrated. Caught on the wind the scent is piercing and delicious but in the confines of a greenhouse or courtyard it becomes thick and oppressive. Included in this group are jasmine, jonquils, stephanotis, lilac and many lilies. Most members have white or cream-coloured flowers like the aminoid plants but their fragrance is intended to appeal to butterflies and moths rather than flies, hence their additional sweetness. Many flower at night to suit the nocturnal species.

The scents in the Aromatic Group are extremely varied and complex, so much so that they seem to have little in common with each other. But the quality that binds them together is their enduring sweetness shaded with degrees of spiciness which remains appealing even in quantity. They are at once the most popular and abundant garden fragrances. Included in the group are the vanilla scents of azara, hamamelis and *Clematis flammula*, the almond scents of choisya, heliotrope and *Prunus yedoensis*, the balsam scents of bluebells and tobacco flowers, the aniseed scents of cowslips and primroses, and the clove scents of carnations, pinks and viburnums. Butterflies are the main pollinators of these flowers and the group encompasses a range of pastel whites, pale yellows, pinks, mauves and blues to please them.

The Violet Group comprises those scents which are so sharply sweet that they fatigue our nerves very quickly and so seem to vanish as abruptly as they arrive. In quality they are as refined as the aromatic scents, in my opinion more so, but because they are so elusive they cannot be properly managed by the gardener to take part in special effects. Violets are not the only plants to exhale such a fragrance; it is found also in mignonettes and in *Iris reticulata*.

Most of the rose scents belong, appropriately enough, in the Rose Group. They are as light and attractive as the violet scents but longer-lasting and usually shaded with a fruity or spicy fragrance. They are as exquisite at close range as at a distance. As well as in the various roses, the scent is found in some tulips, paeonies and irises. Flowers in this group exhibit many different colours but white, pink, red and yellow are the most common; pollination is chiefly by beetles, for roses secrete no nectar.

Many roses fit more comfortably in the Lemon Group and the Fruit Group. Here the dominant fragrance is sharp and refreshing and the violet and spicy notes provide the shading. The scent is always exhilarating and pleasurable. The lemon scent is found in *Rosa bracteata*, waterlilies, magnolias and evening primroses; other fruity smells come from *Cytisus battandieri* (pineapple), philadelphus and some rambling roses (orange), *Rosa wichuraiana* and calycanthus (apple), *R. × dupontii* and *R. soulieana* (banana), and *Iris graminea* (greengage). The colours of the flowers in this group are principally white and yellow, and again beetles are the main pollinators.

Closely related to these two groups is the Animal Group, whose members smell of various mammals. Often the scent is shaded by a fruit fragrance when it is less objectionable, but in its purer forms it can be highly distasteful. Included here are codonopsis, cimicifugas, valerians and some orchids. Fortunately few produce sufficiently powerful scents to dissuade us from planting them.

Finally, there is the Musk and Honey Group whose scents combine a waxy musk-like odour with the sweet perfume of honey to produce a warm, enduring fragrance that is almost always appetizing. As well as the musk roses, buddleias, honeysuckles, sarcococcas and crocuses come under this heading. Butterflies do most of the pollinating and the flower colours keep mainly to white, pink, red, lilac and mauve.

Of course the flower is not the only part of a plant which can release scent. It is encountered in the bark of trees and shrubs, such as sassafras, illicium, fir and Scots pine, in the roots of herbaceous perennials and bulbs, such as *Iris florentina*, *Rhodiola rosea* (*Sedum rhodiola*) and crown imperials, and, most importantly for the gardener, in leaves. Here the function of the scent is not to attract insects but to afford the plants protection against browsing animals, scorching sunshine, infection or pests. Consequently we find few sweet-smelling fragrances and instead a tendency towards the pungent, bitter and medicinal.

Some leaf scents can be classified under the same groups as the flower scents, so similar are they in content. Stinkwood belongs in the Indoloid Group; dog's mercury in the Aminoid Group; certain scented-leafed pelargoniums in the Heavy Group; *Humea elegans* and *Rosa primula* (both shrouded in incense), helichrysum, sweet balsam, bay and fennel in the Aromatic Group; *Hebe cupressoides* and *Juniper virginiana* in the Violet Group; other pelargoniums in the Rose Group; balm, lemon verbena and lemon thyme in the Lemon Group; *Rosa eglanteria* (apple), rue (orange), and *Salvia rutilans* (pineapple) in the Fruit Group; dictamnus, hyssop and *Salvia sclarea turkestanica* in the Animal Group; and olearia in the Musk and Honey Group.

The remainder produce fragrances quite distinct from those breathed by flowers and must be given their own separate groups. The Turpentine Group comprise those scents that are highly resinous and includes all the conifers. Their effect is sharp and refreshing but their potency drowns other fragrances. The Camphor and Eucalyptus Group includes the heavy, pungent scents of artemisia, catmint, santolina, sage, thyme and chamomile. These are often shaded with sweetness or spice and are generally pleasing, though occasionally oppressive when inhaled in quantity. The cool, piercing scents of the mints and *Pelargonium tomentosum* belong in the Mint Group. Few people find them distasteful for their underlying sweetness takes the edge off their keenness. In fact the only truly unpleasant fragrances in the scent groups relating purely to leaves are found in the Sulphur Group. Here the scents are bitter and aggressive and suffer universal disfavour. Included in the group are onions, garlic, mustard and watercress.

Once we have identified the individual character of scent, we must decide whether its introduction will contribute to or detract from the harmonious atmosphere of the garden. Clearly not even the most dedicated bog gardeners are going to introduce foul-smelling members of the Indoloid Group into their borders in great numbers for fear of driving themselves, their families, their neighbours and their pets out of the district during their flowering period. But there will be other specific fragrances within the various scent groups which will bring about similar feelings of nausea in certain people, but which to others will seem quite blissful. I find the steaming curry scent of *Helichrysum angustifolium* the most revolting of garden scents, suffocating and fetid as a Calcutta kitchen, but friends of mine think it is ambrosial, prepared according to the finest Madras recipe, served with coconut and mango chutney. On the other hand, I do not mind the stale smell of *Salvia sclarea turkestanica*, which you only really taste at the end of the season as you are pulling up your plants, but others say it is reminiscent of a room full of sweating Sumo wrestlers (how they would know, I cannot say), and refuse to grow it.

It has been noted that as a nation we seem to favour the softer, subtler scents of the Rose, Violet and Aromatic Groups, while the Latin races prefer the thicker, sweeter scents of the Heavy Group and the Eastern races the heavier, spicier scents of the Musk and Camphor Groups. Climate must play its part in determining our taste in scent just as it does in colour. The moist air of the British Isles is conducive to the more delicate fragrances which are drained of flavour elsewhere by the dry heat, and so we are in a better position to appreciate their qualities. Lavender attains a far richer perfume in England than in France, for instance. Surrounded by such sophisticated scents, we are less disposed to welcome the more potent ones, which seem quite crude by comparison. A parallel can be drawn with our love of pastel shades, which look so well in our soft light, and our fear of intense colours, which can easily look vulgar and brash; in hotter countries such shades seem insipid, and the brighter hues take the stage.

Having prepared a blacklist of plants with scents which we find offensive, we can set about distributing the other scented plants around the garden. The sites we choose for them are determined by the power of their fragrance. Those plants which release their perfume freely can be planted some way from the house and the paths and still be enjoyed to the full. In this category come most of the rambling roses, the rugosas and the musk roses, and the species with scented leaves such as *R. wichuraiana* and *R. primula* whose fragrance engulfs the whole garden after a shower of rain; also the honeysuckles, the mahonias, the sarcococcas, the evening primroses, the tobacco flowers, the sweet rockets and stocks. We have already noted that the scents of the Heavy Group are delicious only in moderation and consequently the most powerful such as those of jasmine and *Lilium regale* should also float towards us from afar. Wily gardeners will make use of the prevailing winds to carry scent in their direction by grouping fragrant plants on the windward side of their gardens but this is easier said than done, for in many gardens the winds seem to attack from all angles and no regular pattern can be established.

The majority of scented flowers need to be within arm's reach so that we can pull them towards us and plunge our noses into them. This is not necessarily because their scent is faint but because we want to drink as deep a draught as possible. I would never grow the viburnums, daphnes, magnolias, abelias, osmanthus or cytisus far from a path, nor any but the most generous of roses. Even a fragrance as sweet and far-reaching as hyacinth does not satisfy many of us unless we can intoxicate ourselves completely by burying our faces in the petals. The smallest plants, such as sweet violets, crocuses, *Iris reticulata* and *Daphne cneorum*, need to be brought above ground-level and grown in troughs or raised beds to prevent you having to drop to your hands and knees to sniff them. It is astonishing how many gardeners overlook this obvious requirement to make their scented flowers readily accessible, and merrily plant a shrub like *Cytisus battandieri* behind a thicket of prickly berberis; the frustration of being denied a wonderful sensuous experience that is so cruelly dangled in front of you is indescribable – it is a punishment fit for Tantalus.

Most plants with scented leaves must also be grown close to paths for they need to be rubbed or brushed against before they can release their fragrance. Fortunately many are attractive foliage plants – rosemary, artemisia, fennel, santolina, mint, lavender, and *Geranium macrorrhizum*, for example – so we do not begrudge them such prominent positions. The smallest scented-leaved plants can actually become an integral part of the path, spilling over the edges of the stone or gravel and erupting from cracks in the middle, but care must be taken to avoid a chequerboard effect which looks highly artificial. The aim should be simply to smudge the firm lines of the path and soften the harshness of its cold surface. Occasionally you may feel justified in dispensing with stone and gravel altogether and construct your fragrant walkway entirely from prostrate varieties of thyme, pennyroyal and chamomile, but this is quite a labour-intensive project and unless it is meticulously maintained it can easily become weedy and untidy. A far more manageable scheme for the amateur gardener is to grow your creeping plants in a raised bed which is converted into a seat by the addition of a wooden back- and arm-rest. As you flop down to rest your aching limbs, a cloud of aromatic scents rises up to refresh you.

Indeed, a seat is the ideal centrepiece for a group of fragrant plants for it encourages you to tarry and down tools for a moment, and in this relaxed state you are most receptive to the mysterious powers of scent. With a foaming rose behind you, a tangle of philadelphus and pineapple sage beside you, and little waves of lemon thyme rippling against your feet, you will doze off into a fantasy world of borogoves and Tumtum trees, and awake full of ideas for new and even more ambitious schemes. A comfortable chair beneath a rose-clad pergola is another marvellous spot for abandoning yourself to fragrant dreams and so is a hammock slung between apple trees which drop with the weight of flowering honeysuckles. Scented plants which bloom in the colder months of the year are not the best candidates for choice positions near seats for you are not likely to want to linger outdoors on many occasions then. Site such plants beside your main paths and close to your front door instead, so that you can catch wafts of scent as you hurry to the garage or wood store.

Night-scented plants such as tobacco flowers, daturas, evening primroses, sweet rocket, *Gladiolus tristis* and *Daphne laureola* should be assembled near the house, where their perfume can glide in through open windows. In high summer they can stray further into the garden, for no doubt you will be wandering in the remotest corners of your property until quite late in the evening, armed with a stiff drink if not a trowel. Jasmines and honeysuckles are especially powerful at night and their perfume will flood into the sitting-room from fifty yards away.

Since scent is never static but is always drifting around on currents of air, it is difficult to predict how much its presence will be felt at any given moment. Sometimes it will be so pervasive that you can scarcely breathe; at other times you will detect only a vague wisp of fragrance that just tickles your nostrils. Gardens that are exposed to the wind have little chance of being drowned in scent because their fragrances are usually blown away as soon as they are released, but sheltered gardens, particularly walled gardens, hold the air captive and here scented plants are more often able to exercise their full potential. You are seldom disappointed by a visit to the walled rose gardens of Mottisfont Abbey or Sissinghurst Castle in June or early July where the air is as rich and exotic as the colours displayed, an infusion of honey and lemon, orange and clove, violet, musk and pineapple. The walls also create a warmer microclimate which encourages the free production of scent, not only by reflecting the sun's beams during the day but by radiating heat in the evening.

The uncertainty surrounding the exact impact of a scent heightens our sense of expectation and deepens the mystery of the substance but it does mean that we cannot orchestrate any fragrant effects in the garden with the precision that we manage colour schemes, and are forced to leave much more to chance. Fortunately scents do not appear to clash with each other with the ferocity of colours, probably because the majority of them have so many elements in common, and the only factor that need really concern us when distributing them around the garden is the suffocation of one fragrance by another. It would be insensitive to plant a drift of mignonette beneath a wall draped with jasmine, for example.

Nevertheless, we must not let this lack of control over precise effects dissuade us from managing scent altogether. Even though we do not know precisely how potent a fragrance will be or how much it will be masked by neighbouring fragrances, its characteristic sweetness or spiciness, nuttiness or fruitiness will always proclaim itself. By concentrating certain related scents in certain areas of the garden, we can thus be confident of establishing distinct zones of fragrance, each with its own mood and flavour. As a result our borders will reveal not only a series of colour impressions but a series of scented delights as well.

There are no end of tricks that we can play on our senses by the thoughtful use of fragrant plants. The pungent aromas of a dry bank planted with cistus and rosemary, thyme and sage will immediately transport us to the dusty hillsides of southern France, where gnarled peasant women tend their ripening vines while their idle sons, mopeds close by, snooze in the shade of olive trees (incidentally, sea buckthorns and silver pears make good substitutes for olives if you are thinking of recreating a miniature landscape; if only we could find some reliable foliage that matches the powdery turquoise of the vine leaves). The sharp resinous scents of pines, junipers and balsam poplars, grouped in a quiet, colourless corner, will carry you off to the deserted forests of Scandinavia with their deep, crystal clear lakes, their black shadows and their haunting silence; the sweet honey scents of a stand of weeping silver limes (*Tilia petiolaris*) to the lazy piazzas of Italy where the young men strut and the young women flirt, and the tourists watch enraptured; and the thick, heavy fragrance of a bed of *Lilium regale* pierced by the clear, fresh scent of *Oenothera odorata* to the shores of the West Indies where tropical nights swim with the perfume of the frangipani and vibrate to the rhythmic grating of cicadas.

But it seems to me that the most satisfying use of scent is as an undercurrent to a colour scheme, where there is perfect accord between the two substances, each echoing and confirming the flavour of the other and contributing to an overall mood. The sharp acid tones of a scheme of yellows is thus matched by the thrilling lemon scents which pervade the air around them; a scheme of tropical flowers and foliage is enhanced by the wild exotic notes struck by the fragrance in its midst; and a scheme of heavy velvet purples and golds pours out a perfume equally luxurious in its spices and sugars. There is a fine example of this unity between colour and scent at Sissinghurst (I make no excuse for continually referring to this property; it is my favourite garden, after my own). Spread out at the entrance to the herb garden is a pair of Chinese rugs, finely woven in pastel pink and white, carmine, lilac and mauve – at least they look like Chinese rugs; close inspection reveals them to be miniature lawns turfed with prostrate thymes. The effect is unmistakably oriental, the handiwork of the most skilled Imperial weaver, and this illusion is strengthened when you walk upon them (not that you must take such a liberty in a National Trust garden; the lawns would never survive the wear from the thousands of pairs of feet), for the scents released are full of the fragrances of the East, aromatic and sweet, shot through with fruit and spice.

Walks down Cottage Paths

The romantic gardener's love of colour and scent is equalled only by a passion for plants. Flowers, leaves, barks and berries are a source of endless fascination and the entire process of growth from shiny seed to sturdy plant, from winter dormancy to spring awakening, summer maturity and autumn decline, is a source of wonder and delight. But, like all passions, once ignited it quickly gets out of control and the appetite for acquiring and growing different plants proves insatiable; greenhouse staging is permanently crammed with a hundred seed-trays, cold frames spring up in unexpected places to accommodate the multitude of plastic pots containing softwood cuttings, borders start bulging at the seams, no longer able to contain the ever-increasing communities, and beds begin appearing even outside the garden gates in an attempt to catch some of the spillage.

As far as modern professional garden designers are concerned, this is the last straw. Not only are our heads filled with all sorts of dreamy nonsense and our attention focused on colour schemes and fragrant groups instead of on important architectural considerations of proportion, balance, mass and elevation, but we are incapable of exercising any restraint in our introduction of plant material and of selecting our plants according to the strict requirements of the overall design. The differences in attitude are irreconcilable and, shaking their heads in despair, they go their separate way. Fortunately, the problem of finding a style of gardening suited to our temperament and interests is easily solved, for there has been a romantic wave rolling through the gardening world for centuries and those caught up in it have been developing and perfecting their own genre, often with total disregard for the activities of their classical counterparts but usually with one eye trained on them in case they unearth any interesting techniques which could be of universal benefit.

The wave gathered fresh momentum in the early nineteenth century as attention was focused on a type of garden which had emerged many years earlier but which had been languishing in obscurity, in the shadow of the Renaissance and landscape traditions which swept the country. This was the cottage garden, a small enclosed parcel of ground surrounding a country dwelling, which had been used almost exclusively for the cultivation of vegetables, herbs and fruit but which was now gradually opening its arms to ornamental plants as well. The qualities of the cottage garden that appealed to the nineteenth-century romantic were its informality of design, its seclusion and tranquillity, and, above all, its carefree and bountiful appearance which so perfectly conveyed the rosy-cheeked ideal of rural life. These qualities have as much appeal today, as we each seek refuge from the regimented, hectic world of the cities, but it is the ability of the cottage garden to absorb vast quantities of plants that has ensured its popularity with today's gardeners. The design is loose enough and flexible enough to cope with constantly growing and changing collections and gives gardeners every opportunity to indulge themselves to the full. This feature was not particularly significant when the range of plants available was small but as plant hunters and travellers brought back more and more exciting specimens, it was this which made the cottage garden style the obvious choice for the keen gardener (on a grander scale, of course, there was the woodland garden style which developed later to accommodate the new species of trees and shrubs).

The best example of the genre is (or was until very recently: the house and garden have just appeared on the market) East Lambrook Manor in Somerset, formerly the home of Margery Fish. Although it was not made until the 1930s, you would think it had been laid out a century ago, so faithfully does it embody all the characteristics of the traditional cottage garden. Uneven, winding paths, littered with seedlings and prostrate herbs, twist their way through beds crammed with double primroses and hellebores, hollyhocks and astrantias, pulmonarias, pinks and campanulas; culinary herbs rub shoulders with aristocratic shrubs and common native plants with eastern rarities; roses and honeysuckles tumble

out of apple trees; curious wallflowers and miniature irises sprout from cracks and crevices; and the house and barn are engulfed in wild foliage. There are no views or vistas in such a garden: the interest is always in the foreground with the plants themselves.

The cottage garden style continues to form the basis of the modern romantic garden. Its exuberance, its riotous spirit and its casual unpretentious design are all qualities that we try to reproduce in our own gardens, and many of its traditional features and plants have found a permanent place in our repertoire. But the style has not survived entirely intact. Although it satisfies our practical gardening requirements and is in perfect accord with our gypsy temperament, it does not always satisfy us as artists or designers. The truth is that what seems carefree and charming in a setting of thatched cottages and cornfields can look chaotic and dishevelled against dwellings with a stronger architectural presence.

This problem was faced at the turn of the century by William Robinson and Gertrude Jekyll, though they were approaching it from a different angle. Their concern was not to bring artistic and architectural cohesion to the cottage garden but to bring the cottager's wealth of plants and his natural informal ways of growing them to the gardens of the larger country houses without detracting from the sense of order and unity between house and garden that had already been established. Attempts to integrate larger plant collections into such gardens had until then proved disastrous – grotesquely artificial carpet-bedding had erupted on the stately terraces of the formal gardens, and the smooth lines of the landscape tradition had been interrupted by the appearance of shrubberies and incongruous flowerbeds. A new style had to be found which would hold a quantity of plants in a strong and coherent design.

If you glance through the illustrations to Robinson's *The English Flower Garden*, you will see that the majority of gardens depicted are essentially cottagey in their composition, with generously planted, mixed flowerbeds, climbing plants scrambling over walls and dwarf herbs spilling over paths. (There are grander features too, further away from the house, which reveal the same desire for the natural and informal – outcrops of rock dripping with alpine plants, irregularly shaped ponds bordered by casual groups of moisture-loving perennials and shrubs, and woodland floors strewn with daffodils and primroses.) But there are elements in the design which you would not find in the traditional cottage garden. Paths often follow clean, straight lines, stone steps and sundials are introduced as features, beds are lapped by neatly mown lawns, and plants are more purposefully grouped and more carefully arranged and sited for their foliage or flower effect. All this is evidence of architectural thought, and in response the gardens, although keeping their carefree flavour, carry the stamp of order and unity.

A sense of architecture is even more keenly felt in the gardens designed a little later by Gertrude Jekyll in collaboration with Edwin Lutyens, but credit for this should not rest entirely with Jekyll. The gardens (of which one of the best examples is Hestercombe in Somerset – recently restored by Somerset County Council) were the fruits of a union between a romantic and a classicist, similar to that between Vita Sackville-West and Harold Nicolson, and the influence of each partner is apparent in their design. Each is a perfectly integrated composition in which the bones of the house are carried by the architect Lutyens right out into the garden through walls and balustrades, stairways and paths, while the plants, in familiar cottage profusion, sweep in from the countryside right up to the house walls, softening the hard lines.

Left to her own devices, Jekyll produced a much looser composition which depended far more on plants than on brick and stone. Her own garden at Munstead Wood in Surrey followed more the Robinsonian model of formal touches near the house, such as straight paths and neat borders, clipped yew hedges and velvet lawns, and a totally informal, natural approach elsewhere. The design betrays the typical romantic preoccupation with colour, scent and the cultivation of plants for their own sake, rather than any special concern about architecture. Nevertheless, it has absorbed enough alien elements to distinguish it from the traditional cottage garden and to show us that the romantic garden style has become more sophisticated. The most important innovation is the assembling of plants into large borders, backed by walls or hedges and fronted by lawns; this enabled the gardener to grow a wide range of plants and yet maintain some semblance of order. It is the construction and management of such borders that has dominated the thoughts of gardeners ever since, for they remain the principal features of most modern gardens.

With Jekyll the large border, called the herbaceous border

because it was composed mainly of herbaceous perennials, not only became the central feature of the garden but also became the stage on which gardeners might display their artistic skills. Plant association began to dominate people's thoughts. The classical gardener concentrated on shapes; Jekyll and the romantics concentrated on colour.

Jekyll may not have been the first person to handle garden colour with sensitivity, but she was certainly the first to maintain that the arrangement of colour is the gardener's single most important concern and the first to convince the gardening public that to use colour skilfully, they should turn to the laws of harmony and contrast for guidance and to painting for inspiration. In the Introduction to her book *Colour in the Flower Garden*, published in 1908, she states that gardening is nothing less than a living branch of painting and gardeners have a duty to treat it as such:

> I am strongly of the opinion that the possession of a quantity of plants, however good the plants may be themselves, and however ample their number, does not make a garden; it only makes a collection. Having got the plants, the great thing is to use them with careful selection and definite intention. Merely having them, or having them planted unassorted in garden space, is only like having a box of paints from the best colourman, or, to go one step further, it is like having portions of these paints set out upon a palette. This does not constitute a picture; and it seems to me that the duty we owe to our gardens and to our own bettering in our gardens is so to use the plants that they shall form beautiful pictures.

With Jekyll the arrangement of shrubs and perennials was raised to the level of a fine art. There was a grand design and a preconceived colour plan for each area of bare soil; the garden was divided into different seasonal sections each of which was expected to give a triumphant display at a particular time of year, after which it could collapse unobserved as attention switched to its awakening successor; and every plant was carefully selected and sited in bold drifts so that it would make a proper contribution to the overall scheme.

Since she had trained as a painter, her understanding of colour was comprehensive. The French colourist Michel Chevreul provided her with the theoretical knowledge – the natural ordering of colours according to their positions in the spectrum, the potency of the hot colours and the recessive nature of the cool colours, the interactions of complementary colours and the importance of white as the colour of light – and the great painters like Monet and Cézanne with the examples. It was in fact J. M. W. Turner whose influence seems to be most apparent in her use of colour and by comparing his colour sequence as used in his later paintings with that employed by Jekyll in her main August border at Munstead Wood, we can perceive how close painting and gardening became.

Turner was fascinated by the colour of light and in his work he set out to capture the gorgeous effects of sunsets and fires and the different ways their brilliance was reflected in sky and water. He devised a scale of colours which would give the impression of movement and changing light, which ran from blue, the colour of distance, through yellow and white, to red, the colour of matter itself. His fires and sunsets dominate the paintings and set the canvas alight with their glowing oranges, reds and yellows, and the eye, having been saturated by their richness, is led away across sky and water by a graded sequence of pale yellows, purples and blues.

Jekyll's main flower border re-creates this same movement towards and away from a central core of fiery hues.

> The planting of the border is designed to show a distinct scheme of colour arrangement. At the two ends there is a groundwork of grey and glaucous foliage – stachys, santolina, *Cineraria maritima* (*Senecio cineraria*), sea-kale (*Crambe maritima*), and lyme-grass (*Elymus arenarius*), with darker foliage, also of grey quality, of yucca, *Clematis recta* and rue. With this, at the near or western end, there are flowers of pure blue, grey-blue, white, palest yellow and palest pink; each colour partly in distinct masses and partly intergrouped. The colour then passes through the stronger yellows to orange and red. By the time the middle space of the border is reached the colour is strong and gorgeous, but, as it is in good harmonies, it is never garish. The colour strength recedes in an inverse sequence through orange and deep yellow to pale yellow, white and palest pink, again with blue-grey foliage. But at this, the eastern end, instead of the pure blues we have purples and lilacs.

(The plants used in this border include, in sequence, *Campanula lactiflora*, white everlasting pea, rue, sea-kale, golden privet, verbascum, meadowsweet, white and yellow snapdragons, *Iris pallida dalmatica*, blue lobelia, blue daisy (*Felicia amelloides*), *Eryn-*

gium × *oliverianum,* pale and dark blue tradescantia, *Thalictrum flavum,* coreopsis, helenium, achillea, yellow cannas, scarlet bergamot and *Senecio artemisiifolius,* orange lilies, orange gazanias, *Lychnis chalcedonica* and *L.* × *haageana,* scarlet salvias and scarlet tropaeolum. The colours then recede through eryngium, everlasting pea and pale yellow calceolaria to delphiniums and *Euphorbia wulfenii.* The border faces south and is backed by a high sandstone wall clothed in wall shrubs and climbing plants, which harmonize in leaf and flower with the colours in front of them – they include roses, robinia, laurustinus (*Viburnum tinus*), nandina, *Abutilon vitifolium,* loquat (*Eriobotrya japonica*), bay, pomegranate, Japanese privet, prunus, chimonanthus, fuchsia, claret vine, magnolia, *Choisya ternata, Cistus* × *cyprius,* piptanthus and carpenteria. It is flanked by yew buttresses and the planting is anchored by groups of yucca and bergenia at either end.)

This border is a masterpiece of composition. The careful gradation of colour carries the eye naturally from one tone to the next, each step a reminder of what has been and a preparation for what is to come, building up to a crescendo of colour and then fading away. Each colour is in harmony with its neighbours and the escalation of strength is controlled so gently that the sharp changes in temperature, from the cool whites, yellows and blues to the hot oranges and scarlets and back down the scale to the cool tones again, are neither unexpected nor disconcerting.

Because each colour group is large, the eye has time to absorb every changing mood before being led forward and this makes for a slower progression to the fiery core than in the earlier schemes, even though they offered periodic relief. By the time the centre of the border is reached, the eye has been so filled with bright colour that it longs to descend the scale back to the cool shades, and by having an inverse sequence of colour this is exactly what Jekyll allows it to do.

This is why the design is so skilful. Although it is composed of harmonious groups, it satisfies the eye's desire for stimulation and contrast by moving up and down the scale, enabling it to seek relief from a colour by providing its complement:

> The whole border can be seen as one picture, the cool colouring at the end enhancing the brilliant warmth of the middle. Then, passing along the wide path next to the border, the value of the colour arrangement is still more strongly felt. Each portion now

becomes a picture in itself, and every one is of such a colouring that it best prepares the eye, in accordance with natural law, for what is to follow. Standing for a few moments before the endmost region of grey and blue, and saturating the eye to its utmost capacity with these colours, it passes with extraordinary avidity to the succeeding yellows. These intermingle in pleasant harmony with the reds and scarlets, blood-reds and clarets, and then lead again to yellows. Now the eye has again become saturated, this time with the rich colouring, and has therefore, by the law of complementary colour, acquired a strong appetite for the greys and purples. These therefore assume an appearance of brilliancy that they would not have had without the preparation provided by their recently received complementary colour.

Jekyll's ideas of colour and on plant association have had a profound influence on the course of the romantic garden this century. Although few people have been sufficiently talented as artists to attempt such ambitious plant paintings as she did, her appeal to gardeners to treat their gardens as a series of colour schemes by grouping plants together which share the same flowering season, by making use of coloured foliage, by exploiting the effects of sunlight and shadow, and by putting into practice the laws of harmony and contrast has been heeded, and the pleasure of composing these living pictures is the main driving force behind our pursuit of gardening today.

But garden design is never static and if we look at the two most important romantic gardens of the early twentieth century, Hidcote, which was made before the First World War, and Sissinghurst, which was made between the wars, we will see that although the Jekyllian influence is strong and omnipresent, the romantic gardener is already departing in another direction. In their overall structure, their formality and symmetry, and their abrupt use of barriers to transform the garden into a number of different rooms, Hidcote and Sissinghurst owe rather more to European gardening traditions than to English ones. The strong axes, vistas and focal points recall the classical gardens of France, the dramatic vertical effects of tall hedges, conifers and poplars are features borrowed from Italy, and the pattern of linked rooms is the basis of the Moorish gardens of Spain.

This return to a more formal structure is coupled paradoxically with a return to the wild profusion of the cottage garden. The high artistry of Gertrude Jekyll has been rejected in favour of the more carefree use of plants; colours are not meticulously graded to produce great crescendos designed to make you gasp; plants are not necessarily arranged in large blocks but are often muddled and their colours diffused; and the different parts of the garden do not restrict their display to one season, though they may have a definite peak, so they are not expected to look immaculate at a given time. The happy consequence of this more casual approach is that the plants themselves surface once more as individuals and are no longer just the blobs of colour which they tended to become in many Jekyllian borders; schemes are more flexible and plants can be chosen and accommodated more on their own merits than on the aesthetic needs of the picture.

Nevertheless, the wide borders crammed with plants and the dependence of every room on colour for its mood and flavour are Jekyll's legacies, and it is they that give the gardens their character. Each part of the garden is given over to different parts of the spectrum. At Hidcote there is a kitchen garden devoted to pastel pinks and apricots, a paved garden devoted to blues and golds, and a pair of borders devoted to reds and crimsons; at Sissinghurst there is a cottage garden of reds, oranges and yellows, a rose garden of pinks and crimsons, a border of violets and purples and, most famously, a twilight garden of greys and whites. The colour schemes are purposeful and distinctive and keep to a definite range of colours; their more natural, spontaneous appearance is achieved not so much by relaxing the rules to let in a wide range of colours but by considering the personality of each plant and associating it with appropriate companions, instead of placing it in the position dictated by an extremely precise, preconceived colour plan.

To many gardeners, including myself, the planting style of Hidcote and Sissinghurst represents an ideal worth striving to emulate. There is just enough cottage garden informality to enable us to pack every corner and crevice with plants and, to a great extent, to allow them to seed themselves where they choose; the division of the garden into colour schemes gives us the opportunity to exercise our artistic talents and to pursue all sorts of fantastic projects while maintaining unity between the ingredients; and the formal touches in the garden's design, the clipped yew hedges, the straight paths, the symmetrical pairs of box bushes, the repetition of junipers down borders and the use of terracotta pots in prominent positions, provide an architectural cohesion which is so emphatic and conspicuous that the garden seems orderly no matter how tangled and riotous are the borders themselves.

There are, however, two essential differences between Hidcote and Sissinghurst and the average modern garden which, though not necessarily affecting our approach to garden design (a room at Hidcote or Sissinghurst still makes a very good blueprint for a garden today), certainly change our approach to planting. Firstly, the modern garden is much smaller. Half an acre is now thought to be a very generous size and most people garden in considerably less. This means that it cannot be conveniently divided into rooms. Thus the whole garden is visible every day of the year and has to be permanently presentable. Huge tracts of decaying foliage in early summer as bulbs are completing their cycle and avenues of dead brown sticks through the winter as herbaceous perennials retreat from the cold cannot be tolerated, and provision must be made for a framework of reliable and substantial material which gives the garden an air of respectability at all times and conceals the undesirable elements.

The lack of space also means that we are denied the chance of composing really large colour schemes unless we are prepared to forego the delights of autumn, winter and spring for the sake of one sumptuous visual feast during the summer. This might suit hearty, devil-may-care gardeners, who prefer to take their drink in one deep draught rather than in a number of little sips, and gardeners who try not to set foot outdoors until the balmy weather arrives, but does not suit tranquil gardeners who take their pleasures in moderation day by day, and plantsmen, who could not bear the thought of having some genera unrepresented. So most of us have to abandon ideas of reproducing the colour sequence of Michelangelo's 'Last Supper' or Botticelli's 'Birth of Venus' and concentrate instead on a series of smaller schemes which maintain interest from January until December, punctuated with the occasional extravagant gestures.

Secondly, the modern garden is generally looked after by one person, working only at the weekend, rather than by a team of full-time gardeners, so borders cannot be too labour-intensive. Think of the work involved in managing a Jekyllian herbaceous border, in terms of staking, dividing, replacing, feeding, pruning, spraying and weeding; it is enough to make today's gardener weak at the knees. Every square yard of soil has to work overtime to ensure a continuous display. Large numbers of annuals have to be incorporated since they perform longer than their perennial colleagues and carry the border through the difficult period of high summer when flowers can be scarce; plants at the back of the border have to be trained forward to hide those which have finished flowering; and pots of reserve plants such as lilies and hydrangeas are plunged into any blank spaces that appear. And in autumn, after straining every muscle, the border collapses, exhausted.

Even the maintenance of borders such as those at Hidcote and Sissinghurst, which do not have such great artistic pressure placed on them and employ many labour-saving techniques, would be beyond the capacity of the weekend gardener. The balance of power is still with the miles of dwarf hedging that needs to be cut, the hundreds of annuals that have to be raised and pricked out, the dozens of tender perennials and shrubs that have to be lifted and stored or wrapped in winter overcoats, the climbing plants that have to be tied back and pruned, and the herbaceous perennials that need to be staked. Plants that are troublesome to cultivate are packed into our borders too (how can we resist their charms?) but they have to be outnumbered by plants which thrive on near neglect and plants which contribute significantly to weed control.

Thus, sadly, we have to limit the number of annuals, biennials and half-hardy plants that we grow; we have to be selective in our choice of herbaceous perennials, largely avoiding those which cannot keep themselves respectable; and we have to introduce into all our schemes those categories of plant which give the longest period of interest for the least amount of work, namely foliage plants, bulbs and shrubs.

Foliage plants, that is to say plants with strikingly shaped or coloured leaves, persist in beauty for much of the year and if they are generously distributed, they will carry a border safely through even the leanest months. They make attractive foils for the flowers and they distract attention when the displays are over. In Jekyll's day they were little more than pleasant additions to a colour scheme, but now they provide much of the scheme's substance, and often form the very nucleus of a group. Bulbs have a relatively short flowering season but they are valuable to the border because they will share the same plot of ground with other plants, thriving under the skirts of shrubs and between clumps of herbaceous perennials, and permit a succession of colour without having to dig anything up and replace it.

Shrubs have also become key ingredients. They need so little attention, keep the ground beneath them comparatively free of weeds, offer ideal sites for early bulbs, contribute flowers themselves, provide the backcloth for the displays of others, and by their stature and bearing bring form and weight to the border. Furthermore, many give a twelve-month period of interest, transforming themselves from gaunt, twisted winter skeletons into wealthy dignitaries who change their costume as the seasons advance – lime green in spring, deep green in summer and flaring scarlet and gold in autumn.

However, being conscious of the need for labour-saving ingredients in our schemes makes us easy prey for the disciples of the trouble-free school of gardening, so we should be vigilant. They would have us turn our gardens into drab wastelands of heather and St John's wort, punctuated by conifers and wizened trees. Their mission is to eliminate labour altogether; ours is just to reduce it to manageable proportions. You cannot hope to create a beautiful garden if you are not prepared to devote a reasonable amount of time to it, and how can you possibly design a garden in these islands which does not include roses and honeysuckles, columbines and delphiniums, foxgloves, violets and asters?

No, we must take care to ensure that the garden is always presentable and that the workload is never oppressive, but we must not let such considerations prevent us from growing anything we choose or from drawing on the full range of plant material available. And what a treasure chest that is! It is crammed with far more precious items now than it was in Gertrude Jekyll's time. New introductions are made every year through nurserymen and plant hunters so we should keep abreast of the contents and be prepared to plunder every compartment.

Although in many respects the romantic garden has changed a great deal since its rustic beginnings, its two most important characteristics have remained constant. It is primarily a garden in which to grow plants and it has always been so; plants have never been an embellishment to the design but always the very core of it. No type of garden that forbids a profusion of plants and discourages a magpie nature is ever likely to win the romantic heart, for the desire to grow as many plants as possible and to immerse ourselves in the hundred and one gardening activities related to them is an integral part of the romantic's enthusiasm for gardening. Thus the latest design trends, obviously the product of disciplined classical minds, which seem to encourage an almost Japanese restraint in the use of plants and which revel in the hard lines of modern materials such as glass and concrete, are destined to pass the romantic by. Meanwhile we are amusing ourselves with gravel borders and peat-wall rock gardens, island beds in the lawn and borders with abstract outlines; we have yet to see whether these will make a permanent impact on the course of romantic garden design.

Secondly, because it comprises such quantities of flowering plants, which perform for comparatively brief periods, the romantic garden has always been a garden of dramatic and constantly changing images. In the past the gardener was content to leave such images entirely to chance, but today, with the example of Jekyll to inspire us, we are more ambitious and enjoy the artistic challenge of devising our own. Through the careful use of colour and scent, sunlight and shadow, shapes, sizes and textures we can fashion a garden which exactly reflects our personality and satisfies our appetite for the rich and exotic, the curious and the intricate, the startling and the subtle. It will be a garden of mystery and adventure, of tranquil scenes, of breathtaking effects, and a garden closely in tune with the mood of each season.

The remaining chapters of this book will attempt to convey the spirit of the romantic garden of the 1980s through its plants, sights and scents and at the same time provide you with the living material with which you may build your schemes. I am not going to draw up any planting plans for whole borders – all the fun lies in devising your own – but I will suggest numerous plant associations and colour groups which you might like to incorporate into your designs and I will assemble the plants, season by season, according to their colour so that you will be better able to see how they might play their part.

Surprising Leaves

It is time to meet the plants and draw up some schemes. But before we get too carried away by intoxicating images of tall groves of sulphur hollyhocks entangled with *Clematis flammula* (a favourite association of Gertrude Jekyll) or arbours of violet and white wisteria dripping down into inky pools of purple irises, we must stop to collect our army of foliage plants.

In many ways the colours and shapes of foliage are, of course, already providing the background and framework of the garden and giving it an architectural cohesion. Hedges delineate boundaries, separate us from our neighbours and subdivide the garden; trees give height and substance, provide focal points and act as links with the countryside or immediate environment; grass gives us our tranquil arenas around which the mixed borders are arranged; and well-placed evergreen shrubs hold the garden together even in the depths of winter. Such features provide the foils for our groups of flowering plants and help to counter the crowded and untidy areas of border which romantic scheming can so easily bring about.

But the borders themselves also need an internal framework of foliage which will provide an appropriate and relatively permanent setting for the flowers and at the same time give some form and weight to the planting. Since leaves persist in beauty for far longer than flowers, the foliage will not only enhance the colours around them but help to conceal and divert attention from plants whose flower displays are over. Naturally many desirable flowering plants also have attractive leaves but to be able to orchestrate the most telling foliage effects we must temporarily

44

ignore floral temptation and concentrate wholeheartedly on the genuine 'foliage plants', that is to say on those plants which are grown primarily for their leaves.

To qualify under this heading a plant must have leaves which are in some way unusual. These may be coloured silver or gold, purple or bronze; they may be variegated; they may be huge and leathery, small and prickly, grassy, palmate or feathery – anything which makes them stand out from the crowd. For convenience I have expanded the conventional scope of the term by also including in this chapter those plants whose main attraction is their leaf scent; their positioning is also dictated ultimately by their leaves and not their flowers.

Foliage plants have many specific roles. They can be employed as architectural anchors at the ends of borders, as a means of carrying a border through a lean flowering season, as softening influences and foils for flowers, or simply grouped together to make contrasts in form or texture. Obviously care must be taken to ensure that the colour of their leaves – and their flowers – blends with the schemes around them. The colours and shapes of some are so eye-catching that they cannot be treated as backcloths for other plants; rather they will need foils themselves and will have to be used sparingly, if a restless and patchy appearance is to be avoided. Strongly patterned plants scattered about the border are the undoing of any garden, as incorrigible collectors like myself know to their cost, but placed intelligently they flatter the colours around them and lighten the dreariest corners.

The importance of foliage has been so fully recognized today that in many gardens flowers have taken second place. I suppose the stark outlines of modern architecture have contributed to the appeal of plants which can hold their own against an unsympathetic background, where the wispy cottage flowers would be out of place. Chunky-leaved hostas and sword-shaped phormiums are enjoying so much popularity that new varieties cannot be raised fast enough. The interest in the less architectural plants, the silvers and the blues, the purples and the golds can only be attributed to a general refinement in gardening taste, the realization that there can be as much beauty in a leaf as a flower, coupled perhaps with the recognition that the modern garden has to contain as many long-lasting trouble-free plants as possible. As a consequence of this new-found public awareness the range of foliage plants available to the gardener is enormous, and suitable subjects can be found for every colour scheme and every position in the garden.

The professional garden designer would no doubt encourage us to distribute our foliage plants about the borders before we become distracted by flowers, but for the romantic gardener this is a hopeless proposition. It is the association of flowering plants which is for us the inspiration for the whole design, and thus we will already have a strong idea of the character and content of the border to be planted by the time we begin thinking about foliage; we will have an impression of colours in our minds, maybe even a combination of scents; we will have chosen all our dominant plants and most of the border's prominent positions will now be occupied. In romantic scheming foliage is always a secondary consideration, albeit an important one, and is admitted entirely as a supplement to the flowers.

Foliage plants must be in accord with the chosen mood of the scheme being constructed in colour, size, shape and character. Usually they will be required to harmonize with the flowers around them, glossy leaves reflecting pale petals or matt leaves softening strong hues, tropical leaves echoing exotic blooms or misty leaves shrouding pastel colours, coppery leaves supporting orange flowers and bluish leaves complementing cool tones. But occasionally they will be required to make striking incidents, perhaps to provide a pool of golden leaves in an expanse of violet or blue or a repetition of bold shapes down the length of a border, which is in turn picked up by groups of imposing flower spikes; or to act as gentle contrasts, as in a silver border where, with a restricted colour scheme, one shape is played against another to bring variety and relieve monotony.

Naturally the most important quality of a foliage plant as far as we are concerned is its colour and this is how I will group the plants in this chapter. But as we look at each individual we will also identify other features which will help us to perceive more easily its precise uses in the border. The reason for including this chapter here rather than at the end of the book is so that foliage association will be nearer the front of our minds as we move through the remaining seasonal chapters, and as we concoct our flowering groups later on we will be able to continually refer back to draw on the fund of material already assembled.

Let us therefore launch ourselves into the world of foliage plants without further delay with an investigation into purple, the darkest of leaf colours. Under the heading purple foliage, the gardener includes a range of tones from maroon and near-black to deep red and near-brown but all produce the same sort of effect in colour schemes, namely an area of warm shadow against which pale colours can be silhouetted or hot colours intensified. There are few colours which do not associate well with purple foliage and so there is a temptation to bring it into every scheme, but we should bear in mind that it can be rather a depressing colour and from a distance large expanses of it tend to look like dark holes in the border. Furthermore, it is not a natural colour of the English landscape, tending to disturb the tranquillity of a sweep of greens, so is better suited to positions near the house; certainly a perimeter group of trees and shrubs should always pass from purple back into green before disappearing into the countryside.

As a background to a border of lively fiery colours, however, it is unrivalled. This might take the form of a collection of large purple-leaved shrubs and small trees or a more formal hedge. For hedging material I would turn either to the copper beech, *Fagus sylvatica* 'Riversii' or the purple-leaved plum, *Prunus cerasifera* 'Pissardii'. Copper beech starts the year a bright reddish-plum but by midsummer has turned sombre and leaden, when, to compensate, the border needs to be very bright indeed. At Hidcote it is woven with common green beech to make a gentle tapestry backdrop for a garden of blues and golds, an especially sensitive association with the blue flowers echoing the plum shades in the hedge and the golds echoing the deep green. The purple-leaved plum undergoes a similar colour change from deep red to dark purple as the seasons advance but has the bonus of white flowers, pink in bud, which appear towards the end of March. They are set off perfectly by their shadowy background which tempts me to suggest other white-flowered subjects which could be allowed to ramble through it. Perhaps a large white clematis like 'Henryi' or, even better, 'Miss Bateman', whose maroon stamens would match the colour of the purple foliage. The clematis would have to be planted on the shady side of its host, some way from its greedy roots, and kept well-fed.

To make an informal group of purple foliage or an isolated incident I would look to more aristocratic plants such as the Japanese maples, among which the two finest varieties are still *Acer palmatum* 'Atropurpureum' and *A.p.* 'Dissectum Atropurpureum'. The former will ultimately form a small tree, 20 feet tall, and its palmate leaves are red when they open but soon fade to a bronze purple. The leaves of 'Dissectum Atropurpureum' are far more deeply divided, the shrub giving the appearance of being composed of tumbling folds of dark lace, which turn brilliant scarlet in the autumn. This shrub may eventually make 10 feet. Both these maples are best in semi-shade and on deep peaty soil. At Kiftsgate Court in Gloucestershire *A.p.* 'Atropurpureum' is the central feature of the golden border and it looks magnificent rubbing shoulders with the golden-variegated *Elaeagnus pungens* 'Maculata'.

Three members of the berberis family deserve to be considered. *Berberis vulgaris* 'Atropurpurea' is the largest at about 8 feet and its deep purple leaves provide the foil for the racemes of yellow flowers which appear in spring. More familiar is *B. thunbergii* 'Atropurpurea', a small-leaved prickly shrub growing to between 4 and 6 feet, which accords well in any blue or silver scheme. At Sissinghurst this shrub sits among mounds of glaucous blue *Acaena magellanica* whose arms wander up to mingle with its purple partner. It is such a good combination that I have repeated it in my own garden, but at the moment the acaena is dominating the berberis and it will be a year or two before the roles are reversed. The smallest barberry, suitable for the rockery or the front of the border, is *B.t.* 'Atropurpurea Nana'. This only grows to about 2 feet and you could achieve a similar partnership with a blue acaena by choosing a smaller species, such as *A.* 'Blue Haze'. All these barberries require full sun to maintain their richest tones.

One of the gloomiest of shrubs is the purple hazel, *Corylus maxima* 'Purpurea', whose large rounded leaves successfully eliminate all light from its black heart. But the gloom is partly relieved by a sort of iridescence, rather like the neck of a pigeon or the breast of an adult starling. It is not shiny but it does contain a hint of emerald and amethyst, which means that it is only properly appreciated in sunlight, where it will grow into a large specimen. The catkins are also purple.

Cotinus coggygria 'Royal Purple' is never sombre and is my favourite purple-leaved shrub. With the sun behind it the small leaves shine red and bright, and are a highlight in any scheme. It grows to about 10 feet and in summer produces a fawn inflorescence which, like the rest of us, greys with age. This is the reason for its common name of Venetian smoke-tree or sumach. I saw a striking association in Peter Healing's garden in Worcestershire where the wine-red *Clematis viticella* 'Rubra' had hoisted itself into the branches of the cotinus. The colours were so well matched that it looked as if the flowers belonged to the shrub.

The purple sand cherry, *Prunus* 'Cistena', is a small shrub which can be used either as a hedging plant or as a foliage feature. Its leaves remain a gleaming red throughout the year, especially when seen with the light behind them, and look well when surrounded by the blue lyme grass, *Elymus arenarius*. The single white flowers appear in spring.

I am not sure if one of my chosen shrubs, *Rosa glauca* (formerly *R. rubrifolia*), is purple at all. I can see it from my desk, and from here it seems reddish grey but I know it will look more purple if I go and inspect it. It is a wonderful shrub which grows to 8 feet or so and is covered in shocking-pink single flowers in June followed, in early autumn, by clusters of scarlet hips. If it likes you it will drop seedlings at its feet, so there is no excuse for not having plants all over the garden. Its glaucous colour makes it particularly suitable for grey, blue and rose-pink harmonies.

The purple sage, *Salvia officinalis* 'Purpurascens', is a very valuable semi-evergreen for the middle or front of the border which needs to be clipped in early spring to keep it to a comely dome of dusky green and purple, although this does mean some loss of its violet flowers. Among pink, purple, white, blue or lemon-yellow flowers it is never out of place and since it roots readily from softwood cuttings you need never be short of plants for new schemes. The greyish tone of its leaves enables it, like *Rosa glauca*, to blend with its background more easily than other purple subjects and makes it an ideal partner for silver foliage. I wish I could lavish as much praise on the variety 'Tricolor', but its leaves are splashed with green, white and purple and, to me at least, just look diseased. It is incongruous in every association and I would urge you to avoid it at all costs. Incidentally the same is true of the similarly patterned bugle, *Ajuga reptens* 'Multicolor', the variety of *Fuchsia magellanica* called 'Versicolor' and, horror of horrors, that ghastly climber *Actinidia kolomikta* whose leaves look as if they have been dipped first in whitewash and then in raspberry juice.

Purple foliage can be used to clothe walls as well so your sombre theme can be lifted above ground level. For this purpose I would choose *Vitis vinifera* 'Purpurea', a true grape vine with typical lobed leaves which begin green and gradually turn to a bloomy purple; its small bunches of black grapes (bitter to the taste – see

Christopher Lloyd's story in his book *Foliage Plants*) are jet black
and against the leaves are scarcely discernible. *Hillier's Manual of
Trees and Shrubs* recommends training this vine through the weeping silver pear for a dramatic contrast. *Parthenocissus henryana* is
another first-rate climber and usefully self-clinging. Its leaves are
more of a greenish-bronze than purple and in shade are promi-
nently veined in white.

Among the few purple-leaved perennials in cultivation the best
known is probably *Ajuga reptens* 'Atropurpurea'. It gives a fine
display of intense violet-blue flower spikes in early summer but
even if it did not, as a prostrate purple ground-cover plant in sun
or shade it is without equal. It spreads quickly by overground
runners and you need to keep a mindful eye on its progress. I have
two stretches of it, one of which is associated with the ferny *Acaena*
'Blue Haze' and backed by the grey-leaved *Achillea* 'Moonshine'
and the other is massed among violet *Campanula portenschlagiana*.

I first met *Euphorbia amygdaloides* 'Purpurea' at Sissinghurst
where, in early April, it was reclining on a bank beside some stone
steps, behind a group of royal-blue grape hyacinths. Racemes of
yellow bracts were held aloft like shepherds' crooks and the plant
made an impressive feature in its bare and rocky setting. When
fully open the flowerheads become quite round like a more dainty
version of the common *E. robbiae*, and the contrast of lime yellow
against the purplish leaves and red stems is striking. The form I
acquired from Powis Castle is distinctly superior to my original
plant, being more upright and more vigorous, although it was sold
under the same name, so it is clearly worth shopping around for a
good specimen. It also associates well with blue grasses.

There is a useful stonecrop, *Sedum maximum* 'Atropurpureum',
whose succulent foliage is dark maroon. It does not flower until
September when it produces typical flat flowerheads of carmine-
red stars, supported on 2 foot stems, but for the whole of the
summer it is a good dark component of the border, particularly
effective among the strong reds, pinks and lavender blues. It does
not make such fat clumps as *S.* 'Autumn Joy' which it resembles.

Heuchera micrantha 'Palace Purple' is a more versatile border
plant for it will thrive in sun or shade (the sedum needs sun). In
shade it becomes quite dark and bronzy but in sun it is far redder
and makes a smouldering groundwork for the various scarlets and
crimsons, as in the red borders at Hidcote. There are no better
front-line components of warm schemes, for the solid domes of

broad scalloped leaves are always presentable and the plants benefit from close scrutiny since if you lift the leaves you will find that
they have bright carmine-red undersides, a feature normally only
revealed by the wind.

The purple variety of the New Zealand flax, *Phormium tenax*
'Purpureum', will play a prominent part in those tropical schemes
that you compose in summer, comprising cannas and kniphofias,
hedychiums and yuccas, but in my part of the country it is not at
all hardy. It makes an imposing stand of sword-shaped leaves
which in some areas may reach 6 feet in height. It is useful in
places where you want your scheme to come to an abrupt full-stop
or suddenly turn from border into shrubbery.

I know of only one black-leaved plant in cultivation. It is the
black spider 'grass', *Ophiopogon planiscapus* 'Nigrescens', which resembles a spider not just because of its dumpy body and arching
legs but because it feels its way stealthily around the garden. The
parent does not move of course, but it sends out youngsters to
investigate the surrounding territory for it. Every time I look at
my plant there are more offspring, sometimes a foot away from
their mother. It is so small and dark that it needs a bright companion to show it up. In shade you could try the silver deadnettle, *Lamium maculatum* 'Beacon Silver', and in sun a low-growing
artemisia like *A. schmidtiana* 'Nana' or the feathery *Chrysanthemum
haradjanii*, sometimes known as *Tanacetum densum amanum*.

Bronze foliage is closely allied to purple and has similar garden
uses, but its particular forte is among orange and creamy yellow
flowers, where really brown shadows are required. Some bronze
foliage is very dark but some is so pale as to be almost tan. This is
the colour of *Acaena* 'Copper Carpet' ('Kupferteppich'), a prostrate sun-lover which finds its way into every area of border
containing orange. It spreads rapidly like most of its relatives so it
must not be sited next to timid plants. In summer it covers itself in
copper-coloured burrs as an apology for flowers and these harmonize well with the leaves. It is especially effective with lime-
green alchemilla and apricot violas, and also with the bronze-
leaved sedge *Carex buchanani*. This sedge is the perfect candidate
for desert schemes which need a short wiry accent, for it only
grows 2 feet tall and keeps in a tight clump. Visitors to your
garden generally assume it is one of the casualties of the previous
winter but if they looked closely they would see the cheery glow of
life in the orange bases of the brown stalks.

51

Trifolium repens 'Purpurascens' is, I suspect, another comparatively recent introduction to gardens. It is a typical creeping clover, but its green leaves are blotched with chocolate. It has a definite preference for full sun where it will meander through blood-red violas to great effect, and it is also a suitable ingredient for growing in the cracks between paving stones, upon which you set pots of scarlet pelargoniums or apricot mimulus. It spreads rapidly, rooting as it goes.

But perhaps the most dramatic bronze foliage plant is the bronze fennel, *Foeniculum vulgare purpureum*. This comes very easily from seed and in a very short time you have fountains of misty foliage, 6 feet tall, which carries the typical pungent smell of aniseed. If you do not want your plants to flower you can keep cutting them down: otherwise they will bear lacy umbels of mustard yellow. Its feathery foliage makes it an indispensable plant for contrasting with large and solid leaves, while its colour is a marvellous antidote to the fiery oranges and yellows.

Purple and purplish-brown foliage combine attractively with the various blues, the powdery blues and ultramarines of flowers and the glaucous silvery blues of leaves, and if you wish your border to change gear from the warmer to the cooler tones such associations are delicate ways of achieving it; as deep purple gradually gave way to clear blue among the foliage, so among the flowers the buttery harvest yellows could fade imperceptibly to moonlight white.

Like purple and bronze foliage, blue foliage is essentially sun-loving, and no matter how tempting it may be to have its glowing shapes in the murky shadows of walls and trees, your plants will seldom achieve the same degree of blueness as those bathing in full sun. Blue leaves enhance most flower colours, contrasting superbly with the strong reds, yellows and burning oranges and gently harmonizing with the pinks, violets, mauves and whites, so it is a great shame that there are so few blue-leaved plants in cultivation.

There are only two large shrubs to interest us, and one of those is really a tree. The charm of *Eucalyptus gunnii* is in its round, succulent, blue-grey leaves which unfortunately only appear on juvenile plants. To keep your plants young, you need to cut them down in late autumn, after which they will clothe themselves in blue and form eye-catching shrubs 6 feet high. If that sounds too easy to be true, you are right. The problem is that the eucalyptus is not completely hardy and in a severe winter will be killed outright or given such a shock that only a few stems will tentatively surface in the spring. Nevertheless, it is worth a gamble, and because this plant is easily grown from seed, it need not be an expensive one.

You will find *Berberis temolaica* extremely hard to locate because it is a menace to propagate. But it is one of the most attractive of all shrubs, making a glaucous blue dome 10 feet high, bearing lemon-yellow flowers in early summer and red oval berries in autumn. It is hardy, and can be grown in sun or part shade. I have seen it surrounded by yellow, orange and red flowers to great effect and there is a notable association in John Treasure's garden in Worcestershire where the deep purple *Clematis* 'Etoile Violette' is trained through its upright branches, making a delicate pattern of summer shadows.

The dwarf *Hebe pinguifolia* 'Pagei' makes dense, 'evergreen', weed-resistant carpets of greyish-blue under almost any conditions and is covered in short spikes of white flowers in late spring. Because of these virtues, it has been adopted and misused by many of our municipal authorities who include it in the dingiest and most unimaginative plantings. But give it a bit of sunlight and a shrubby partner such as a yellow potentilla and it will look superb.

A plump mound of *Melianthus major* looks decidedly exotic and makes an attractive ingredient for warm, tropical schemes, its cool blue-green pinnate leaves being particularly striking with blazing orange. It seems to be hardy once established, although it still appreciates a thick winter overcoat of bracken; in the coldest areas it would be advisable to take cuttings in late summer. It normally grows to between 3 and 4 feet before being cut down by frost. It is a delicious foil for damson-red *Cosmos atrosanguineus*.

Most of the acaenas have bluish ferny foliage and can make effective ground-cover. The largest, *A. magellanica*, is also the most spectacular with long inquisitive stems of pinnate leaves which penetrate all their neighbours up to a height of 2 feet. There are many smaller species but 'Blue Haze' with very fine purplish-blue leaves and *A. caesiiglauca* with greyer and more rounded foliage are probably the best known. All are worthy of extensive use in border and rockery, and the smaller ones delight in colonizing the cracks in paving or the risers in steps. They will tolerate sun or shade.

We are always looking for spiky-leaved plants to provide contrast in form, and more often than not it is members of the grass family which are pressed into service. *Festuca glauca* is the most common blue variety, forming small clumps of erect leaves, which keep their colour well into the winter. It needs to be divided every spring for the strongest hue to appear, and replanted in groups. Connoisseurs prefer the larger and bluer *Helictotrichon sempervirens* (syn. *Avena candida*), which is more of a steel blue in colour and more spiky in shape. The tallest blue grass, at 3 feet, is *Elymus arenarius*. Its leaves are broader than those of the others and it does not confine itself to a hummock, preferring to explore underground. It was one of Gertrude Jekyll's faithful standbys. All three species need positions in full sun and starved soil to bring out their finest blue, and this can be made to look even more intense by putting them next to something very silver such as lamb's lugs or the furry rosettes of *Salvia argentea*.

Some of the bluest effects in the border are provided by the hostas, particularly *H. sieboldiana* 'Elegans' whose glaucous leaves can be a foot across. This form is infinitely preferable to *H. sieboldiana* itself, although it is a little slower to establish itself. The flower spikes, which appear in summer, are the palest lilac, almost white, and look well against the blue-green foliage. *H.* × *tardiana*, which has narrow pointed leaves is smaller and even bluer (the variety to choose is 'Halcyon'), but you need to have several plants to make an impact. Both these will flourish in sun or part shade but be vigilant in guarding them against the depredations of slugs, who will leave your plants looking like a stack of Emmental cheese.

How the cottage garden would suffer if denied the presence of the blue rue, *Ruta graveolens* 'Jackman's Blue'. All through the year (apart from just after its annual tidy-up in spring) it is a compact mound of steel-blue rounded leaflets, pungently scented of orange, and in midsummer it produces heads of greenish-yellow flowers which, although unspectacular, complement the foliage well. It needs sun but is otherwise easy to please and has an infinite number of uses in associations involving orange and yellow, purple and pink or blue and white. It is also very easy to propagate by softwood cuttings in late summer.

You will rarely go wrong when placing blue foliage. It is not as cold and stark as silver or grey, which needs to be positioned as thoughtfully as purple, so it lends itself for use in both warm and cool schemes. It combines well with gold, silver and purple foliage, and do not overlook its role as a contrast with fresh green. I am thinking of that classic cottage garden association of blue rue with the lady's mantle, *Alchemilla mollis*.

Silver foliage plants are the most popular of all, and there is one well-known nursery that sells nothing else: Ramparts Nursery (Bakers Lane, Colchester, Essex). No small part of their rise to fame is due to the work of Mrs Desmond Underwood who experimented tirelessly with her subjects, testing their constitutions and their manners and eventually producing a treatise on them called *Grey and Silver Plants*, which is unfortunately now out of print. All of the silvers are sun-lovers and most require sharp drainage.

One of the more impressive is the weeping silver pear, *Pyrus salicifolia* 'Pendula', which is such a feature of the White Garden at Sissinghurst, sheltering the statue of a Vestal Virgin. It will make a silver waterfall of willowy leaves which can rise to over 20 feet, adorned in spring with typical pear-like bunches of white blossom. The branches are often wild and wavy and may need encouragement to grow downwards in early years by being attached to the ground. I grow pale lilac *Campanula persicifolia* at the base of mine, followed by mauve colchicums and the combinations work well. I would like to train a purple clematis to peep through its branches, or even one of those bright magenta varieties which are so difficult to place.

The Jerusalem sage, *Phlomis fruticosa*, makes a sprawling evergreen shrub, 5 feet tall, and in early summer is covered in whorls of clawlike flowers the colour of English mustard. Unfortunately, it is not as silvery as one would like, being more often just a dirty grey-green, and it is often better to plump for its cousin *P. chrysophylla*, which is whiter and narrower in leaf and has a more golden flower. My plant hardly ever flowers and so remains respectable throughout the summer when its cousin is looking rather bedraggled. Both shrubs need to be given a sheltered spot or they may surprise you by not coming through the winter.

If my garden was damper (and a lot larger) I would grow a forest of willows. There is an enormous range of these trees and shrubs, many of which are as valuable as foliage plants as for their spring catkins. Most will thrive perfectly well in ordinary garden soil, and a number are quite dwarf enough for inclusion in rock gardens or at the front of the border. I am always admiring the

woolly willow, *Salix lanata*, which has round silky leaves and erect
woolly catkins. It only grows to about 4 feet and although it
requires full sun, it prefers the soil to be cool and moist. There is a
related willow called 'Stuartii' which is a little smaller and has
larger catkins. *S. repens argentea* is smaller again, being semi-pros-
trate, and has leaves which are heart-shaped and silky grey. My
favourite silver willow is *S. helvetica* which forms a small dense
shrub clothed in narrow, soft grey leaves, and whose catkins appear
with the young foliage in spring. All these willows are particularly
suitable for inclusion in early schemes of green and yellow, colours
which echo the shades of their catkins and allow the fresh greys
and blues of their leaves to glow unopposed.

The best small silver shrub is undoubtedly *Santolina neapolitana*.
It makes a hummock of feathery foliage 2 feet high which is
exceptionally pale and silvery, and in July bears button-like
flowers of bright creamy lemon. This is as subtle a combination as
one could imagine and I keep meaning to reproduce it elsewhere:
cream tulips rising from mats of *Stachys lanata*; pale yellow violas
among *Helichrysum petiolatum*; lemon evening primroses behind
Artemisia arborescens; the list is endless. But santolina would be
grown for its leaves alone, since finely cut silver foliage capable of
surviving an English winter is something to be treasured. The
plants need to be pruned in spring to retain their shape, and I
usually replace mine altogether every third year with young plants
raised from summer cuttings. I much prefer this species to the
ordinary lavender cotton, *S. chamaecyparissus*, with its mustard
flowers.

So many people have got an old plant of *Senecio* 'Sunshine' once
known as *S. laxifolius* or *S. greyi* somewhere in their garden, an
untidy sprawling shrub with grey-green leaves and corymbs of
scruffy yellow daisies in summer. If they cut it back in spring,
preventing it from flowering in the process, and removed some of
the overhanging branches above it, they would be surprised to find
they owned quite a different plant which formed a compact mound
of bright silver, lasting right through the winter, and was a very
imposing addition to their silver schemes. There are several other
good senecios. *S. cineraria* 'White Diamond' is the whitest of all with
large, deeply cut leaves and the usual yellow daisies. Two plants
out of five survived the ferocious winter of 1981–2 unprotected in
my clay soil, so it is fairly tough. The variety 'Ramparts' is
very lacy and supposed to be equally hardy, but if I grew it I

would play safe by taking autumn cuttings. Then there is the tender *S. vira-vira* (syn. *S. leucostachys*), which has very finely cut white foliage and the useful habit of linking arms with its neighbours in the manner of helichrysum, making it an indispensable part of summer bedding. Again, autumn cuttings will ensure that you retain a population.

Members of the genus *Artemisia* will provide the nucleus for most silver foliage schemes, as they give a brightness and filigree texture unsurpassed by any other plants. They have a reputation for having a delicate constitution but this is only true of a small number; most will survive very low temperatures providing they are given sharp drainage and full sun. The only species I lost in the 1981–2 winter was *A. canescens*, and I am sure I was to blame.

A. absinthium 'Lambrook Silver', named after Margery Fish's home in Somerset where it first appeared, is a sub-shrub, growing to about 18 inches tall. Its very finely cut bright silver leaves appear to cascade down the plant, and it carries yellow mimosa-like flowers in July. It is completely hardy, even on clay soil. Unfortunately, the same is not true of *A. arborescens*, the most attractive of all silver plants, whose filigree foliage has a silvery sheen which makes it shimmer in sunlight. It needs perfect drainage and is not capable of standing much frost either. Luckily, there is a hardy variety 'Powis Castle' which is more compact and less prone to flower. Mine is clipped in April to form a spreading plant 2 feet high and 5 feet across and it makes one of the most telling effects in the garden. I have grouped the double red helianthemum 'Mrs Earle' in front and weaving through it is the herbaceous potentilla *P. atrosanguinea*. The artemisia is so light and silvery that the deep reds glow like rubies.

A. canescens rarely reaches more than a foot in height and sprawls around with its long woody shoots clothed in curly, wiry leaves. Mrs Underwood likened it to an aluminium pot scourer. With such a bizarre appearance, it is a problem to find suitable companions for it, and it is perhaps best used as a spot feature on the corners of borders, where it will provide contrast for more conventional foliage. *A. ludoviciana latifolia* looks more like a senecio than an artemisia. It is an invasive and floppy perennial with broad, white, deeply cut leaves and plumes of nondescript silvery flowers. The plant is presentable only when it carries its young upright growth, so it is a good idea to cut it down in midsummer and wait for another crop. Alternatively, you could grow it in a patch of wild garden where it will be seen at a distance and can luxuriate to its heart's content. It disappears completely in winter. Another hibernator is *A. nutans* which has delightfully lacy leaves on thin erect stems thrown up from the ground. Unusually, it revels in clay soil and creeps about underground, sending up new 18-inch shoots between its neighbours and decorating everything in a cloud of grey-green. Both these artemisias are completely hardy.

Anaphalis triplinervis is another of the valuable silver flowering plants, making a neat clump of silver white leaves which is covered with pearl-white everlasting flowers from September onwards. It will tolerate clay soil and some shade. My group grows among the billowy green *Euphorbia cyparissias* at the top of a flight of steps, making a contrast of colour and texture which lasts for months, but its uses are legion in the late summer border.

I often wonder why one does not see *Ballota pseudodictamnus* planted more frequently. Perhaps its name frightens people away. I made its acquaintance several years ago since when we have become firm friends. Its appearance is unique, its rosettes of rounded white leaves and its upright stems being clothed in wool, which is soft and irresistible to touch. Young plants quickly turn into dense sub-shrubs 2 feet high and whenever they begin to look scruffy, which they will do after flowering (tiny mauve flowers on whorls of pale green bracts), they can be cut down and new growth will begin at once. You can plant them with abandon among pink, purple, white and blue and they will make your schemes permanently bright and lively; alternatively, for a simple contrast in foliage, they look dazzling in front of something grey-green, such as southernwood, *Artemisia abrotanum*. Cuttings taken in summer and put in an electric propagator root faster than anything else I know, so you can be generous in spreading them about the garden.

From an angel to a devil. Beware of *Cerastium tomentosum*. As it sits in its pot on the nursery bench, it looks like the remedy for every dreary rockery: evergreen ground-cover of bright silver; sheets of white flowers in June; impenetrable by weeds. Perfect. In it goes and you retire smugly to your drawing-room for a large gin and tonic. That will be your last restful evening. The cerastium, having settled in nicely in its new home, is now getting down to business. 'A carpet of silver, you said you wanted, and a carpet you are going to get,' it scoffs, and begins smothering everything in sight. It chokes your alpine treasures and does battle with its

perennial peers, murdering or maiming all in its path. Not content
with that it decides to seed itself as well, scattering its progeny far
and wide to wreak havoc in greener pastures. The day will come
when you must prove you are man not mouse, take it forcibly by
the throat and rip it from the ground. Wondering what to replace
it with, you may like to know it has a mild-mannered relative *C.t.
columnae* with none of its cousin's vices; more likely, you will
decide to leave the whole family well alone.

The silver foliage plant with the largest leaves is the cardoon,
Cynara cardunculus. They are often 5 feet long and are broad and
heavily toothed to boot. The whole plant will grow 8 feet tall, but
if you remove the flowering spikes as they appear you can keep it
to a 5 foot mound of arching silver foliage. If grown from seed, the
young plants will need protection their first winter but thereafter
will prove quite hardy. This is one of the most spectacular foliage
plants and well worth a place at the back of the border.

Helichrysum petiolatum is one of those indispensable bedding plants
which can be used to fill gaps in the border from late May onwards,
and looks as if it has been there forever. It sends out long searching
shoots of small heart-shaped grey leaves which weave their way
sideways into neighbours, upwards into shrubs or even downwards
from pots or hanging baskets, but always quite harmlessly as the
shoots are firm and woody. It is not at all hardy and cuttings
taken in the autumn should be overwintered in a frost-free
greenhouse. Helichrysum is a wonderful partner for pelargoniums,
easily coping with the harsh pinks and scarlets as well as the
salmons and peaches. Once you have acquired it, you will wonder
how you ever managed before.

The tallest of the silver border plants is the cotton thistle, *Onopordon acanthium*, which can reach 8 feet with six months' growth.
The silver-white leaves are woolly and extremely prickly but they
are a great ornament until the end of July when the purple
flowerheads begin to appear. The plant then rapidly becomes
unsightly and needs to be pulled out and discarded. New plants
are raised from seed in June and transferred to the border in the
autumn to perform the following year. If you have a suitable
space and do not mind a gap in the latter part of the year, they
are worth growing, since they have an architectural quality which
few plants can rival. A dark yew hedge at their back and a sea of
silver and grey at their feet and they will not let you down.

The lamb's lugs, *Stachys lanata*, is one of the best-loved cottage garden plants. Its close mats of silver-white woolly leaves make the perfect edging for sunny schemes of pink, white, violet and blue and a shimmering underplanting for wine-crimson roses. It tends to sprawl about untidily in July when its stems reach out to display their pink flowers, but I find this eruption of arms quite appealing – set against a deep purple cotinus, they shine like beacons. This does mean, however, that it is not suitable for planting beside a lawn and in such positions you would do better to choose the non-flowering variety 'Silver Carpet'. During spells of wet weather plants are apt to dissolve into soggy heaps but they soon recover.

Silver foliage is at its most seductive in the twilight garden, among the black-greens of yew, the ghostly whites of delphiniums and lilies, tobacco flowers and yuccas and the moonlight yellows of oenotheras, kniphofias and potentillas. It is also an obvious companion for the pink and purple flowers of summer, many of which, such as dianthus and lavender, have silver leaves themselves, and a lively contrast for some of the oranges, reds and yellows (silver-leafed plants with flowers from this side of the spectrum include gazanias, senecios, helianthemums, horned poppies and verbascums).

Because silver foliage is always a source of brightness in the border, it has a tendency, as does white, to dilute the impact of schemes of which it is not the dominant member. The eye is carried to a source of light first and then sees other colours in relation to it. In practice this may not cause you any problems for if you have a small garden you will probably have only one area sunny enough to grow silver plants. But if you have plenty of options, I would suggest that you allow your silvers to take charge of one or two schemes and exclude them from everywhere else.

Since we are already in the realms of silver, let us now look at some of the silver-variegated foliage plants, which have a similar effect of bringing light to colour schemes, though in a subtler, more diffuse way. Their especial value is that they will tolerate shade, enabling us to illuminate areas which were previously overcast and gloomy.

Most gardeners grow dogwoods for their winter stem colours but several have striking variegated leaves. *Cornus alba* 'Elegantissima' (syn. *C.a.* 'Sibirica Variegata'), which has leaves painted with broad white margins and stems of thrilling scarlet, and the more vigorous *C.a.* 'Variegata', whose leaves are grey-green with a narrow margin of cream, are the most common. They need some darkness to glow effectively but they must be sited so that they can be reached by the winter sun, without which their branches will fail to ignite. For the best stem colour they must be hard pruned in early spring.

The aristocrats of the genus are *C. alternifolia* 'Argentea', whose branches grow out horizontally, forming tiers of foliage like a cake-stand – I saw a perfect specimen growing beside the lake at Pusey House in Oxfordshire, where its delicate, almost skeletal form was silhouetted against the murky green of the water – and *C. controversa* 'Variegata', which is also tiered but with coarser leaves, larger and more heavily splashed with cream. Both are, alas, expensive and difficult to obtain.

Variegated euonymus is often the answer for those dingy, north-facing beds, backed by dusty ivies and emaciated privet. *E. fortunei* 'Silver Queen' is the short form, at around 3 feet, though it often decides to climb up walls in a gingerly fashion; *E.f.* 'Variegatus' is more vigorous. I must confess that I cannot summon up much enthusiasm for these shrubs and were it not for their bright ever-green appearance and their tolerance of the most miserable sites, they would not find refuge in my garden.

More variegated wall cover is offered by the ivies. *Hedera helix* 'Glacier' is one of the most distinguished of the silvers. Its leaves are small and glaucous grey with a narrow white margin; planted against a shady wall, it will make a modest 4 or 5 feet. Quite similar but even less vigorous are the cultivars 'Marginata Ele-gantissima' and 'Silver Queen', which have a more marked creamy margin which turns rose-pink in winter. I have these ivies along a wintry stretch of border behind groups of shiny green sarcococcas, which fill the frosty air with their honey scent. It is important to remember when placing ivies that it is in the cold bare months that they will be most appreciated, for there are far more exciting things to look at in summer.

We have become so used to seeing the privet in its suburban role as a neat hedge that we have forgotten what a marvellous shrub it is when left to its own devices: wild and wavy branches weighed down with scented white blossom; fast-growing and virtually evergreen; tolerant of nearly all aspects and soils. Given all that and silver variegation as well, why is *Ligustrum ovalifolium* 'Argenteum' not found in every garden? I gather there is a variety called *L. sinense* 'Variegatum' with leaves grey-green and white but I am not sure that I have met it.

There is a beautiful variegated mock-orange, *Philadelphus coronarius* 'Variegatus', whose light green leaves have a striking cream margin. The flowers, produced in summer, do not disappoint either, being white and richly fragrant. All philadelphus tend to become rather untidy after flowering, so pruning can be undertaken in August.

I battle with *Rhamnus alaternus* 'Argenteovariegata' because it is one of the most attractive of all variegated shrubs, but it is not reliably hardy here in North Wales even with wall protection and in a severe winter we can be sure of losing it. Fortunately, it roots easily from summer cuttings so you can always keep a plant in reserve. Its leaves are small, dark green, with grey patches merging into a wavy cream margin, and are unusual because the veins protrude on the upper surface rather than the underside. It prefers a shady position, and the largest specimen I have ever seen, at Denmans in Sussex, nestles at the junction of two shady walls, where it has reached 10 feet in height.

Weigela florida 'Variegata' is another of the variegated plants which produces a superb display of flowers to complement its foliage. They appear in May and are pale pink, tubular, and scented, and with the fresh green and white leaves make as sugary a picture as you can imagine. Planted at the centre of a pink and white scheme, it would be sensational, and it is eminently suitable for the border since it only grows 6 feet tall and forms a dense compact shrub.

In addition to the purple bugle, there is a fine variegated form, *Ajuga reptans* 'Variegata'. It is flatter and more ground-hugging than its relatives and its leaves are attractively splashed in green, grey and cream. It can be trusted in places where the others would be too rampant, and associates well with white dicentras whose pendant flowers and ferny foliage combine effectively with the bugle's stout leaves and erect, blue flower spikes which appear in May.

I cannot resist mentioning *Arum italicum* 'Pictum' although it has limited uses in colour schemes since it disappears underground from June until September. The dark green leaves are veined in white and are the shape of large arrow-heads, but they are replaced in summer by drumsticks of orange berries. It is really a shade-loving woodlander, and its leaves are the perfect foil for snowdrops. They also associate pleasantly with pulmonarias and plum-coloured hellebores.

Not far away from my colony of arums (or ara?) lives another woodlander which is guaranteed to raise a few eyebrows when shown to visitors. It is the variegated strawberry, *Fragaria vesca* 'Variegata', which makes good variegated ground-cover in shade. Apart from its cream-splashed leaves, it looks and behaves like any other self-respecting strawberry, sending out runners in the usual way and even bearing fruit. I have tried it in dry shade but it was not very successful, and seems to be much happier in a fairly retentive soil. It makes a lively contrast to the dark green sword-shaped leaves of the Gladwyn iris, *I. foetidissima*.

The best silver-variegated hosta is still *H. crispula* whose leaves are large and pointed with a broad margin of white. The flowers are pale lavender and appear in July. This is one of the shade-loving species, where it stands out importantly, bringing life to the dingiest of borders. *H. undulata* is another shade-lover, whose narrow twisted leaves have a broad cream centre and whose flowers are pale lilac. It needs to be planted in a generous group, for it is not an imposing plant. There is a variety, *H.u.* 'Univittata', which has straight, white-centred leaves.

From broad shields to slender spears. There are three excellent variegated irises. The most useful is *I. foetidissima* 'Variegata', the white-striped version of our native species. It thrives in deep shade and on the driest of soils, though it develops the lushest foliage in the more hospitable sites. Try it with variegated strawberries. Another evergreen iris is *I. japonica* 'Variegata' which has a wide creamy stripe down one side of its leaf fan and lilac flowers which appear in June. It is rather floppier than its cousins and seems to enjoy a little sunshine. More striking is *I. pallida* 'Argentea Variegata', whose glaucous green leaves are striped with white and held on upright fans, making it a very eye-catching subject for the front of a dry, sunny border. I have seen a pleasing association with electric-blue *Salvia patens* but all the whites, blues and pinks harmonize well.

Most of the deadnettles are too warlike to be unleashed on to the main border but they are indispensable in those dry shady places where you have failed with everything else. There are two large copper beech trees beside the main lawn in my garden, and the dusty sunless soil underneath their branches had clearly been the despair of the previous owners. We found remnants of

63

hypericum, phlox, paeonies, daylilies, campanulas and even monardas; only groups of male fern, *Dryopteris filix-mas*, had become established. We decided not to waste time and tears over this unpromising site, and turned to the deadnettles. The variety we selected was *Lamiastrum galeobdolon* 'Variegatum', the yellow archangel (at last I know why it is called this); now, several years later, there is a carpet of silvery leaves surmounted by spikes of lemon-yellow hooded flowers in spring. This plant spreads at an enormous rate, weaving its way into anything in its path in a most appealing manner.

The pink-, white- and magenta-flowered varieties of *Lamium maculatum* have a white flash down the centre of their leaves, but in the variety 'Beacon Silver' (with magenta flowers) and the variety 'White Nancy' (with white flowers) the central flash becomes silver and extends over the whole leaf, leaving just a margin of green. The leaves of all these forms of *L. maculatum* are small and soft, and the habit of the plants is to creep stealthily rather than sending out long shoots to cover great distances, as does *L. galeobdolon*. They also seed themselves about with gay abandon.

Miss Jekyll thought that the variegated applemint, *Mentha rotundifolia* 'Variegata', was one of the best underplantings for schemes of yellow and white. Its leaves are round and fresh lime green, splashed with white, and it grows about 12 inches tall. I have only just acquired it and have a propagator full of cuttings so that I can try out some associations next year. I fancy it grouped behind *Viola* 'Moonlight' and in front of some pale yellow *Aquilegia formosa* for an early scheme, and perhaps a later group with the stronger yellow of *Coreopsis verticillata* 'Grandiflora' and some white gypsophila.

There are a number of grassy plants with variegated leaves. Everyone is familiar with the ordinary gardener's garters, *Phalaris arundinacea* 'Picta', whose clean white-striped foliage is an arresting border feature from spring until autumn, but you may not know the equally dazzling *Glyceria maxima* 'Variegata' whose stripes are in Devon cream. This makes a splendid foil for blue- and yellow-flowered spring bulbs. It begins to look unsightly in July, its leaves turning brown and murky white, but if the stems are cut down it will reclothe itself in young growth. Both these grasses are extremely invasive and need to be divided every spring. It is important never to disturb grasses in the autumn if you want them to establish themselves quickly.

The aristocrats of the family are found in the genus *Miscanthus*. These do not share the territorial ambitions of their cousins and are content to make neat clumps of gracefully arching leaves. The finest silver form is *M. sinensis* 'Variegatus' which grows to around 5 feet in height, much the same size as phalaris. It is outstanding as a specimen plant, either as a focal point at the end of a border or as an apparition rising out of a misty carpet of violet and grey-blue.

Variegated plants seem to catch our attention in nurseries and garden centres as surely as they do in the garden and most keen gardeners rapidly build up sizeable collections of them. Absorbing them into the garden is not always easy. Some people, myself included, are unable to pass a dark evergreen without wishing to plant something variegated in front of it. As an individual scheme this is invariably successful, but when repeated all over the garden it becomes tiresome. Just like silver foliage, variegated foliage is distracting and we are generally better to use it boldly in a few carefully chosen places rather than scattering it about in a haphazard fashion. Remember also that variegation tends to look artificial and should be excluded from all those natural, wild green corners where you go to snooze away the cares of the world.

In the border, silver variegation harmonizes attractively with all the whites, pinks, salmons, mauves and violets; for schemes of oranges and yellows we will usually turn to the golden-variegated plants. The most striking colour for use with silver-striped leaves is scarlet: go and plant some *Lychnis chalcedonica* in front of your gardener's garters and you will see what I mean.

Let us now cross the treasury floor, and move from silver to gold. Immediately we can see and feel that we are dealing with a different medium. Gold is mysterious, warm and inviting, the colour of a hot summer's day, a log fire and a harvest moon. It can warm the cockles of your heart in the garden too. Unfortunately, there is not such a wide range of golden-leaved foliage plants as there is of silver, so our choice of good subjects is restricted; and, what is more, since golden foliage plants tend to dislike full sunlight, which scorches their leaves, we do not have great freedom in distributing them about the garden either. It is for these reasons that deep purple often takes its place in the hottest flame-coloured groups, the gardener having despaired of finding a golden backdrop.

There are some fine golden-leafed trees available including a maple, *Acer japonicum* 'Aureum', a honey locust, *Gleditsia triacanthos*

'Sunburst', and a false acacia, *Robinia pseudoacacia* 'Frisia', but if you are short of space you might like to grow the golden indian bean tree, *Catalpa bignonioides* 'Aurea', as a shrub by pruning it back each March. You are then rewarded with the most impressive foliage, huge, round and soft yellow, which will make a notable contribution to those tropical schemes you plan for high summer. Any good soil suits it and it will keep its colour in sun until the autumn. If you allow it to become an adult it will bear panicles of foxglove flowers in summer and long runner beans later.

Gertrude Jekyll used the golden privet, *Ligustrum ovalifolium* 'Aureum' in her main border at Munstead Wood with groups of rue, verbascum, meadowsweet and white everlasting pea in a scheme of yellow and white, but it is of course more commonly seen now as a hedge. Imagine it as a background to a fiery border of orange and red or highlighting a quieter one in shades of mauve and violet or white and blue. As a free-standing shrub it will grow very large and if you site it far enough away from a path, you will not notice that the golden-yellow leaves have a green centre. It is a cheery sight even in the depths of winter.

Another evergreen which can be grown as a hedge or specimen shrub is *Lonicera nitida* 'Baggessen's Gold'. The leaves are small, oval and bright gold but turn a greenish yellow in late summer, and it makes a squat bush, 4 or 5 feet high. It does not grow naturally into a neat dome but rather bulges here and there, which gives each plant a unique appearance; you can prune it into a rounded shape, when it would serve the same purpose as clipped box, giving formality to warm-coloured borders. I use it as a feature at the end of a yellow scheme and have planted the scarlet *Aquilegia canadensis* in front, a tempestuous scene for early summer.

Not only is there a silver-variegated form of *Philadelphus coronarius* but also a splendid golden-leaved one, 'Aureus'. It grows to the same size as 'Variegatus', about 6 feet, but its leaves are the brightest gold, and make a striking feature in semi-shade. I say semi-shade advisedly because it needs sunlight to dazzle you with its brilliance and yet the full strength of the sun will scorch its foliage. But its leaves are only half the story; in June there appear the most deliciously fragrant white flowers, and the white and yellow together make a very pleasing picture.

The golden elder, *Sambucus racemosa* 'Plumosa Aurea', is the most graceful and feminine of all the golden plants. Like all ladies of quality, she cannot bear much sun on her face and prefers it filtered through a light canopy of leaves; and then again she will take a little sun providing it is in the early morning or late afternoon, since a little is good for her complexion. She does not mind company provided it is in harmony with her costume which, needless to say, she is continually changing: copper in spring, bright yellow in summer, old gold in autumn. In summer she is prone to wearing jewellery, how much she cannot tell but it will definitely be rubies, huge sumptuous brooches of burning red. Her dress is always finely textured, lacy at the edges, and does not reach much below her knees. She may grow to 8 feet or more, and then again she may not.

I am not sure what to think of *Spiraea japonica* 'Goldflame' (syn. *S. × bumalda* 'Goldflame'). There is no doubt that its brilliant gold foliage is one of the most spectacular features in the spring garden, but trouble starts in early summer when the flowerheads begin to emerge. Their colour is the brightest carmine pink and this, in association with the burning gold, is perfectly hideous. It makes a reasonably compact shrub, about 3 feet tall, but do not ask me where to place it. Mine keeps moving every autumn, a nomadic misfit.

Of the two worthwhile golden climbers, the most vigorous is the golden hop, *Humulus lupulus* 'Aureus', which will drape an unsightly shed in a mantle of bright golden-yellow in a single season. The leaves are hoplike, large and coarsely toothed and the plant attaches itself by twining through the available support. This hop is truly herbaceous, disappearing below ground for the winter and producing fresh shoots the following spring. It is easily grown from seed. If you want to grow it in the border but feel it might be too powerful to risk with a shrub, you could always train it on to a tripod of stout posts wrapped in wire mesh, which it would rapidly conceal. Most positions suit it, but the leaves do not colour well in shade.

The other climber is an ivy, *Hedera helix* 'Buttercup'. It also needs sun to produce the richest yellow hue, but even then there is usually a trace of lime green in the leaf. It is one of the least vigorous of ivies, rarely reaching more than 5 feet in height. If you do not have a spare wall, remember that ivies make effective ground-cover among trees and shrubs; 'Buttercup' would associate well with some of the purple-leaved subjects as well as the dark green ones.

The queen of the golden-leaved perennials is a form of the

meadow sweet, *Filipendula ulmaria*. The variety 'Aurea' has the same delicately divided leaves as its parent, but its colour is bright golden-green. The flowers are unremarkable and their removal serves the dual purpose of encouraging the plant to produce fresh new growth and of preventing it from seeding. It prefers semi-shade and moist soil, when it will make a dense clump of foliage 2 feet high.

The yellow-leaved hosta, *H. fortunei* 'Aurea', turns from fresh lime-yellow to a disappointing green by midsummer, when its pale lilac flowers appear, which is a pity because the combination would be very pleasing. It is not a large hosta, reaching scarcely a foot in height, so you will need three or four for a lively spring picture. It will tolerate sun or shade.

A very eye-catching plant for the front of the border is the golden marjoram, *Origanum vulgare* 'Aureum'. It makes a compact mound of golden yellow leaves, 9 inches high, which remains bright for much of the summer, and in spring is startling. If you cut it back in summer you are rewarded with a repeat of the spectacle, and in the process lose the clashing pink flowers. It contrasts pleasantly with blue rue, and enjoys full sunlight and a well-drained soil.

Bowles's golden grass, *Milium effusum* 'Aureum', is also at its best in spring and looks well with the brick-red cowslip flowers of *Pulmonaria rubra*. It grows to a height of 18 inches and thrives in partial shade where it will seed itself around; this is very welcome for the clumps do not increase quickly. It is stunning in combination with bluebells and blood-red polyanthus.

There is a golden-leafed form of *Helichrysum petiolatum*, 'Aureum' (syn. 'Limelight'), whose leaves are a bright primrose-yellow. It can be used to fill all the gaps which appear in your warm-coloured schemes during the summer, where the silver forms would be out of place and looks especially brilliant beside bronze foliage such as that of *Acaena* 'Copper Carpet', bronze fennel or the coppery leaves of *Crocosmia* 'Solfatare'.

You may think that this is a feeble list of golden foliage plants but I have racked my brains to think of more to no avail. Of course there are others in existence, a weedy feverfew called *Chrysanthemum parthenium* 'Aureum', for example, and a dreary golden yew, *Taxus baccata* 'Aurea', but I would never choose to grow them. Perhaps it is just as well that we are not offered as great a range of golds as we are of silvers, for if we had an entirely free hand our gardens would soon resemble the heaped stall of a market jeweller, its metals flashing and glaring and blinding our eyes. Gold is a rich colour and is more digestible when balanced with plainer fare.

In the border it combines well with deep green, purple and bronze foliage, and helps to carry potent schemes from sunlight into shadow without losing any brilliance. The contrast with silver is for me rather abrupt but I do like associating it with silver variegation, perhaps as a background to violets and lavender blues or as the supporting foliage to a monocolour group of yellows.

To supplement the golds on our palette we have a choice of golden-variegated plants, though these are on the whole less striking, for the gold is often insufficiently distinct from the green to make a strong impression of colour. Another problem is that leaves mottled or suffused with gold tend to look diseased, since this is how green-leafed plants often react to unsuitable conditions. Consequently we ought to be more than usually particular about our selection.

One of the dogwoods makes a lively plant for the wilder part of a garden. It is *Cornus alba* 'Spaethii', which has its leaves edged with yellow. It is very vigorous and soon grows into a large shrub, so it will outgrow a position in the border unless you chop it down annually. If you are growing it for the winter beauty of its red stems, this will be what you are doing anyway.

The varieties of *Elaeagnus pungens* are unquestionably the best golden-variegated shrubs in cultivation. They are evergreen, vigorous and tolerant of nearly all positions and their colouring is bright and clearly defined. As a result you see them everywhere, and I should think in a hundred years' time the elaeagnus will be as despised as the spotted laurel is today. But do not let that dissuade you from planting it and giving it a good spot. It will grow to about 9 feet in quite a compact manner so it will not be out of place in a large border. Its leaves are dark green and leathery, and have a bright golden-yellow flash down their centre, which accords well with yellow-flowered plants. There is a variety 'Limelight' whose central flash is lemon yellow instead of gold. I have seen this elaeagnus effectively teamed with a blue ceanothus, though it needs no more exotic backdrop than a dark green hedge to dazzle you with its colour.

The golden-variegated holly, *Ilex* × *altaclarensis* 'Golden King', is similar in effect to elaeagnus. Its leaves are also shiny and smooth-edged, although the positions of the green and gold are reversed. I can imagine this shrub would be striking among scarlet reds, perhaps a stand of *Lychnis chalcedonica* in front and a strong red form of *Clematis viticella* threaded through its branches for a later display. The hedgehog holly, *I. aquifolium* 'Ferox Aurea' is a curiosity and worth including. It even has spines down the golden centres of its leaves. Mine is teamed with bronze fennel and the early yellow rose *R.* × *cantabrigiensis*.

The purple sage has a counterpart in green and gold called *Salvia officinalis* 'Icterina'. Just like its cousin it is a quiet border ingredient, harmonizing well with all the limes and yellowish greens, so does not have to be placed quite as deliberately as the more strident golds. A mound of it is pleasant behind *Alchemilla mollis* and in front of a generous clump of lemon-flowered *Hemerocallis flava*.

Hedera helix 'Goldheart' is my favourite ivy. Its leaves are usually quite small and have a yellow heart-shaped centre, which is sometimes bright gold and sometimes primrose. It colours well even on north walls and is moderately vigorous, reaching about 5 feet in height. For a winter picture it makes a striking backcloth for the dark green mahonias.

Another bright climber is the honeysuckle *Lonicera japonica* 'Aureo-reticulata', though its variegation is only apparent at close range. But we can overlook this fault because the leaves are so delicately pencilled in gold, following the veins on the upper surface, and the plant has the enchanting habit of threading its way harmlessly through its evergreen neighbours, displaying its diminutive shields to great advantage. The flowers are sparse and will probably pass unnoticed.

Mr Bowles has been busy with golden-striped grasses as well as with those of pure gold. *Carex stricta* 'Bowles's Golden' is slightly taller than a golden grass and has arching leaves lined with bright yellow. It prefers a damp position, being one of the pond sedges, but grows quite happily in full sun. Its brilliance is also lasting, so you can invent all sorts of spring and summer schemes around it. It is marvellous with *Astilbe* 'Fanal' and scarlet *Aquilegia canadensis*. A smaller grass for the front of the border is *C. morrowii* 'Aurea Variegata', which has the advantage of being evergreen. It forms a dense arching mound, about 9 inches high, which increases in size slowly but surely, and can be divided in spring. I have it on a right-angled corner in my main border, serving as a full stop to a line of purple bugle on one side and a drift of white willow herb, *Epilobium glabellum*, on the other.

For the aristocrats we must look again to the genus *Miscanthus* and to the bamboo family. The variety *M. sinensis* 'Zebrinus' is probably the most bizarre of all grasses. It is striped with gold, but the stripes do not run vertically with the vein of the leaves. They run horizontally in broad lines, about 6 inches apart, and need full sun to encourage them to appear. The plant is most graceful in form, rising upwards in erect fashion to about 5 feet and then curving over in all directions, making it a useful focal point to a yellow border.

An even brighter feature, but only 3 feet high, is the dwarf bamboo, *Arundinaria viridistriata*, whose leaves are often entirely golden yellow, but more usually streaked with lime green. It wants full sun to give of its best. I think this bamboo prefers the warmer south, but it seems to survive the winters in the Midlands without any trouble, and deserves a good spot. Gardens in sunnier climes will no doubt be tempted by the variegated phormiums to make their spiky incidents. *P. cookianum* 'Cream Delight' and *P. tenax* 'Yellow Wave' seem to be good varieties.

From the many golden-variegated hostas on the market I would select *H. fortunei* 'Aureomarginata', which has green leaves edged in pale yellow, *H. sieboldiana* 'Frances Williams', which has a lime-yellow margin to its glaucous blue leaves, and *H. ventricosa* 'Variegata', which has huge leaves and a luxurious golden edge. This last has purple flowers and the others lilac, though in 'Frances Williams' they are so pale as to be almost white. You might try associating them with some of the fiery crocosmias and daylilies, which will accord with their leaf colours but provide dramatic contrast in form.

They make a bold contrast with iris foliage as well. *Iris pseudacorus* 'Variegata' enjoys exactly the same moist conditions; indeed it is usually seen half-submerged in water at the edge of a pond. The upright, yellow-striped leaves turn green during the summer, alas, so they are only available for golden schemes early in the year. The golden-variegated form of *Iris pallida*, called 'Aureovariegata', however, holds its colour and will thrive at the front of any well-drained sunny border. Its flowers are lavender; those of *I. pseudacorus* 'Variegata' are yellow.

One of the deadnettles, *Lamium maculatum* 'Aureum', has a special role in shady schemes because it is variegated in gold and white and has no green at all. It is far less vigorous than its relations, and you will have to take cuttings if you want to cover an area quickly. Its mauve flowers are a disaster, and are best removed, if this is feasible.

Golden-variegated plants serve the same purpose as silver-variegated plants in that they enable us to devise schemes with brightly coloured foliage even in the deepest shade. A well-positioned group produces the illusion that sunlight is after all filtering down through the canopy and reaching the plants below, and it is worthwhile emphasizing this effect by adding pools of primrose and cream flowers. Of course, they also team up well with the white and blue shade-lovers, so there are endless pictures to paint.

There ought to be one or two areas in your garden where strong colour is entirely excluded and where there is an atmosphere of peace and a sense of silence. There may be a few pastel colours present, a few misty blues or creamy yellows, but the dominant colour will be green, the most restful of hues. It is here that the green foliage plants will come into their own, away from multi-coloured competition, and it is here that gardeners, rocking in their hammocks, will be able to give undivided attention to their shapes and structures.

We ask a lot more of the green foliage plants than of the gold and silver. Their colour alone is unremarkable; so they must have some additional quality of form or size or texture which gives them the ability to stand out even against a green background. Their leaves might be narrow, round, corpulent or skeletal, pinnate, dissected, minute or grotesque – anything which makes them strikingly different from their green brethren. Now there are a number of subjects which qualify for inclusion but which have been omitted from this list because the architecture of their leaves is more than matched by the beauty of their flowers. I am referring to such plants as the mahonias, the acanthus, the hellebores and the kniphofias. They will all be described in later chapters.

The delicate palmate foliage of the maples is always discernible, contrasting with the more solid leaves around them. Many species and varieties have green foliage, but two are exceptional. *Acer palmatum* 'Dissectum Viridis' is very similar to 'Dissectum Atropurpureum', having very firmly cut leaves which are displayed as a curtain of lace, but their colour is the brightest lime green. Although it will ultimately reach 10 feet in height, it is so slow growing that you will probably get away with treating it as a small shrub. It needs a position in semi-shade to avoid scorching, and looks magnificent at the top of a small bank, perhaps in association with a yellow-flowered berberis and drifts of blue forget-me-nots.

A. japonicum 'Vitifolium' is far more vigorous, and may eventually grow to over 40 feet, making it one of the largest Japanese maples. The leaves are broad, quite large, and not so deeply dissected and they take on the most brilliant autumn tints of scarlet, green and gold.

Strangely, people are still surprised when they see the false castor oil plant, *Fatsia japonica*, growing happily outdoors in northern gardens. But it is a tough old thing, coming through every winter without turning a hair, and making an imposing evergreen shrub, 7 or 8 feet tall. The huge leaves are dark, glossy and palmate and bring a tropical flavour to their surroundings. In more sheltered gardens this can be used to advantage by planting cordylines, agaves and even palms nearby, but you could still conjure up an exotic scheme in colder areas with yuccas and bamboos and summer bedding of cannas, melianthus and ricinus. The fatsia's flowers are also unusual, panicles of cream drumsticks held aloft which have the perfect foil in their smooth green backcloth.

Griselinia littoralis, as is its names suggests, is usually seen in coastal districts, but it is fairly hardy inland if given wall protection and a well-drained spot. The smooth oval leaves are a dazzling lime-green, and this colour is retained throughout the year, making a unique contribution to the winter garden. It will grow 10 feet tall in a favourable location, but will also respond well to pruning and makes a good seaside hedge.

There are two large-leaved, vigorous climbing plants which can be used to give body to wall plantings or to bring life to listless evergreens. One is the kiwi fruit, or Chinese gooseberry, *Actinidia chinensis*, whose huge heart-shaped leaves are dark green above and grey below, and covered in hairs. The flowers are pleasing too; they appear in summer, opening white but changing to buff. The fruits will need no description, having become a familiar constituent of fruit salads, but you will need a male and a female plant to obtain these. Actinidia grows rapidly to about 30 feet by twining through its support and prefers a position which is shaded for part of the day.

The other giant is a vine, *Vitis coignetiae*, which is even more vigorous, rapidly clambering to the tops of tall trees. Its leaves are also large and heart-shaped but the dark green upper surface is complemented beautifully by a rust-coloured undersurface which is very noticeable from below. It is in autumn that it will be most appreciated for it turns sumptuous shades of crimson and scarlet, making yew trees and hollies rival the maples in the intensity of their colour.

Some of the bamboos make splendid green specimen plants. *Arundinaria murieliae* (now called *Thamnocalamus spathaceus*) has small, fresh green leaves and narrow canes and grows to about 9 feet. I like to use it in tropical schemes with cannas and kniphofias or blue and white agapanthus. More dramatic is the Chilean bamboo, *Chusquea culeou*, which has proper stout canes and thick clusters of pencil-shaped leaves. Both create a misty, oriental atmosphere and if you site them beside a pond full of golden carp, you will need little more to complete the picture than a couple of dwarf maples, some moss-covered stones and perhaps a golden pheasant in the distance.

The old cottage garden favourite, the lady's mantle, *Alchemilla mollis*, does not need a description and is, I am sure, already established in the shady corners of your garden, but just in case I will say that its leaves are soft, round with a wavy edge, and are covered in tiny hairs which always seem to have just captured raindrops, even when it has not rained for days. It makes a thick clump of foliage 12 inches high, from which the clouds of tiny greenish-yellow flowers emerge during summer, and seeds itself with abandon: you will find its progeny all over the garden, especially in the cracks of paving or at the bottom of walls. The fresh green of the leaves harmonizes well with all the warmer colours and the solid compact form is always useful for setting against the feathery foliage of rue and fennel, as well as the slender leaves of iris and hemerocallis. It begins to look dishevelled in late summer and the flowerheads and old leaves can be removed to make way for the new growth.

I grow several other species of alchemilla, but the only other notable foliage plant is *A. conjuncta*, whose leaves are darker and more divided than *A. mollis* and have an undersurface of shiny silver which looks and feels like silk. It is also much smaller, rising to no more than 6 inches. It increases in a methodical way and does not seem to seed itself, making it a trustworthy subject for the rock garden.

The fresh green, mossy growth of chamomile, *Chamaemelum nobile* (syn. *Anthemis nobilis*), releases its fruity scent when rubbed and is an ideal ingredient for the cracks in paving stones. The daisy flowers are fragrant too, especially in the double form 'Plena', but for those who would make a chamomile lawn and keep their plants tidy there is a non-flowering variety called 'Treneague'. Plants are susceptible to heavy frost and in colder areas a covering of bracken is advisable, at least in their first winter.

Gertrude Jekyll was so fond of the bergenias (called megaseas in her day) that they became one of her trademarks. She liked to use them beside stone paths where their stout leathery leaves could conceal and soften the edges and provide a permanent architectural feature to contrast with the smooth surfaces. They remain the best plants for this purpose, but there is now a greater number of varieties from which to make a choice. *B. cordifolia* is probably the most common with its large leaves which turn the colour of ox-heart in winter, and its shocking magenta flowers; the variety 'Purpurea' has carmine flowers. *B. purpurascens* has even better leaves which are held in a more purposeful way and its reddish-purple flowers are carried on a taller, branching spike. But my favourite bergenia is the deciduous *B. ciliata*, whose flowers are far superior to those of its cousins. They are soft pink and carried above the dark hairy foliage rather like Beauty escaping from the Beast. All these varieties will thrive in sun or shade and can be underplanted with bulbs or associated with something which will flop over them, such as *Aster divaricatus* or *Clematis recta*.

The euphorbias number some of the most architectural of green foliage plants. The largest in general cultivation is *E. wulfenii* which, if persuaded to grow upright, will reach 6 feet. Left to its own devices, it will start to sprawl after 3 feet, stretching out in the most tortuous of shapes. The leaves are narrow and glaucous sea-green and they are arranged on the stems like one of those bristly tools you use to clean chimneys. The flowerheads are magnificent too, large domes of fresh lime-green in the most intricate design. It likes a well-drained position in sun or shade. *E. characias* is shorter and darker in leaf.

E. robbiae has an entirely different habit. It is small and compact, rising to $2\frac{1}{2}$ feet and is constructed of rosettes of dark green leaves which completely hide the stems. The flowers, which appear in early spring, are bright greenish-yellow and combine well with all the blue-, white- and yellow-flowered bulbs which are out at that time, but the heads are best removed in early summer before they turn an unpleasant brown. This species is rather rampant, but not sufficiently terrifying to be excluded from the border; it makes excellent ground cover for dry shade.

E. mellifera is one of the rarer euphorbias, appealing not only because of its foliage, which is a bright sea-green, but because its flowers breathe a powerful honey scent. It needs a sheltered position and plenty of sun, and will be cut to the ground by frost in most winters, forming a mound 3 feet high the following year. In mild areas it may be unharmed and grow up to 6 feet. It seeds itself, just like *E. wulfenii*.

To my shame, I do not grow many ferns. I think the main reason is that they are never at the front of my mind when I am ordering plants from the autumn catalogues. And yet every spring I regret my oversight as I watch the unfurling fronds of the male fern, *Dryopteris filix-mas*, which has seeded itself into one of our retaining walls. There is always something to entice you to examine them – the growing fronds, the rust-coloured spores, the smell of dry woodland in their foliage – and then, when they begin to wither in late autumn, they give you the material with which to protect the more tender plants in the garden. Wall shrubs wrapped in an overcoat of fronds or herbaceous subjects nestling under a blanket of them will usually emerge unscathed from the sharpest winter.

The broad, ribbed, fresh lettuce-green leaves of *Hosta plantaginea* 'Grandiflora' remain appetizing throughout the summer, standing out refreshingly against all the tired greens around them. But this is not the plant's only charm, for in September the clumps are surmounted by stems bearing crisp white trumpet flowers which exhale the sweetest perfume. If you removed the stem from its base, most people would attribute the flowers to a lily, so bewitching are they in appearance and fragrance. Unlike most hostas it revels in full sun and is an indispensable plant for the white garden.

I have already written about the variegated form of *Iris foetidissima*, but the type is a worthy plant itself, being evergreen and tolerant of all conditions from full sun to deep shade. It makes clumps of shiny, deep sword-shaped leaves which are covered with violet flowers in early summer, followed in autumn by large pods of orange berries which last through the winter. What more can you ask for? Scent. Well, if you break a leaf, the smell released is of roast beef (this is the standard descripton – some think it smells of old socks). There is a form called *I.f.* 'Citrina' which has pale yellow flowers and larger pods.

Lemon balm, *Melissa officinalis*, can become a menace in the garden unless its flowerheads are removed for they seed themselves wildly. It grows to around 3 feet and prefers a sunny, well-drained spot. The leaves are rather like those of a nettle, and are preferable in the golden and golden-spotted forms, 'Allgold' and 'Aurea'. The fragrance is that of a cheap lemon-scented soap, unrefined but overwhelmingly and sharply citrous; there is no attempt at the fine infusion distilled by such as oenothera or frangipani.

A wild corner devoted to the different mints would be a refreshing spot. It would have to be wild because mints are rather ungainly when in flower and have invasive roots. As well as the variegated applemint, we would have the common spearmint, *Mentha spicata*, the eau de Cologne mint, *M. piperita citrata*, the variegated ginger mint, *M.* × *gentilis* 'Variegata' (green with gold down its veins), Bowles's mint, *M. villosa* (the tallest mint), pennyroyal, *M. pulegium* (prostrate for most of the year), the white and black-stemmed peppermints, *M. piperita officinalis* and *M. p. piperita* and a carpet of *M. requienii* with its minute peppermint-scented leaves. All prefer a retentive soil and thrive in sun or part shade.

The ornamental rhubarb, *Rheum palmatum*, has its drawbacks but is a most impressive foliage plant for the back of the border or beside a stream or pool. Its leaves are large and deeply cut, red when they emerge in spring but changing to green in late adolescence, and the flowers which appear in early summer are borne on large panicles which rise 6 feet tall. Its drawbacks are that its foliage begins to collapse in late summer, leaving a gap in the border, and that it is apt to be feasted upon by slugs. The two best varieties are 'Atrosanguineum' and 'Bowles's Variety'.

Another plant which likes wet feet is *Rodgersia pinnata*. It only grows to about 2 feet and its large pinnate leaves are arranged in pairs. The erect feathery plumes of flowers are creamy white in the type and bright pink in the variety 'Superba'. They are produced in summer. *R. podophylla* is similar but slightly taller and has palmate leaves which are always tinged with bronze. Its flowers are also cream.

Tellima grandiflora 'Purpurea' should perhaps have featured at the beginning of this chapter but its round, hairy leaves are green for most of the year and only assume their liverish purple in winter, when they are an excellent foil for snowdrops. Plants make solid clumps in any shady site and lose their neatness only in May and June when a forest of long thin stems, bearing tiny greenish-yellow flowers, erupts from their midst; but you will be inclined to overlook this fault, for the flowers are sweetly and penetratingly scented, more than compensating for their unremarkable appearance.

Thymes can be pushed into the front row of borders to spill out over paths throughout the garden, so that everywhere we walk an aromatic cloud floats behind. All the species and varieties flower during the summer in various shades of pink, purple or white, so provided we keep them out of strong yellow and orange mid-summer schemes we can site them for their scented impact without too much thought about colour scheming. Their scents do vary dramatically. In the lemon thyme *Thymus* × *citriodorus*, and its less hardy variegated form 'Silver Queen', which bear mauve flowers, the fragrance is powerfully citrous; in *T. fragrantissimum*, also with mauve flowers, it is of oranges; in the dwarf, half-hardy *T. herba-barona*, with deep pink flowers, it is of caraway; and in *T. vulgaris*, its purplish-flowered, golden-leafed form 'Aureus', its lilac-flowered, silver-variegated form 'Variegatus' and its pale pink-flowered 'Silver Posie', it is more of a true thyme scent, shaded with a hint of balsam.

For our Chinese carpet, composed of different coloured prostrate varieties, we must look to the forms of *T. serpyllum*. The species itself, which has a true thyme scent, has flowers of lilac-pink; there is a white variety, *T.s. albus*; and there is a form with bronze foliage and deep purple flowers called 'Coccinea'. If you grow this thyme from seed you will obtain all sorts of colour variants to add to the scheme, and to vary the scented composition we could also include the lemon-scented 'Lemon Curd' and the fruit-scented 'Pink Chintz'. We could even weave in some prostrate creeping mint, *Mentha requienii*.

We have passed through the world of foliage plants at breakneck speed, and I hope that you have not been too irritated by the hasty glances at your favourite leaves. We have now completed all the preliminary groundwork. We have absorbed the essential principles of colour combination, we have probed the mysteries of scent, we have some idea of how we are going to arrange our plants and we have amassed a stock of coloured leaves. Let us now enter the romantic garden just as spring is drawing breath and linger there for a complete year recording the plants as they make their appearance, drawing them together into schemes and establishing the different moods of the changing seasons.

Promise of a Warming Air

There comes a day, sometime in late March, when you realize all of a sudden that spring has arrived. Slowly and imperceptibly the sun has been getting warmer, the hedgerow greener and the dawn chorus noisier. For the past three months you have been buried in rugs in front of a roaring fire, venturing outside only to collect essential provisions and, on the occasional crisp sunny days, to admire your groups of winter-flowering plants at closer quarters. But now, sleepily peering out of your bedroom window, you find that the world is awake once more and a new year has begun. The first daffodils have opened, the quinces are in flower, carpets of coloured primroses are unfurling in your shady borders and the air is heavy with the honey scent of mahonias.

You will also notice that a colour change has begun to take place. The whites, pinks, purples and browns which have dominated the garden for so long are now being challenged by brighter and sharper hues. The blues, reds and oranges are making their first appearance and the yellows are now really asserting themselves – every day more are revealed, and by the middle of April they will reign supreme. You will certainly want to emphasize this change in the colour groups that you plan for early spring by concentrating on those hues which are fresh and cheerful and bring warmth to the garden. Fortunately, there are plenty of excellent plants with which to fill your palette.

Corylopsis pauciflora is one of my favourite early spring shrubs. Its soft yellow cup-shaped flowers hang in tassels from its bare branches and smell sweetly of cowslips. It is not reliably hardy in cold areas so you may like to plump for its relative *C. spicata* which is rather more spreading and has flowers of a stronger yellow. Both shrubs grow slowly to about 6 feet and look superb when set in a pool of rich blue scillas and backed by a tangle of naked brown shrubs and tree trunks.

The Oregon grape, *Mahonia aquifolium*, is itself a worthless garden plant but the leaves of some of its offspring, notably 'Atropurpurea', colour well in winter and spring to coincide with their dense clusters of yellow flowers. Purple and yellow is an unusual combination for this time of year and is worth picking up by grouping plum-coloured hellebores and some clumps of strong yellow daffodils at its feet.

I intend to omit the rhododendron family from these short plant portraits at the risk of incurring your wrath. I do not grow any rhododendrons myself (well, I inherited two large plants but their days are numbered) and do not consider them comfortable occupants of the sort of cottagey romantic garden which I am trying to evoke. They belong properly in woodland, lurking as at Bodnant in North Wales or Crarae in Argyll on steep hillsides under a canopy of tall trees, with perhaps a torrential stony river somewhere below, where one can picture brilliantly coloured Himalayan pheasants and tragopans drinking at dusk. In the confined space of the average garden, among all the more re-strained border perennials and shrubs, their huge and heavy flower trusses, so spectacular in a grand and majestic setting, look outsized and vulgar, as awkward and disoriented as wild heather removed from its barren moorland home to take its place among the lush greens of meadow flowers.

So let us pass over the lemon-yellow *R. lutescens* and instead consider the best known of all the yellow-flowered spring shrubs, the forsythias. I do not know why people confine themselves to strong canary-yellow forms like *F.* × *intermedia* 'Spectabilis' and *F.* × *i.* 'Lynwood' when they could associate them with paler forms such as the primrose *F. suspensa*, its purple-branched clone 'Nymans', and the dwarf early-flowering *F. ovata*. Imagine a thicket of sharp and soft yellows against a clear blue sky, the entire group underplanted with blue and white anemones. The only disadvantage of massing forsythias like this is that you are left with a mound of coarse foliage for the rest of the year, though this could always be disguised by giving them a summer overcoat of vines or clematis.

At ground-level the wild primrose, *Primula vulgaris*, is already decorating the borders with mats of sulphur. Around trees, down grassy banks and under the skirts of deciduous shrubs it spreads, the very herald of early spring. Being such a simple and delicate flower it is easily overpowered by robust companions and needs to be kept on its own against soil or grass or grouped with other plants which have a similar character such as forget-me-nots and chionodoxas.

Certainly it should be kept away from its more flamboyant relatives which are appearing now. They come in every colour from midnight blue to china pink, from apricot to vermilion, and their arrival is for me the greatest excitement of the spring garden. They are all easily raised from seed so new strains can be tried out every year, the only danger being that your collection grows so fast that other plants are elbowed out. Barnhaven Nursery (Brigsteer, Kendal, Cumbria) stock a mouthwatering selection – strains of polyanthus called 'Harvest Yellows' and 'Rustic Reds', 'Spice Shades' and 'Violet Victorians'; strains of dainty *acaulis* primroses called 'Butterscotch' and 'Tartan Reds', 'Candy Pinks' and 'Coral Island'; dwarf *juliana* primroses in crimson, ivory and plum; double primroses in rose, apricot and bronze; and, most delicate of all, gold-laced polyanthus with deep crimson and black petals painted with gold and silver. There is a colour and a form for every spring scheme. They have to have a shady spot for the summer months but can be grown in full sun during the spring and moved afterwards. They enjoy this nomadic existence but if you do not have the time for such an operation, leave them in semi-shade and split the clumps now and again.

Narcissus bulbocodium is the first of the early daffodils to open in my garden. It does not have a conventional daffodil shape, its trumpet being like an old-fashioned ball dress and its petals short and pencil thin. Normally a lively golden-yellow, it does have a primrose-coloured relation, var. *citrinus*, and it is this which carpets the famous alpine meadow at Wisley. It is happiest in grass where its fragile-looking flowers glow above the rough green sward like giant buttercups. Following close on its heels are the *N. cyclamineus* daffodils; the species itself, tiny and bizarre, its petals totally reflexed which make the whole flower look like a Christmas cracker; and the hybrids, sturdy but exquisite, their heads slightly bowed and their petals floating behind their long trumpets. These last are the gems of the daffodil world, and the finest varieties are 'Dove Wings', with cream petals and sulphur trumpet, 'Jack

Snipe', similar but shorter, 'Charity May', a gentle bright-yellow, 'Peeping Tom', a strong golden yellow, and an outstanding white called 'Jenny' which I am growing among blue chionodoxa, silver-leaved deadnettle and large granite rocks on the slope above my rock garden. None is more than a foot in height and if you can somehow raise them so that they can be seen from below or at least nearer eye-level then so much the better.

The earliest large daffodils are the so-called trumpets, and there are some outstanding varieties among their ranks – rich golden-yellows like 'King Alfred' and 'Golden Harvest', yellow and white bicolours like 'Magnet' and 'Queen of Bicolours' and pure whites like 'Empress of Ireland' and 'Mount Hood'. Blended together in generous drifts they will provide the first waves of an ocean of yellow which in a few more weeks will have consumed your garden. Plant the strong yellows as deep troughs and the whites as foaming crests, the whole mass seething and swirling across the wilder parts of the garden and advancing into the borders, leaving land-locked shrubs and islands of brown earth. This is our main opportunity to produce a powerful image at this time of the year. Daffodils are reliable, cheap to buy and easy to please and, with careful management, they increase readily.

Grass is the ideal environment for most of them, giving them the perfect foil when in flower and a good hiding-place for their dying leaves afterwards, but it must be left uncut for six weeks after the flowers have finished so you have to choose your areas thoughtfully. Drifts will look more natural if the bulbs are grouped quite densely in one place and thinly elsewhere, as if they have seeded themselves away from the main company; and each drift should flow into the next at its least congested point so that the two varieties can mingle gently. Do avoid the temptation to buy mixed collections of bulbs or to cram too many sorts into a small space; the results are always disappointing.

Unless you have an orchard attached to your garden, you will never find enough rough places to grow all the daffodils that inspire you and you will have to admit them into your mixed borders. Many of the small forms look better here anyway in company with tulips and grape hyacinths. The important point to consider when placing them is how their foliage is going to be concealed after flowering. If they are concentrated towards the back of the border around shrubs and between tall perennials (these are not tall now, of course) then there will probably be enough greenery between you and them by early summer to allow them to collapse in peace. But if you want to have them nearer the front of the border, you have to devise proper partnerships with perennials. Gertrude Jekyll favoured ferns as companions for these are only beginning to unfurl in early spring but there are other contenders such as hostas, daylilies, paeonies and ornamental grasses like phalaris and glyceria, which all grow up fairly rapidly in late spring and arch over near ground-level.

Tulips are not such a problem, since they do not form a tuft of long leaves. The first group to open in early April are the *T. fosteriana* hybrids. They offer an assortment of colours but the most exquisite are the three emperors, 'White Emperor' in cream, 'Orange Emperor' in pure orange and 'Red Emperor' in glistening scarlet. This last one is spectacular among dark greens or beside white daffodils and silver-variegated foliage, while the orange and white varieties in company with the clear yellow 'Candela' make a fine self-sufficient group, all being of similar form but slightly different heights. Gaudier flowers are provided by the *kaufmanniana* tulips which open a little later. These are the waterlily tulips, so called because they flower close to the ground and have large star-shaped blooms. Many have maroon stripes on their leaves as an additional attraction. 'Early Harvest' and 'Stresa' are patterned scarlet and yellow, 'Heart's Delight' carmine and white and 'Shakespeare' salmon and orange. For those people who, like me, find these hybrids a little vulgar there is a gem called 'Franz Lehar' in purest sulphur. Float this in a pool of blue muscari, half close your eyes and you will be transported to Monet's garden at Giverny where from wisteria-draped bridges you look down on cushions of pale yellow water-lilies scattered carelessly across the quiet waters of the River Epte.

The single early tulips also begin to open in the first week of April. Like the *fosteriana* hybrids they are shorter than the May-flowering strains but share their aristocratic bearing. 'Bellona' is a lively yellow and 'Diana' a good pure-white, 'Princess Irene' a strong orange painted with deep red feathers and 'General de Wet' a superb golden-orange, but my favourite is 'Couleur Cardinal' in 'blood-shot crimson' which is often the centrepiece of the Cottage Garden at Sissinghurst at this time of year. They are all ideal bulbs for the front of your mixed borders where, associated with forget-me-nots or grouped with other tulips, they contribute large splashes of colour without occupying too much space.

Tulips are especially valuable because they bring such quantities of orange and red to the garden. These colours quickly warm up the borders after the long cold winter and are, of course, just the right companions for all the yellows and blues. Fortunately, there are some fine shrubs in this same colour range. *Berberis darwinii* explodes into a dome of brilliant orange in early April and although many think it overpowering, you will welcome its cheerful glow on dull days. Put it near your primrose forsythias and your cream and ice-green polyanthus. *B. × stenophylla* is more of an orange-yellow and is a little later to flower. Both species grow to over 6 feet but there are dwarf forms if space is a problem.

The ornamental quinces, formerly called japonicas, provide some more strong red. These popular shrubs can be grown either in the open or against walls and carry their clusters of cup-shaped flowers along the twiggy branches for months on end. The most commonly seen is *Chaenomeles × superba* 'Knap Hill Scarlet' which is a dazzling flame-red but you will not want to grow this if you have seen *C. speciosa* 'Sanguinea Plena', a deep crimson, or the dwarf *C.s.* 'Simonii', a true blood-red, which are quite sumptuous. They look superb among yellow daffodils but if you are tired of yellow groups try some white arabis, white tulips and pulmonarias and arrange the whole group around *Magnolia stellata*.

Photinia × fraseri does not have red flowers but its young leaves, glowing copper-red, rival anything in this part of the spectrum. The best clones are 'Birmingham' and 'Red Robin' although *Hillier's Manual of Trees and Shrubs* maintains the hardiest is 'Robusta'. This photinia is an evergreen shrub with smooth leathery leaves and grows to ten feet; all clones will need some protection in cold areas. *P. serrulata* is apparently a tougher species altogether and has identically coloured toothed leaves but I do not know it.

I like the idea of a red and green scheme for early April; both colours, in their less brilliant shades, belong more to the dignified palette of late summer and make a refreshing change from the brassy tones of spring. I have been saving some polyanthus for just such a scheme. They are the 'Garnet Cowichans' in shades of the blackest red. They have no eye to speak of in the centre of their velvet blooms and even their leaves are suffused with smoke. Another ingredient will be a patch of *Pulmonaria rubra*. The leaves of this lungwort have only the faintest trace of pale blotching, which is the main feature of the rest of the tribe, and are a dull grass-green, while the cowslip-like flowers are brick red.

Incidentally, pulmonaria is a useful ground-cover plant for any area which is not too dry, although it prefers shade.

I shall mass the polyanthus and pulmonaria underneath the photinia and interplant with paeonies – these are not in flower until early summer but their young foliage is a rich mahogany-red during April. A few stands of crimson tulips will bring some height to the front of the group and if the whole scheme looks too sombre I might introduce some cream primroses and ivory tulips; but since the idea is to have a corner which contrasts with the rest of the garden I would prefer to leave other colours out.

The predominant mood of the spring garden should be one of warmth and cheerfulness. Yellows, oranges and reds should be assembled in quantity and used boldly to make schemes which are rich and radiant. Now is not the time for painting in pastels. It is a time to enjoy the brilliance of colour after a winter of deprivation. Harmonies should be gorgeous and inspiring and contrasts sharp and striking. The role of the cooler colours, the blues, violets, pinks and whites, is to complement, flatter and enhance the qualities of those colours on the other side of the spectrum not to rival them. But even though the cool colours must play second fiddle, it is they which convey more clearly the feeling that another year is beginning. The crisp blues, the fresh whites and the tender pinks display in their delicate tones all the fragility and purity of new life, and there ought to be the occasional scheme in the spring garden which emphasizes this.

It is a pity that all the blue flowers of spring bloom at ground-level. How exciting it would be to have billowing clouds of ultramarine and cobalt floating above an orchard of golden daffodils. Instead we must be content with an assortment of small bulbs and perennials which can be used only as underplanting for larger plants or as companions for other dwarf plants; we have to rely on clear skies for effects on a grander scale.

Chionodoxa luciliae is the first of the bulbs to open. Commonly called the glory of the snow, it was this plant that Beverley Nichols colonized in his rock garden. The flowers are shaped like stars, bright blue with white centres, and open six inches above the ground. It flourishes in the poorest soil providing it gets some sun, and in my garden has spread rapidly along cracks in the paving stones, pushing its spearlike leaves up through aubretia and polygonum. *C.l.* 'Gigantea' (syn. *C. gigantea*) has larger flowers in pale violet-blue.

86

Anemone blanda 'Atrocaerulea' also opens in March but has a quite different apearance. The flowers are like large deep-blue daisies and the leaves are ferny. It thrives in sun or shade and I grow mine beneath a mat of grey *Hebe pinguifolia* 'Pagei' which makes a fine foil for the flowers. It is also a good plant for naturalizing in grass and under trees where it can be massed on its own or mixed with its white form 'White Splendour'. Even more beautiful is *A. apennina* which has larger flowers, sky-blue and starry, decorated with white hairs inside. This is a plant for semi-shade, perhaps in association with the snowdrop windflower, *A. sylvestris*, in pure white. Blue and white anemones make charming companions and I have seen them scattered among maroon hellebores and red paeony growth in a north-facing border where they looked magnificent.

The most electrifying blue is that of *Scilla sibirica*. The flowers nod like snowdrops on top of thin dark stems four inches above the ground, and are such a brilliant shade that they could pass for gentians. The variety 'Spring Beauty' (syn. 'Atrocaerulea') is more widely grown than the type because of its larger flowers and its more intense colouring; it is delicious with dwarf daffodils like 'Dove Wings' and 'Peeping Tom'. Scillas flourish in light shade as well as sun, so you can devise some ice-cold schemes with *Daphne mezereum* 'Alba' and white pulmonarias under silvery willows like *Salix exigua* and contrasting schemes with warmer hues in sunlight. You cannot have too much of this plant.

For a stouter blue carpet you can turn once more to the Barnhaven polyanthus and primroses, where colours range from Prussian blue to cornflower. I am not as fond of these as of the other strains because the contrast of strong blue petals with glowing golden centres is rather crude, but if you sow enough seed you will raise some good forms. I have just noticed that the catalogue lists a strain of blue cowichans, inky velvet with black eyes. I do not know how I could have overlooked this before, and will dispatch a late order.

All the purple-flowered plants of spring bloom at ground-level as well. *Corydalis solida* used to be one of the commonest but you do not see it so often today. It is a very worthwhile addition to the early spring garden and increases rapidly in shady corners. The long purple funnels are tinged with mauve and held in dense upright racemes above the grey-green foliage. It looks wonderful underneath pale pink cherries in association with pulmonarias, and silver-leaved deadnettles.

Two members of the primula family open in March. *P. denticulata* is a curious plant which supports its tight ball of flowers at the top of a long stem as if it is going to attempt a circus trick. Its normal colour is pale lavender-purple, a rare shade at this time of year, but you can obtain dark purple and white forms. It associates extremely well with its relative *P.* 'Wanda', a small primula in intense reddish-purple. 'Wanda's' is a difficult colour to place and it is never happy among yellows where *P. denticulata* excels.

The pulmonarias are some of the most valuable of garden plants and are found in every cottage garden, where they are relied upon to cure the most fearsome lung diseases. Even if you would rather put your faith in the National Health Service, you will not want to omit these plants from your borders. They are foliage plants par excellence; they are useful as ground cover; and they bear very attractive bell-shaped flowers like cowslips in early spring. *P. officinalis* is the most common. Its flowers open pink and fade to lilac blue and its leaves, broad and hairy, are dark green spotted with white. A superior species is *P. saccharata* whose flowers fade to a clearer blue and whose foliage is more heavily splashed in murky white. This latter species has produced some highly desirable offspring, notably *P.s.* 'Alba', the clear pink 'Pink Dawn', and the best variety for foliage, 'Margery Fish' (although I have seen this attributed to *P. vallarsae*), on which the silvery spots and splashes join up to cover almost the entire leaf. There are purer blue-flowered species and varieties but they tend to flower later in the spring and we will postpone meeting them for a while.

I cultivate over a dozen forms of this plant and the only problem I have encountered is that some are quite susceptible to mildew, but this is easily cured by spraying with a fungicide. They all enjoy rich soil and a shady position, and in return supply near-evergreen foliage at ground-level, suppress weeds and flower for months on end. What more do you want?

The pasque flower, *Pulsatilla vulgaris*, opens its first mauve-purple chalices in early April. At their base they are filled with golden stamens which contrast brightly with the petals and this association can be picked up by making a scheme of mauve and lilac aubretias and some dwarf yellow daffodils. Pulsatillas need well-drained soil and full sun to give of their best and are ideal in an open position in the rock garden among slate-grey boulders and gravel. Their ferny leaves and the silky silver hairs around the flowers are as attractive as the blooms themselves.

Sweet violets, like all the old-fashioned cottage plants, are enjoying a revival of interest at present and are beginning to appear in larger numbers on nurserymen's lists. A particularly good stock is maintained by Careby Manor Gardens (Careby, Stamford, Lincolnshire), who always exhibit at the early RHS shows at Vincent Square. Many people grow them under glass and bring potfuls into the house at flowering time – this is clearly the way to enjoy their fine perfume to the full – but of course they flower very happily outdoors, their blooms often opening in January and the displays reaching their peak in March. Some even flower sporadically during the summer, and most give a second burst in the autumn.

In rich retentive soil they are properly at home, and will send out runners in all directions from their tight clumps of heart-shaped leaves. There are single, semi-double and double-flowered plants to collect. Fine cultivars include, among the singles, 'Coeur d'Alsace' in rose pink, 'Norah Church' in deep blue, 'John Raddenbury' in clear blue, 'Princess of Wales' in violet-blue, and 'The Czar' and 'Governor Herrick' in pure violet; among the semi-doubles, 'Duchess of Sutherland', a violet-blue with a pink centre, and 'Mrs David Lloyd George', a blue with a golden centre; and among the doubles, 'Mrs J. J. Astor' in rose pink, 'Comte de Brazza' in white, and 'Marie-Louise' and 'Duchesse de Parme' in lilac. Mass them in mixed colours with primroses and pulmonarias.

Of all the horticultural events of spring, none is more evocative than or looked forward to with so much sentiment as the eruption of groves of cherry trees into blossom. The main flush of pink and white does not come until later in April and May but there are a number of varieties which flower now and whet our appetite. Among them is the queen of all cherries, *Prunus sargentii*. Its single pink flowers open at the end of March and when silhouetted against an azure sky and underplanted with chionodoxas there is no lovelier sight. Its leaves, which begin a glowing copper-red, catch fire in early autumn with orange and scarlet flames licking the burnished branches and making the tree the centrepiece of the garden once more.

P. subhirtella 'Autumnalis' has been bearing its blush-pink blossom intermittently since November and is now giving its final performance, but its numerous cousins are only just entering the stage. It is difficult to decide which is the most attractive. *P.s.* 'Ascendens' makes a small upright tree, clothed in pale pink in early spring and red and yellow in autumn; 'Rosea' is similar but more graceful in shape and its flowers are a brighter pink, though still pale and delicate; and 'Pendula Rubra' is shaped like a small weeping willow, showering its blossom like a rosy pink fountain on to plants growing beneath it. This last tree looks delightful near a pond or lake, its outline making an effective reflection throughout the year but quite breathtaking in April when its petals drip off the slippery twigs and for a fleeting moment cast a spell on the water.

Apart from all the cherries, there are almonds and plums to bewitch us. The common almond, *P. dulcis*, flowers at the beginning of April and is another favourite flowering tree. The type has bright pink flowers but there is a fine white variety, 'Alba', and a blush-pink one called 'Praecox' which blooms in early March.

I mentioned *P. cerasifera* 'Pissardii (syn. *P.c.* 'Atropurpurea') in the previous chapter as a valuable foliage plant but now it is displaying its creamy white flowers against its young purple foliage and makes a splendid foil for other pink and white flowers like tulips and daffodils and, even better, for lavender flowers like *Primula denticulata* and forms of *Anemone blanda*.

Perhaps the most common of pink-flowered shrubs which bloom in early spring is the flowering currant, *Ribes sanguineum*. Not everyone likes the raw colour of its rose-pink lanterns but they do hang elegantly from the tips of the branches and look well in schemes with white magnolias and pink and purple tulips. The clone called 'Albescens', in pale pink, will appeal more to the gentle gardener, perhaps incorporated into a scheme of bright blues and plum-coloured foliage. Both these currants are quite happy in shade and poor soil but do not neglect them too much because they respond well to a little feeding and pruning.

I have already included many perennials and bulbs with white and off-white flowers – daffodils, tulips, polyanthus, anemones and pulmonarias – which we can use in our colour schemes. To complement them there are very few white-flowered shrubs of quality. You will find some among the ornamental quinces, the flowering currants and the cherries and almonds. But the most exciting you will find among the magnolias. *M. stellata* rarely grows more than 6 feet tall, but with its untidy white flowers fluttering along its bare branches it becomes a focal point of the spring garden. It is the first of its genus to open, the wild petals breaking out of their furry cases towards the end of March and delicately scenting the air around them. Even though it appears so early it is not as liable to wind damage as its relations and you need not search around for a sheltered site. It does not really require flowering companions to enhance its beauty and looks stunning all alone among deciduous shrubs which are still half asleep. But if you want to build a scheme around it you can look to any part of the spectrum and plant away.

As April advances into its second week, all thoughts of winter are forgotten. From every part of the spectrum flowers are arriving. Day by day their numbers swell and for the first time the borders are beginning to look properly furnished. We can now indulge ourselves to the full. Our palette is varied and the treasure-chest of plants well stocked; the only limitation is our imagination. We still want a preponderance of sunny schemes to bring a sense of warm well-being to the garden and a scattering of schemes which celebrate the arrival of the clear fresh tones of a new year, but as the season progresses into summer our pictures gradually become more subtle and more ambitious.

Yellow and blue confirm their supremacy among spring colours during April and most schemes will centre on them. Many of the shrubs, perennials and bulbs which opened in late March maintain their display until early May and can be incorporated into all our spring schemes, but many more outstanding plants delay their appearance until April is well under way. Among yellow-flowered shrubs none is more popular than *Kerria japonica*. Every cottage garden has one, usually in its double-flowered form 'Flore Pleno', which makes a tall thicket of narrow green canes amply studded with scruffy golden buttons. Far more worthwhile is the variety 'Variegata', a shorter shrub with arching growth, single flowers and white-splashed leaves. I have it behind a row of purple bugle at present but rather fancy it among other dainty whites and yellows such as dicentras and corydalis.

At the end of the month the first of the shrubby potentillas begin their long display. They are without doubt one of the most valuable groups of shrubs for the small garden, tolerating almost any aspect and soil, growing in a dense compact manner and producing their simple single flowers intermittently until October.

Furthermore, they have quite unassuming characters and are perfectly content to step out of the limelight when other more refined plants decide to take the stage. As a consequence they can be planted all over the garden. I use them as punctuation marks down the path through my main borders and also in places where there is little in flower from July onwards. They are just the sort of plants which you could grow outside the kitchen window to give you a perpetually cheerful scene to look out on.

There are numerous varieties of potentilla on the market but the three I would select for an early display are 'Elizabeth', a neat and low-growing hybrid with flowers as bright as a border canary, 'Moonlight', a small upright shrub with flowers of soft primrose, and a white-flowered form called 'Abbotswood', which is short and spreading. I enjoy seeing these plants near rich blue ceanothus and beside hummocks of blue grasses, and 'Moonlight' is superb when underplanted with blood-red violas or wallflowers.

Plenty of cream has been stirred into the yellows of spring and every opportunity we have to pour some of this produce into our schemes should be seized. One family which provides this colour in quantity is the brooms. In contrast with the potentillas, their beauty is fleeting. For a couple of weeks in early May they shower us with pea-shaped flowers and engulf us in their heavy, almost claustrophobic, scent. But in spite of this brief flowering period everyone should try to find room for them, because their display is so spectacular. They need full sun and a well-drained soil.

Cytisus × *kewensis* is like a large insect, with long arms arching away from a central mass, and is an ideal broom for the rock garden, being dwarf and well-behaved. Its frothy appearance can be matched by associating it with forget-me-nots or it can be opposed by associating it with something firm and upright such as muscari. *C.* × *praecox* is a larger shrub, about 5 feet tall, and although there are white and pure yellow forms, its normal creamy colour is the most desirable. Imagine it backed by the lavender-blue *Clematis alpina* and surrounded by cushions of purple sage and wine-black tulips. The common broom, *Cytisus scoparius*, has sired a number of outstanding offspring and if you have the space for one more form I would grow 'Cornish Cream' to complete your May picture.

I have just been browsing through an old book on rock garden plants and have come across a photograph, obviously taken in April, of a titanic struggle between battalions of golden-yellow alyssum and hordes of invading aubretia. I would like to think that it was included as a warning to those who would recklessly play with bright colours but I fear it is meant to stand as a shining example of the gardener's art and one worthy of emulation. April is a dangerous month in the rock garden. There is an eruption of colour in a relatively small area and unless you are careful you can be knocked over by the flying particles. Alyssum and aubretia are likely to be your most potent ingredients. They do not need to be kept apart but a thoughtful selection of their different shades and a firm hand in positioning them are essential.

The ordinary, dazzling yellow *Alyssum saxatile* does look well among the softer purplish tones of aubretia, the lavenders, violets and lilacs, providing that the purples are dominant and the alyssum sits on a carpet of them. For associations involving the more aggressively coloured aubretias, the reddish purples, mauves and carmines, I would always choose the creamy lemon form of alyssum called 'Citrinum'. In these partnerships either 'Citrinum' or the aubretias can dominate, depending on what sort of effect you want – a channel of cream or a massif of purple. The leaves of alyssum are quite silvery and make a good foil for later flowers.

To haughty gardeners *Corydalis lutea* is nothing but a weedy native which they would not dream of admitting through the garden gates. But it really is one of the most exquisite spring plants with its delicately divided ferny leaves and its dainty spikes of clear yellow flowers. It enjoys shade and will seed itself into crevices and cracks and places where you could never have planted anything yourself. The seedlings are easily extracted if they have chosen unwelcome sites. I grow a group of corydalis in a shady part of my main border close to a stretch of silver *Senecio cineraria* and because they are in such a prominent position I cut them to the ground at the end of June to obtain mounds of fresh green foliage in late summer, a time when most greens are quite sombre. Corydalis is hardly ever out of flower and can be relied upon to participate in schemes throughout the year. It is marvellous with other small, choice plants such as lemon and apricot violas, and when backed by plants with equally well-fashioned foliage such as *Santolina neapolitana* and blue rue.

By early April *Euphorbia robbiae* and its cousin *E. amygdaloides* 'Purpurea' are in flower and in blue schemes they are most effective. Far more flamboyant, however, is *E. epithymoides* (syn. *E. polychroma*) which bears flat heads of brilliant lime-yellow bracts throughout April and May. It only rises eighteen inches above the ground but makes a plump tuft of stems and is very eye-catching. Its colour is not one which mixes well with other yellows but it does stand out effectively among the bright oranges and scarlets of tulips and the browns and tans of wallflowers and polyanthus.

The beauty of the species paeonies is sung by every gardening writer, and the one which is always placed on a pedestal above all the others is *P. mlokosewitschii*. The very strangeness of its name encourages you to conjure up a picture in your mind of something fashioned by a sorceress to beguile and enslave you. When you see this paeony you are not disappointed. Its milky lemon cups are large enough to drink from and are filled with a shock of golden anthers; they rest above a mound of rounded grey-green leaves on stems tinged with crimson; and late in the summer, when the cups have long vanished, the seed pods open to reveal an assortment of beads in scarlet and jet black. At the beginning of April the leaves are suffused with copper and plum and associate well with spice-coloured polyanthus. Alas, the flowering itself is brief, only a few short days in early May, but if you have some in part shade you can enjoy the flowers for longer. Alternatively, you can prolong the display with similar species such as *P. wittmanniana nudicarpa* and the whiter, larger flowered *P. sterniana*.

From an exotic aristocrat we turn once again to a humble native. *Symphytum grandiflorum* has, like all comfreys, coarse hairy leaves and bell-shaped flowers. But it is a low-growing plant and does not have to be confined to wild parts of the garden like its larger relatives. Its bells are creamy yellow and look well in association with the lime-green leaves of *Alchemilla mollis* and the light blue funnels of its cousin *S. caucasicum*.

Of course, the greatest quantity of yellow in the spring garden is provided by bulbs. Most of the early daffodils maintain their display throughout April and now they are joined by their sleepier cousins. The short-cupped daffodils open in early April and, in my garden at least, they are the first varieties to open with orange centres. 'Barrett Browning', with its flame cup and pure white petals, is one of the finest forms; 'Sempre Avanti' is similar but cruder in shape and colour; 'Birma' is also striking with bright sulphur petals and a potent orange cup; and 'Edward Buxton' combines lively colouring with grace – its petals are a rich Devon cream and its cup a furnace. They are all stiff and slender daffodils which are quite at home in the border in schemes of white, orange and yellow. I never think that bicoloured daffodils are so effective when used as contrasts with blues – the juxtaposition of the three strong hues, four if you include the fresh green of the foliage, is uncomfortable and you need an intermediary to unify the group. They are seen at their best when their neighbours pick out one of their colours, ideally the colour of their cup or trumpet.

Out in the orchards and shrubberies and at the back of wide borders the rest of the large trumpet and long-cupped daffodils are making their appearance. There are golden yellows like 'Unsurpassable' and 'Rowallane', clear whites like 'Vigil' and 'Desdemona', and bicolours like 'Trousseau' in yellow and white, and 'Kilworth' in white and orange-red. Here is the material for our second wave of yellow which has been gaining momentum behind those first troughs and crests and now rises above them, towering over erythroniums and anemones and breaking its back against the trunks of gnarled fruit trees.

All waves must end in seething foam and we can look to the jonquils and the *poeticus* narcissi to provide it. The jonquils have tiny heads, rushlike leaves and a strong fragrance. They flower towards the end of April in shades of soft yellow. *N. jonquilla* itself is bright and pure, 'Lintie' has larger, rounded petals and an orange cup, 'Baby Moon' and 'Trevithian' are clear lemon. Because they are small and fragile, jonquils are best used in the more cultivated positions and can mark the shores of the daffodil sea in the borders and shrubbery. In grass the *poeticus* narcissi can take their place. They are also delicate in appearance and are deliciously scented but their shape and colouring are different. Their petals are large and laundry white and their cups tiny and flame orange. The two I recommend are 'Actaea' which is as perfect as bone china and 'Pheasant's Eye' which is simpler and more rustic.

For our tamer schemes the most valuable ingredients throughout April and May are likely to be the tulips. In about the third week of April they start to arrive in quantity, coming in every conceivable colour from ivory white to damson black. The first group to appear are the triumph tulips, a family of sturdy plants with longlasting flowers in many superb colour forms. 'Reforma' is sulphur yellow, 'Bestseller' a blend of salmons and oranges, 'Tambour Maître' deep ruby, 'First Lady' magenta purple, and 'Lady Diana' rose pink. They all grow to a height of 16–18 inches and are thus rather shorter than the Darwin and cottage tulips which open around the first week of May. These two groups

contain so many splendid varieties that unless you are very disciplined you will find yourself plundering children's piggy banks
and emptying grandparents' purses as soon as the autumn bulb
catalogues arrive. I am not going to preach moderation. Buy,
buy, buy, and next May revel in your ill-gotten gains. Choose
'Clara Butt' in peachy pink, 'Dawnglow' in apricot and rose,
'Holland's Glory' in scarlet and carmine and 'La Tulipe Noire' in
sooty purple from among the Darwin hybrids, and 'Maureen' in
cream-flushed white, 'Mrs John Scheepers' in acid yellow,
'Kingsblood' in cherry red and 'Queen of the Night' in damson
black from among the cottage varieties.

These tulips succeed the polyanthus as the providers of an
abundance of strong clear colours from both sides of the spectrum
but they do need a little more care in their distribution and siting.
They are formal flowers, tall, dignified and well groomed. The
polyanthus are lowly, homely and gregarious, relishing the
company of a thousand friends sharing their bed beneath nut trees
or beside a winding garden path. Tulips prefer a more select
gathering where they can maintain their individual character. I
have no wish to see the bulb fields of Holland with all those hapless
plants marshalled into mile-long rows. No doubt it is this spine-
chilling spectacle which continues to encourage gardeners to
arrange tulips in columns and squares and phalanxes. I can see the
temptation. They are easy to place in a regular pattern and have
a uniformity of size, shape and colour, and there is always that
urge in the gardener to chisel a straight line through his plot and
prove his dominance over wild nature.

But plants are not just blobs of colour. We have to show some
sensitivity to their personalities. Either plant your tulips in small
groups among other plants where they can provide contrast in
form or plant them in thin irregular lines to make streams of
bright colour which meander through your colour groups. You
can mix varieties to make harmonious teams, and contrasts are
often effective as well. The classic spring associations are those
consisting of tulips, forget-me-nots and wallflowers and with these
ingredients you should be able to devise some memorable
pictures.

If such associations are to cover quite a large area of ground, it
is better to make a harmony with the tulips and wallflowers and
let the forget-me-nots supply the contrast. Acid-yellow tulips,
primrose wallflowers and bright blue forget-me-nots is an obvious

team, but you could also try forget-me-nots with pale pink tulips and deep red wallflowers or white tulips and creamy wallflowers.

The best tulip association I have seen was at Nymans in Sussex where a plum-red variety, possibly 'First Lady', had been grouped at the base of *Magnolia* × *soulangiana* 'Anne Rosse'. The flowers of both plants are shaped like chalices and the magnolia's deep pink is flushed with a vinous purple which exactly matched the tulip. The partnership was sober and ascetic but against the azure of an April sky not at all severe.

Those gardeners who like to grow something a little unusual will be tempted by other May-flowering tulips. There are the Rembrandt tulips, streaked and splashed in colour combinations which are sometimes gaudy and sometimes highly sophisticated. There are the Parrot tulips which resemble bundles of ruffled feathers – try 'Black Parrot' and the copper-red 'Bird of Paradise'. And there are the Lily tulips, slender and feminine with tight bowls and pointed tips – these are the most graceful of all tulips and the finest among them are 'China Pink', a shocking sugary pink, 'West Point', a clear yellow and 'White Triumphator', a pure white.

With so many lovely varieties of tall tulip available, it is easy to pass over the little species tulips. To do so would be to deprive yourself of a number of exquisite plants for the rockery or front of the border. Among the April-flowering species I recommend *T. batalinii*, sulphur globes from thin shrivelled leaves and only 4 inches tall, *T. clusiana*, slim and dashing flowers, milk-white and cherry-red, held nearly a foot above the ground, and *T. chrysantha*, smouldering yellow and flame-orange flowers, long and narrow and 8 inches tall; among the May-flowering species *T. kolpakowskiana*, another name to wrestle with, with squat round cups of pure yellow and rusty carmine and *T. linifolia*, blazing scarlet flowers with pointed tips, which does not flower until the end of May. These last two species are only 6 inches tall.

Let us return from this excursion among multi-coloured tulips and recover that path which leads us quietly through the spectrum. There are still more yellow flowers to consider. Those American cousins of the dog's tooth violet, *Erythronium dens-canis*, open in April. In fact they do not look American at all, having the graceful shape and delicate colouring of inhabitants of an Oriental tea garden. *E. tuolumnense* has a sheaf of broad, smooth green leaves from which rise stems dripping with bright yellow flowers. The whole plant is only 6 inches tall, the same size as the best white-flowered form *E. revolutum* 'White Beauty' whose pendant blooms have a chocolate-brown ring inside them and whose leaves are marbled in olive and greenish white. 'White Beauty' is a little later to flower than the others, arriving towards the end of April. I have not attempted to describe the shape of the flowers of these two varieties because this is conveyed by the name of my third choice *E.* 'Pagoda'. No plant has been named as expertly as this hybrid. Its flowers slope exactly like a pagoda's roof, from a pointed apex down to upturned corners, and to a greater or lesser extent all these erythroniums follow this design. 'Pagoda' is taller than the others, being nearly a foot in height, and its colour is pale sulphur.

All erythroniums enjoy a peaty soil and semi-shade but otherwise present no cultural difficulties. I liked the associations I saw in Beth Chatto's garden in Essex, where white varieties were grouped with intense blue pulmonarias or the lavender-blue form of *Anemone nemorosa* 'Robinsoniana'. In my own garden the pale yellow forms are associated with the bronze-leaved *Saxifraga fortunei* 'Rubrifolia' which thrives in the same conditions.

The crown imperial, *Fritillaria imperialis*, is a plant of one's childhood. Did you ever push your finger into its giant bells and collect the drops of sweet nectar at their base? I still do it, just as I still pop open snapdragons and balloon flowers and set fire to burning bushes. The old varieties of crown imperial remain the best – 'Lutea Maxima' with its fresh green leaves and stems and bright yellow flowers, and 'Rubra Maxima' with its maroon-brown stems and rusty orange flowers. The flowerheads resemble giant pineapples with tufts of leaves above the clusters of hanging bells, and the whole plant grows to 4 feet. They are such imposing plants that I like seeing them isolated in the border with only the new foliage of herbaceous perennials at their feet and a dark hedge at their back, but you could mass forget-me-nots or wall-flowers around them to make a billowing foil.

Crown imperials flower at the end of April and prefer a sunny well-drained position. They can prove difficult to establish. Plant them with a little sand to ward off slugs and prevent the bulbs from becoming waterlogged, make sure the soil around them is rich and healthy, and hope for the best.

There is an orange-flowered climbing plant which you could grow near your crown imperials because it too enjoys full sun.

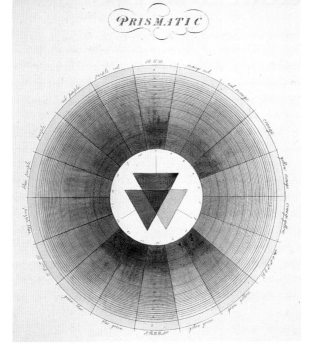

PRISMATIC

1. (top) Prismatic colour wheel from Moses Harris, *The Natural System of Colours*, 1811
(bottom left) Ice-cool colours at Coates Manor, Sussex
(bottom right) The Jekyll/Turner border at The Priory, Kemerton

2. (top left) *Magnolia stellata* and a coppice of coloured willows
(top right) *Narcissus* 'Peeping Tom' among *Scilla sibirica*
(bottom left) Clouds of *Brunnera macrophylla* and yellow *Epimedium perralderianum*
(bottom right) The Christmas Rose, *Helleborus niger*

3. (top left) Massed daffodils at Hodnet Hall, Shropshire
(top right) A fine ruby seedling of *Helleborus orientalis*
(bottom left) *Prunus* 'Cistena' behind scarlet tulips and dusky polyanthus
(bottom right) A rich carpet of polyanthus at Sissinghurst Castle, Kent

4. (top left) A bluebell wood in Surrey
(top right) Oriental hellebores at The Dower House, Boughton
(bottom left) Pale scillas under the dwarf *Salix apoda*
(bottom right) Naturalized *Crocus tomasinianus* and snowdrops at Maidwell Hall

5. (top left) Orange *Mimulus aurantiacus* with silver *Teucrium rosmarinifolium* and plum-coloured sedum
(top right) The mourning widow, *Geranium phaeum*
(bottom left) The honey-yellow torches of *Eremerus bungei*
(bottom right) Venidio-arctotis, *Artemisia pontica* and lavender, backed by *Salvia sclarea turkestanica* and *Rosa glauca*

6. (top left) *Lavandula stoechas* hovering among *Sisyrinchium striatum* and
catmint at Yoxford
(top right) A copper beech provides the foil for this *Rosa hugonis*
(bottom left) A play on verticals with *Ajuga pyramidalis* and
Iris pseudacorus 'Variegata'
(bottom right) Ceanothus behind irises and white and lilac comfreys

7. (top) A pastel scene in Beth Chatto's garden in Essex comprising
cardoons, bronze fennel, centaureas and apricot foxgloves
(bottom left) A rustic setting for this rambling rose
(bottom right) The drumsticks of *Arum italicum* next to glaucous *Euphorbia wulfenii*

8. (top left) *Rosa longicuspis* in the late Margery Fish's garden
(top right) Violas 'Jackanapes' and 'Irish Molly' with woolly *Ballota pseudodictamnus* in the foreground
(bottom left) Bronze-leaved *Crocosmia* 'Solfatare'
(bottom right) *Clematis* 'Henryi' wandering through a variegated ivy

9. (top) The laburnum walkway at Haseley Court underplanted with orange wallflowers
(bottom left) The gallica rose 'Tuscany Superb'
(bottom right) *Clematis viticella* 'Royal Velours' in the branches of a golden
catalpa at Burford House

10. (top left) The bourbon rose 'Madame Isaac Pereire'
(top right) *Lychnis flos-jovis*, stachys, catmint and white irises teamed with
a purple smoke bush
(bottom left) A jumble of old roses with variegated *Iris foetidissima* in front
(bottom right) The alba rose 'Koenigin von Danemarck'

11. (top left) *Liatris spicata*, *Allium sphaerocephalum*, clary and lavender in the Purple
Border at Sissinghurst
(top right) *Polemonium foliosissimum*, *Dicentra formosa*, *D. spectabilis* and a lilac viola
(bottom left) An old-world mixed border at Hidcote Manor, Gloucestershire
(bottom right) *Astrantia major*, an invaluable plant for pastel groups

12. (top left) An edging of *Geranium* 'Johnson's Blue' and *G. endressii* with catmint
(top right) *Lychnis coronaria* 'Alba' with *Malva* 'Primley Blue' behind, and
Corydalis orchroleuca and spotted-leaved pulmonaria in front
(bottom) The alba rose 'Félicité Parmentier'

13. (top left) Scarlet zauschneria with silver *Helichrysum petiolatum* and
artemisia and a variegated yucca
(top right) *Lychnis chalcedonica* with a pale blue delphinium
(bottom left) *Perovskia atriplicifolia* silhouetted against fiery kniphofias
(bottom right) An untamed rose, away from the bustle of the border

14. (top left) *Euphorbia palustris* departs in a burst of lemon
(top right) An autumn scene in the Scott's garden at Boughton House
(bottom left) *Euphorbia cyparissias* peering out of *Berberis thunbergii*
'Atropurpurea Nana'
(bottom right) A tangle of *Clematis tangutica* and *Eccremocarpus scaber*

15. (top left) A bronze view of the Savill Garden, Windsor
(top right) *Salix wehrhahnii* knee-deep in the fallen leaves of *Prunus sargentii*
(bottom left) *Galtonia candicans* in front of *Fothergilla monticola*
(bottom right) *Acer* 'Osakazuki' makes a stunning autumn feature

16. (top left) Echoes of spring with colchicums, cyclamen and *Hosta undulata*
(top right) *Helleborus foetidus* half-buried in snow
(bottom left) A solitary witch-hazel, *Hamamelis mollis*
(bottom right) The frosted stems of *Salix alba* 'Britzensis'

Eccremocarpus scaber is a supposedly tender perennial but in sheltered spots it comes through all but the most severe winters without turning a hair. Even if it does succumb, it is easily raised from seed and will flower in its first summer. I can think of no climber which gives a longer display. For ten months its racemes of bright orange funnels hang from its slender stems, the whole plant clinging by means of tendrils to its support. Although a vigorous plant, it does not produce quantities of foliage and if planted alone against a wall can appear thin and weedy. Far better to let it ramble through a wall shrub or a stouter climber such as a rose. For a spring combination try it with a deep blue ceanothus and the glaucous blue foliage of *Euphorbia wulfenii*, and for a summer combination with a yellow rose like 'Lawrence Johnston' or 'Paul's Lemon Pillar'. There are honey-yellow and cherry-red varieties of eccremocarpus but I cannot comment on their hardiness, since I have never grown them.

Before we cross over to the cooler side of the spectrum, let us look at two large groups of plants which provide colours for every scheme, hot and cold. Wallflowers, *Cheiranthus cheiri*, bloom in April and May and you can obtain them either in named, single-colour strains or in mixed colours. Both have their uses. There is nothing more welcoming than long beds in front of a house packed tightly with wallflowers in every shade from mauve and plum to cream and bronze. There are never any colour clashes because there are no aggressive colours present; all the tones are gentle and velvety. The effect is of a richly woven carpet from Bokhara laid out to greet visitors and to encourage them to make the transition from garden to house. Indeed, Suttons call their mixed strain 'Persian Carpet' and this is probably the one to grow – certainly you should avoid strains which include the gaudier yellows and scarlets. Do not be tempted to add other plants to your scheme because you will only succeed in damaging the carpet and interfering with the image.

Away from the house much of this evocative quality is lost, so you are better to paint with single colours. Again, Suttons have plenty of good strains – 'Fire King', a rusty orange-scarlet, 'Primrose Monarch', 'Blood Red', 'Ivory White' and a deep crimson called 'Vulcan'. You can have a lot of fun blending these strains into colour schemes, and into spring bedding schemes in particular. It was Beverley Nichols's garden which first showed me that you do not need to devote large areas to bedding; rather, you can have small patches in between shrubs and groups of perennials. Any pleasing associations that you see in public gardens or parks (these are few and far between, I know) can thus be adapted and reduced in scale for your own purposes. Let me make three suggestions – deep red wallflowers with purple ajuga and scarlet tulips; primrose wallflowers with bronze fennel and orange tulips; and a triad group of orange wallflowers, plum-coloured *Euphorbia amygdaloides* 'Purpurea' and lime-green polyanthus. Wallflowers should be sown in May, transplanted in June and transferred to their flowering positions in September.

If you really cannot be bothered with growing biennials then there are a few perennial wallflowers which might interest you. They have a long flowering period beginning in early April and they come in some attractive colours. 'Harpur Crewe' is double, bright yellow and scented; 'Moonlight', a variety of *Erysimum*, is a lively lemon-yellow; and 'Wenlock Beauty' is parti-coloured in red and tan. Another old treasure which you will not find so easy to locate is an untidy scarlet and yellow variety called 'Old Bloody Warrior'. It is a plant that I have loved and lost.

There are probably more blue-flowered plants around now than at any other time of the year, so if you wish to devise a scheme made up of all the different shades of blue, April and May are the months to plan it for. One group of shrubs which you could not omit are the ceanothus. In early May the first evergreen varieties open, spraying south- and west-facing walls with their tight panicles of flowers. Lack of suitable sites is the only factor which will stop you acquiring every available form, and making a decision in favour of just one or two varieties is likely to be your most painful horticultural dilemma. The spring ceanothus display many different tones of blue and each is breathtaking in the right setting. Of the paler powdery blues 'Cascade' with its long clusters of flowers and 'Delight' which is one of the hardiest forms are outstanding; of the mid-blues I favour 'Puget Blue' with its small dark leaves and brilliant blossom; and of the deep blues I especially admire the species *C. impressus*, with its short clusters of intense dark ultramarine, and the variety called 'Italian Skies' which is even more luxuriant.

Ceanothus have such a bountiful flowering and make such dense and rapid growth that it is worth planting them even in cold areas. Such audacity will generally be rewarded with a triumphant display of flowers the following spring, but occasionally there will be a sudden death to prevent you from becoming complacent, in which case you just mutter under your breath and replace the casualty with another ceanothus. The chances of suffering two harsh winters in succession are slight.

The smoky blue ceanothus associate particularly well with pink flowers. At Wisley there is a delightful marriage between 'Puget Blue' and the climbing rose 'Pompom de Paris', a very early rose smothered in tiny heads of clear pink. This feminine colour group is worth expanding, perhaps by adding china-pink tulips and some finely cut silver foliage in the form of *Artemisia* 'Powis Castle'. Incidentally, a ceanothus is just the job for planting against those harsh new red-brick walls which can be the despair of the sensitive gardener. The foliage conceals a large section of brickwork and the colours do not fight.

The second essential group of blue-flowered spring shrubs are the rosemaries. In London I have seen plants in flower in January but in most areas they open in early May. The common rosemary, *Rosmarinus officinalis*, and its superior clone 'Miss Jessop's Upright' are a very pale washed-out violet-blue and do not make an important contribution to a colour scheme. There are, however, deeper blue forms. 'Benenden Blue' is smaller than the type but its leaves are darker and its flowers much more intense; dwarfer still is 'Severn Sea' ('Seven Seas' in some nurseries) with similar coloured flowers; but the deepest blue of all comes from the true Tuscan rosemary which you will have to collect on your Italian travels. Its foliage is very narrow and its scent is rich and spicy. I acquired mine from the garden of an old priest near Cortona, where it sprawled with wild cistus and helianthemum.

A gnarled and twisted rosemary contributes much to the overall mood of the garden. It is a sign of age and permanence, of well-being and of an informal carefree style of gardening. It can either flop over a path alone or be incorporated into the border, but whatever sunny spot you choose make sure it is within reach so that you can enjoy its scent. Rosemaries look well in blue and silver schemes for most forms have grey-green leaves or grey on the undersides of the leaves. I particularly enjoy seeing them with hyssop because although their flowers are long over by the time the hyssop's appear their upright growth echoes the hyssop's blue spikes, making a harmony of verticals.

Clematis alpina gives us its violet-blue lanterns throughout April and May. I think it is the most attractive member of a family blessed with many beauties. It is not a particularly vigorous species and is ideal for a low wall, except that then you cannot easily look up its skirts and see the white stamens (properly called staminodes) huddled inside. There is a larger flowered form called 'Frances Rivis' and a rather pleasing reddish-purple one called 'Ruby' which associates well with the dwarf iris 'Sissinghurst' which is a similar shade.

If you are wondering what to give *C. alpina* as a partner, look no further than that curious twining climber *Akebia quinata*. The idea for this team came to me at Wisley where the two were growing close together, though not side by side. The association is perfect, the chocolate-purple flowers of the akebia being a wonderful foil for the blue clematis. The akebia has other attractions as well. Its foliage is interesting in that its leaves comprise a group of long rounded leaflets spread out like a fan and its flowers have a vanilla fragrance.

I may as well deal with the dwarf irises here because most of the finest varieties are from the cool side of the spectrum. They are short versions of the bearded iris, flowering in April and May and enjoying the same hot dry conditions as their June-flowering cousins. 'Tinkerbell' is a good sky-blue with a deep violet beard; 'Austrian Skies' is a lavender-blue flushed with violet; 'Blue Denim' is a pure blue with a white beard; 'Pixie Plum' is a velvet purple; and 'Tomingo' is a reddish purple. Among the warmer colours I especially like the creamy 'Lemon Flare' and the canary yellow 'Pigmy Gold'. The most unusual is that of the variety 'Green Spot' which has grey-white petals and lime-green markings on the falls.

All these dwarf irises sit comfortably at the front of the border with other low-growing plants. At Sissinghurst I saw a pale blue iris associated with the variegated ajuga, which is also in flower now, and this worked well. Other combinations might play on that power of suggestion which connects the iris with summer and so encourages us to imagine that summer is already upon us. The species paeonies and plants like *Geranium malviflorum* are also vanguards of their tribes and could contribute to this springtime summer.

One group of ground-cover plants gives us startling blue flowers in April and May. If your early varieties of pulmonaria were disappointingly tinged with purple or mauve, the late forms quickly bring redress. Grow *P. angustifolia* and its cultivars

'Azurea', 'Mawson's Variety' and 'Munstead Blue' which all have plain green leaves and the brightest flowers, and *P. longifolia* with narrow white-splashed leaves and late flowers. They are all superb as an underplanting to magnolias and cherries or in company with cream comfrey, golden grass and the lime-green *Helleborus corsicus*.

What on earth should you do with hyacinths? Their flower spikes are preposterously overweight and look as if they are made of plastic, two factors which make them quite unsuitable for growing among other spring flowers. And yet their colours are rich and appealing and their scent is one of the sweetest and most penetrating of the plant world. You must have bowls of them in the house, of course, but are there no places for them in the garden? I have tried pale pink forms under magnolias and vivid blue forms under forsythias but neither scheme was very satisfactory, and now I just grow them in tubs near the front door. Outside, the first varieties open at the end of April – 'Delft Blue', deep blue 'Ostara' and pure white 'L'Innocence' – and the rest towards the middle of May – indigo 'King of the Blues', pale blue 'Myosotis', clear pink 'Lady Derby' and primrose yellow 'City of Haarlem'.

For providing rich blue at ground-level there is no more reliable plant than the grape hyacinth, *Muscari ameniacum*. Its tight cones of little bells reveal their colour in early April and are magnificent under *Magnolia stellata* but they can also be allowed to march along the front of the border, pushing their spears up between primroses and dwarf daffodils and threatening orange tulips. I would not bother growing the white-flowered variety, *M. botryoides* 'Album', which is undistinguished, but am tempted to acquire the two bicoloured species *M. latifolium* and *M. tubergenianum* which have the top half of their flower spikes composed of pale blue sterile flowers and the lower half of indigo fertile flowers. I would grow them in front of my dark *Ceanothus impressus*.

It is a mistake to introduce the common bluebell, *Hyacinthoides non-scripta* (syn. *Endymion n-s.*, *Scilla nutans*), into the border. I am still battling away to rid my rock garden of this pest which seeds itself merrily and shows no respect for the foreign aristocrats which share its soil. It is easy to pull the bulbs up but you will not find them all for they hide in all sorts of unexpected places. In fact they have teamed up with another menace, the Welsh poppy, *Meconopsis cambrica*, which is a far more fearsome weed. Together the bluebells and poppies maintain a constant barrage and regularly break through my defences. In a wilder part of the garden they would be a delight because the two plants complement each other well both in shape and colour, and indeed I am trying to tempt them to make the move. So far they have remained hostile to the idea.

A great many gardeners find daphnes difficult to grow. I am sure this is because plants are cosseted too much. It is true that some species have a well-deserved reputation for being troublesome to establish but the majority really are very accommodating, and require no more attention than any other hardy shrub. The three purplish-flowered species that I want to include here are all evergreen, low-growing and exceedingly fragrant so they should have positions at the front of the border, preferably beside a path. *D. collina* flowers at the beginning of May. It is a tiny shrub, often less than 2 feet tall, but is so completely smothered in clusters of deep rose-purple flowers that it becomes a prominent feature. It prefers a sunny position and a retentive soil and looks well backed by a deep blue ceanothus. *D. retusa* opens a week later and is another dwarf plant. Its flowers are pinkish purple tinged with white and it thrives in almost any soil, even in shade. *D. tangutica* is taller than both the others, growing up to 4 feet or more, and is covered with rose-purple and white flowers throughout April.

There are no other shrubs with purple flowers to tempt us this season but there are a few perennials. I mentioned aubretia earlier in the chapter as a companion to yellow alyssum but it is very successful left isolated in its different colour forms to make a mat of lavender, mauve, purple and pink. Gertrude Jekyll recommends including cerastium in the group as a light contrast and this would certainly help to harmonize some of the brasher shades.

If you are a snooty gardener you will not be wanting aubretia in your garden, with cerastium or without, so you will have to find your purples in other quarters. One plant which is bound to catch your eye is the perennial wallflower *Erysimum* 'Bowles's Mauve', and a first-rate plant it is. It flowers non-stop from April until November and makes a neat woody hummock of dark grey-green leaves. It likes full sun and dry soil and I have it in a small bed with purple sage, silver *Salix helvetica* and white lavenders where its shocking lilac-mauve flowers can shout as loudly as they like. They must be kept away from other bright purples and blues.

Two members of the geranium family are also contenders, because they too flower during April and May. *G. malviflorum* (syn. *G. atlanticum*) is a chirpy plant with large lilac-blue, veined flowers and beautifully cut foliage. Like most geraniums it thrives in sun or shade and since herbaceous perennials are not much in evidence at this time of year has many useful roles to play, among bulbs and under shrubs. It associates well with its taller relative *G. phaeum*, the mourning widow, which is a sombre plant with small reflexed maroon-black flowers and large leaves, which themselves often carry purple blotches. *G. phaeum* is also good against silver and glaucous blue foliage such as *Ballota pseudodictamnus* and blue grasses. Against a dark green background its flowers are almost invisible.

A mantle of pink blossom gradually descends on to the garden during April. Early in the month the first cherries, almonds and plums alert us to the forthcoming spectacle and before we have quite registered its proximity it is upon us and we are drowned in petals. *Prunus* 'Hokusai' throws out its great bunches of fragrant shell-pink blossom from its upright spreading branches; 'Tai Haku' floats large, single white flowers from its copper-red leaves; and 'Shirotae' showers us with almond-scented flowers, white and semi-double, from branches erupting in pale green. A little later, at the end of April, comes our native wild cherry, *P. avium*, dripping with white-cupped flowers; *P. serrulata* with white double flowers; and *P.* 'Ukon' with bronze foliage and primrose-green flowers. And finally in May comes the white-flowered bird cherry, *P. padus* and *P.* 'Shirofugen' erupting in white and purplish pink.

It may be that you have no room for any of these cherries, having lost your heart to *P. subhirtella* or *P. sargentii*, in which case you must content yourself with their tiny counterpart, the dwarf Russian almond, *P. tenella*. This suckering shrub only grows to 4 feet and its erect stems are wreathed throughout April with blossom in a delightful shade of rose pink. There is a white form, 'Alba', and a smaller and more brilliant pink variety called 'Fire Hill'. I first saw this plant in the borders of New College, Oxford, near silver clumps of cardoon and it made an immediate impression. Several stands of it made the border look quite furnished, even though there was hardly anything else in flower.

One of the most popular flowering trees for late spring is the Japanese crab apple, *Malus floribunda*. It is perfect for the small cottage garden, having none of the sophistication of the Japanese cherries, just a simple rustic charm which makes it instantly endearing. The blush-pink flowers open from rosy crimson buds and the branches are rough and twiggy. A quite different impact is made by the hybrid 'Profusion' whose flowers are reddish purple and whose young leaves are copper red, but it too deserves a place in schemes which must preserve a rural flavour. Plant hellebores and pulmonarias beneath them, and close by a *Daphne retusa* and some *Geranium malviflorum*. The best setting for the group would be a crumbling wall of grey stone and a view beyond of purple hills, but if all you have is a prospect of your neighbour's house then your imagination must provide the rest.

The pink mantle does not rest only on trees. Shrubs too slip under its folds, and the noblest group to succumb are the magnolias. They are essential members of the spring garden, their huge exotic flowers a symbol of the exuberance and bounty of the season. *M.* x *soulangiana* is the most familiar. Its stout spreading branches support huge white goblets filled and stained with wine, and this display is maintained for over a month from mid-April. Happily this magnificent shrub has given rise to many equally desirable clones, from which I would single out 'Alba', a creamy white with hardly a hint of purple, 'Lennei', a rose-purple with a white interior, and 'Rustica Rubra', a rose-red and white. If you want something more unusual plant *M. liliiflora* 'Nigra' (syn. *M. quinquepeta* 'Nigra') whose goblets are a very dark vinous purple and make the plant look quite funereal.

The best associations involving magnolias usually centre upon tulips because the match between their upright cup-shaped flowers is so perfect. Drifts of pink, white and purple tulips grouped beside them look as if they are collecting every drop of wine or milk which spills over from the cups above. The magnolias cast very little shade at this time of year, so the tulips can be planted quite close.

A spring garden without scent is unthinkable and we must have plants to entertain our nose at every turn. We have already assembled a fair number – corylopsis, mahonias, daffodils, cherries, brooms, wallflowers, rosemaries, akebias and daphnes. The magnolias are also scented, a deliciously fruity fragrance reminiscent of custard apples. You need to push your nose right into the flowers to appreciate it fully. But there is a further assembly of plants which we have not yet considered and which are longing to release their perfume in our gardens. So powerfully scented are they that they have no energy left to colour their flowers and they must remain white. I am speaking of choisya, osmanthus and viburnum.

Choisya ternata, the Mexican orange blossom, produces its open clusters of white flowers in early May. Its scent is heavy and citric, the sort of smell which is pleasant to inhale but does not encourage you to linger. The shrub itself is exceedingly handsome and is a valuable evergreen foliage plant for sun or shade. The leaves are glossy, rounded and trifoliate and do look faintly tropical, associating well with fatsias, cordylines and bamboos. Unfortunately, choisya is not completely hardy and needs wall protection. In a hard winter it may be cut to the ground, although it can be relied upon to shoot again from the base. Its shiny foliage shows up white flowers so successfully that it is worth composing a predominantly white scheme around it by planting white tulips and pulmonarias for spring and lilies and *Hosta plantaginea* 'Grandiflora' for summer and autumn.

The scent of *Osmanthus delavayi* was once likened by a friend of mine to that penetrating smell of cheap sun-tan lotion which overwhelms you on English beaches. I am afraid the similarity is unmistakable though the knowledge of it cannot lessen your enjoyment of its sweetness. Osmanthus is also an evergreen shrub but its leaves are small, dark and toothed like a holly and its flowers are long like a jasmine's. Even more appealing is the hybrid × *Osmarea* 'Burkwoodii' which is the result of a cross between the osmanthus and *Phyllyrea decora*. It differs most markedly in its foliage which is pointed like daggers. It flowers a few weeks later than osmanthus, in May, so it pays you to grow both. Osmanthus and osmarea are very tight compact shrubs and you often see them as specimens marking the corners of a border or enclosed garden, taking the place of box in fact.

The viburnums rival the daphnes as the finest scented shrubs of spring. Their fragrance is similar, a sophisticated French perfume, sweet with a touch of spice. But they are much coarser shrubs than daphnes and are better suited to sites out in the border rather than close to the house. *V.* × *burkwoodii* is evergreen and can contribute to the border's backbone. It grows to around 6 feet and its leaves are glossy and dark above and felted and grey below. The clusters of white flowers begin to appear early in spring but the shrub reaches its peak at the end of April.

V. carlesii is deciduous but its leaves are more attractive, being grey-green throughout the summer and taking on rich tints in autumn. Its flowers are very pink in bud and this quality has been emphasized in its three superb clones, which I would always plant in preference to the type. 'Aurora' and 'Diana' produce shell-pink flowers from their rosy buds, and 'Charis' the purest white. *V.* × *juddii* is quite difficult to distinguish from *V. carlesii* when out of flower, but it is a tougher plant and its flowers are blush pink.

Pink is the colour to highlight in the viburnum during April and May. Plant *Prunus* 'Hokusai' near by or a flowering crab, and group red wallflowers, pink tulips and plenty of white anemones in front. Apart from *V. carlesii* 'Charis' none of the whites are clean enough to appear in a crisp white scheme.

Not all white-flowered shrubs are scented, of course. The bridal wreath, *Spiraea* × *arguta*, more than makes up for a lack of perfume by its arching grace. It grows to 8 feet and makes a dome of slender branches bristling with tiny leaves and studded throughout April and May with tight knobs of white blossom. These low flowers have the unfortunate habit of clinging mainly to the upper surface of the branches and as a consequence the shrub often looks as if it has served as the overnight roosting-place for a flock of sparrows. Nevertheless, this shrub has a cottage feel about it and deserves to be included in spring schemes with wallflowers and forget-me-nots. It is pretty next to a pink Japanese cherry.

If you live in a relatively mild area and have some spare space on a warm wall you may like to plant the vanilla-scented *Clematis armandii*. This is an evergreen climber, vigorous and handsome, with large, deep green leaves and waxy flowers. Although the blooms are often flushed with pink, it is their creaminess which is most striking and they have a perfect foil in the bronze young leaves. I enjoy seeing it behind green euphorbias and bronze fennel, and it is effective with orange berberis and tulips.

We enjoyed anemones earlier in the season but a second wave of them arrives in April. The common wood anemone, *A. nemorosa*, makes the best spring carpet of white that you could hope for and is in flower from early April to mid-May. The single flowers are held 6 inches above the ground and the beautifully cut foliage disappears entirely in July. It thrives in semi-shade and spreads rapidly under trees and shrubs. I came across the variety 'Vestal' for the first time last year in a garden near Banbury and acquired it at once. It is a double version of the type, but instead of having an untidy mop head of large petals, it preserves its six or seven large petals and fills its centre with a cloud of tiny petals.

The wood anemone is marvellous under yellow shrubs because its yellow stamens harmonize so well, and the same is true of *Paeonia emodi*, a prince among paeonies, whose large white cups are filled with gold. This paeony is a first-class border plant, for apart from its sumptuous flowers it has beautiful leaves and a fine scent. In early May it can be the central feature for a group of white and yellow tulips, primrose wallflowers and variegated foliage, and later in the summer when its bracts turn red and its leaves yellow it can take part in a hotter scheme of oranges and scarlets. It is a plant which likes some shade.

The only other pure white perennial that I would like to mention is that well-known rock garden plant *Iberis sempervirens*. There is nothing subtle about this plant. It forms a mound of dazzling white, 9 inches tall, which stuns the garden during April and May. But it is evergreen and it is useful for powerful schemes. Try it with blazing scarlet tulips or flame-orange wallflowers, in front of berberis or beneath a blood-red quince.

Let me conclude this springtime walk through the spectrum with three plants which have the most unusual and elegant colouring. Each has white flowers which are in some way decorated in green. The first is the summer snowflake, *Leucojum aestivum*, which opens not in summer but in April. It resembles a snowdrop, but is much taller at nearly 2 feet and has a tuft of fresh green leaves like a daffodil. The flowers hang down like lamp-shades and each jagged tip bears a green spot. The form to grow is 'Gravetye Giant'. The snowflake tolerates sun or shade providing the soil is moist.

The second green and white plant is *Ornithogalum nutans*, another April-flowering bulb. Its star-shaped flowers are held on 18-inch spikes in the manner of a bluebell. They are essentially white but are so generously shaded in grey-green that the plant looks quite silvery. Ornithogalum is suitable for naturalizing in grass but there its delicate colour is not seen to its best advantage. Plant a drift behind blue muscari and in front of a bulging ceanothus and you will see the difference.

The third plant is the most striking. It is a tulip called 'Angel' which flowers in early May. It has a perfect shape, a full round bowl tapering up to pointed tips, and a primrose-white colour streaked with apple green. Both it and the summer snowflake are exquisite against silver and white-variegated leaves and among pure white flowers.

The Realm of June

As spring ebbs into early summer, gardeners should find a moment to set aside their forks and trowels, pull up a wooden seat and a low support for their wellingtoned feet, and count their blessings. This is a blissful time of year. The early excitements of spring are still fresh in our memory and just ahead lie the velvet delights of summer. The garden continues to wear its youthful coat, the beech trees are but thinly clad in their lime-green veils and tulips stand proud beneath magnolias and cherries. And yet midsummer's day is only four weeks away and most cottage gardens will then be at their peak.

The vast army of spring bulbs has now begun its great retreat and in its wake come troupes of shrubs and herbaceous perennials. They arrive as the outriders and heralds of a long and multi-coloured caravan which, from the middle of May until early July, trundles merrily through the garden. Its carriages overflow with silks and perfumes, and somewhere in its midst, resting on velvet cushions, are the four rich sovereigns which together establish the exotic mood and the Eastern character of the June garden, the iris, the paeony, the poppy and the rose.

Before we allow ourselves to be bewitched by the gypsy charm of these foreign princes, we must focus our attention on their early attendants. There is no dominant colour among them; they hale from all parts of the spectrum, flashing yellow banners and purple pennants, silver torches and scarlet plumes, amethysts and garnets. Most are small plants, not daring to challenge the majesty of their rulers, but some tower over their companions and give us a taste of the extravagance that is to follow.

The largest newcomers are the lilacs. Towards the end of May they open their dense cones of flowers, some single and some double and all drenched in scent. I would love to persuade you to plant a grove of these small trees but the only reason for my encouragement would be that I could then come to your garden to enjoy the frothy colour and sweet fragrance and would not have to plant a grove myself. The truth is that after its brief display the lilac becomes a dreary shrub clothed in coarse foliage and withered flowerheads – these do not fall naturally and have to be snipped away with secateurs. In a very large garden you could find a remote spot and weave a bower of early summer blossom which you could turn your back on afterwards but in the small garden space is valuable.

But one or two bushes you must have, and you can select your varieties from extensive lists. Among the single-flowered forms choose 'Massena', a deep reddish-purple, 'Primrose', a pale yellow, or 'Souvenir de Louis Spaeth', a dark wine-red. Among the double-flowered forms choose 'Charles Joly', a dark reddish-purple, 'Katherine Havemeyer', a deep lavender-pink, or 'Madame Lemoine', a sumptuous, deliciously fragrant white. Lilacs are best kept out of the main flower borders because of their size and short flowering period. They are not easy to disguise and their greedy roots drain the soil of moisture. The most satisfactory positions for them are in the wilder parts of the garden, perhaps at the edge of a shrubbery, or in narrow borders beside the drive, which are not inspiring enough for a full-scale scheme.

You need have no reservations about planting the small species lilacs. It is astonishing that they are seen so infrequently in gardens, for they have so many valuable qualities. They are all compact, sun-loving shrubs, about 5 feet tall, highly fragrant, and have a long flowering period, some going on intermittently through the summer. *Syringa meyeri* has flowers of violet purple, *S. microphylla* 'Superba' of rosy lilac and *S. patula* (syn. *S. palibiniana*) of lilac pink. All have that old-fashioned, rosy character and colouring which enables them to fit so well into cottage garden associations of wine-dark iris, violet lupins and pink columbines. Many nurseries sell them at exorbitant prices, presumably because they are so slow-growing, but it is worth breaking the bank to acquire them.

I am not sure whether the lilacs have led me into the pink or the purple sphere of influence but my notes are pointing me towards

Daphne × *burkwoodii* 'Somerset', so let us plump for pink. I omitted this daphne from the last chapter because it flowers rather late in May, but to omit it from the garden would be folly. The quality that makes it so desirable is not so much its strong scent or its easy-going nature but its combination of clear pink flowers with blue-green foliage. Few plants have this handsome colour scheme, so it is worthwhile designing a pink-flowered, blue-leaved group while you have the chance, as there are two other plants in flower now with the same tones, namely *Allium karataviense* and *Dicentra oregana* 'Langtrees'.

Dicentras are indispensable. Some will have been in flower since early May but the majority make their main contribution in the second half of the month. The tallest, at 2 feet, is the bleeding heart, *D. spectabilis*, which has handsome cut foliage and long arching stems dripping with strong rose-pink lockets. I am not particularly fond of this shade of pink and much prefer the rarer white form *D.s.* 'Alba'. Its flowers collect like raindrops on the undersides of the stems and are an interesting addition to white schemes; yet its foliage, which is a fresh lime-green, begs for associations with yellow. Try it with yellow tulips, cream violas and variegated applemint.

Another dicentra which could be included in the group is the dwarf *D. eximia* 'Alba' whose lockets are tiny and lipped. Like all small dicentras its leaves are beautifully ferny, and plants creep slowly and cautiously between their companions at the front of the border. *D. eximia* itself is a dusky rose and blends happily with other pinks; *D. formosa* is a little larger, at about 18 inches, but is not dissimilar; and in the variety 'Bountiful' the flower colour tends towards crimson; *D. oregana* 'Langtrees' has glaucous blue leaves and pale pink flowers. All these plants prefer shady, moist positions.

Geraniums make obvious bedfellows for dicentras. They are also relatively low-growing, are happy in shade, and have colours from the same part of the spectrum. The advance party, comprising *G. phaeum* and *G. malviflorum*, are still in flower but now they are joined by representatives of the main body. It is impossible to have too many geraniums, and among their ranks there are contenders for every early summer scheme. *G. maculatum* is perhaps the most seductive with its cut foliage and pale lilac-pink flowers. It grows to 2 feet and is splendid among purples such as aquilegias, violas and lupins. *G. macrorrhizum* is better known. It makes a first-rate ground-cover plant and its aromatic foliage takes on scarlet tints in autumn. The form to grow is 'Walter Ingwersen' (syn. 'Ingwersen's Variety'), in rose pink, and there is a superb white, 'Album' whose flowers are held in red calyces and are perfect for pink and white groups.

The best pure white geranium is *G. sylvaticum* 'Album'. With its fresh, dissected leaves and nodding flowers it offers itself as an ingredient for any cool scheme, either among lemon yellows or violet blues, such as that of its cousin *G.s.* 'Mayflower' or the hybrid 'Johnson's Blue'. This last is another must for early schemes. Its flowers are a brilliant blue and glow among pale colours. *G. renardii* is quite distinct. It only grows 9 inches high and loves a dry spot where it can bask in sunlight in the company of silver-leaved plants which complement it well. Its own leaves are scalloped, a greyish sage-green, and its flowers are dusky white with purple veins. It is good in front of alliums, and dark purple columbines.

Late May sees the arrival of a delicious knotweed, *Polygonum bistorta* 'Superbum'. It thrives in damp soil in semi-shade and although its leaves are as coarse and ungainly as a dock's, they make a surprisingly successful background for the soft pink bottle-brushes, which rise to over 2 feet. My group did not enjoy the drought of 1984 and all but disappeared, only to emerge again in the autumn apparently none the worse for their ordeal. I have associated them with purple polemoniums and dark-leaved bugles, but I have seen them happily teamed with the blue bells of *Symphytum* × *uplandicum* and the airy sprays of *Brunnera macrophylla*.

Of all the purplish-flowered plants of May the most spectacular is the wisteria. Its racemes of pea-like blooms fall like a late spring shower on to the plants beneath them, drenching geraniums and columbines and bushes of pale pink lilac. The heaviest honey scent comes from the Chinese species, *W. sinensis*, which has mauve flowers, and its white form 'Alba'. Neither of these need be confined to walls for they are quite vigorous enough to clamber over fruit trees and can even be trained as standards when they could echo and balance a golden-yellow laburnum growing in another part of the garden. There is a variety called 'Black Dragon' which has flowers of deep purple and one called 'Prolific' which has longer racemes.

If I had to choose just one wisteria, however, it would be none of these. It would be the Japanese species, *W. floribunda*, in the form 'Macrobotrys'. Although it has less scent and is far less vigorous than *W. sinensis*, its lilac-blue racemes can be over 3 feet long. Ideally you would grow it over water, as in Monet's garden, where its reflections would put those of the weeping willows to shame, but you could also use it to smother a pergola. Here it would be more confined and trained more vertically, and you would expect the effect to be just as dramatic and thunderous as the Victoria Falls.

I hope it does not surprise you to learn that there are lavenders in flower in May, and trust that *Lavandula stoechas* is safely installed in your garden. The flowerheads are very strange and look like ribbed seed pods from whose clutches frantic flowers are making their escape. The only petals are in a wild tuft at the top – they are purple in the type and reddish purple in the subspecies *pedunculata*. The leaves are narrow, grey-green, and highly aromatic. *L. stoechas* hails from the Mediterranean and likes a hot, dry position. It goes on flowering throughout the summer, and forms a neat dwarf shrub for the front of the border.

Columbines are starting to open now and the first to do so are usually the common species, *Aquilegia vulgaris*, and its varieties. They bring a flighty grace to the border and should be permitted to sow themselves around; they take up very little room and often land in just the right places. The only caveat I would add to this carefree piece of advice is that if you intend to grow more than one species or form of aquilegia, and I shall do my utmost to ensure that you do, then you must keep your varieties apart. Columbines are notoriously promiscuous and if they are grown in mixed company, the result is offspring in horribly wishy-washy colours.

The most attractive colour forms of *A. vulgaris* are plum black, pale pink and pure white. The dark forms combine well with 'Queen of the Night' tulips and the mourning widow geranium, and if you gathered some deep purple foliage as well you could contrive a sinister scheme. The finest white form is called 'Nivea' and has greyish foliage. It was a favourite of Gertrude Jekyll and is valuable for early white associations, but it is now exceedingly rare.

Another familiar occupant of cottage gardens is the mountain knapweed, *Centaurea montana*. There is no doubt that it is still worthy of a place for its large blue cornflowers, stained reddish purple at their centre, have few rivals in this part of the spectrum.

But it considers the production of flowers to be a sufficient contribution to the early summer garden and makes no effort at all to improve its general behaviour, sprawling about in the most slovenly manner. It seems to resent having its stems cut back after flowering, but this is essential if the border is to be kept respectable. The answer is to grow it in a wild part of the garden as an underplanting to a reddish-purple lilac. The combination is arresting.

Solomon's seal, *Polygonatum multiflorum* (strictly *P.* × *hybridum*) and the frothy heads of *Smilacina racemosa* are now glowing in the shade among yellow trollius and daylilies but elsewhere there is a more unusual white-flowered perennial in bloom. It is called *Libertia formosa*, and it makes a sheaf of evergreen rushy leaves, 2 feet high, from which emerge long sprays of open flowers, clear and white like dishes of milk. It is a delightful and unexpected member of the early summer garden, splendid against the rising bristles of variegated grasses or, a little later, next to blowsy white paeonies and cistus. It needs a well-drained soil and plenty of sun; mine did not produce a single flower in semi-shade. I have just acquired an orange-leaved form called *L. ixioides* 'Gold Leaf' which promises to be a valuable ingredient for bronze Turkish schemes and seems perfectly hardy.

The sweet scent of lily of the valley, *Convallaria majalis*, begins to waft through borders towards the end of April, and the plants are obvious companions for Solomon's seal, since both bear bell-shaped white flowers and enjoy moist shade. In some gardens it becomes a rampant weed and seems to flourish everywhere, in full sun, in part shade and even in those dry dusty strips of earth between privet hedge and tarmac drive, while in other gardens it repeatedly fails to establish itself. In dappled shade it is at its most seductive, its spikes of snow-white bells gleaming in their vases of broad foliage during May, and its scanty strings of vermilion berries glinting in late summer. There is a superior form called 'Fortin's Giant' which has larger bells and is slightly later to flower, and a yellow-striped form called 'Variegata' which needs plenty of sun.

Two large groups of plants epitomize early summer and play an important part in exciting our senses and stimulating our colour schemes so that we are ready to receive the Eastern visitors in a few weeks' time. They send up rockets and beacons and unfurl thick rugs and carpets and between them they replace the delicacy and simplicity of the spring garden with the opulence and luxury of a sultan's palace. From now on we will not be satisfied just with purity of colour and elegance of form; we will want diamond-studded blooms, heavy in scent and spices, outlandish in shape and wickedly deep in colour and we will want a garden floating in petals, tangled in growth and flowing with milk and honey. All this we are promised by the multicoloured torches of the lupins and the velvet cushions of the violas.

We have come a long way since the days of the straggly blue lupin, *Lupinus polyphyllus*. Stout spires crowded with pea-like flowers now come in every conceivable shade turning the borders into magnificent firework displays. There are the yellows of 'Chandelier', the whites of 'Noble Maiden', the pinks of 'The Chatelaine', the reds of 'My Castle' and the bicoloured blue and whites of 'The Governor'. All these are seed-raised strains which lack the proneness to disease of the vegatatively propagated forms. There are also a number of mixed-colour strains available which you can blend yourself.

Let them parade towards the back of the border, behind phlox for example, where their foliage can be concealed afterwards (this is easier if they are planted in thin drifts). They do not flower for very long but when the old flowerheads are removed, as they must be to prevent seeding, a new crop of shorter spires appears. Try clear yellow forms behind schemes of silver and white, or purple forms behind silver and lavender blue.

At the front of the borders the violas and pansies are well under way. It is worth assembling a good collection of these plants for many of them flower for months on end and with a large stock you will never be without low-level colour. Many can be raised from seed – velvet crimsons like 'Arkwright's Ruby' and 'Crimson Queen', royal blue 'Ullswater' and clear, perpetual flowering 'Azure Blue', soft oranges like 'Chantreyland' and 'Sutton's Apricot', and jet blacks like 'King of the Blacks' and tiny 'Bowles's Black' which seeds itself everywhere. The seed merchants tell us to treat them as biennials but you can usually get three safe seasons from your plants before you have to replace them.

Other varieties must be bought from Richard Cawthorne (Lower Daltons Nursery, Swanley, Kent) who has the most extensive list. His small stand at Chelsea is the most bewitching in the show. It is quite impossible to reduce your order to a sensible and affordable size. So far I have had, among the larger, black-faced violas,

'Dobbies Bronze' in mahogany red, 'Irish Molly', an extra-ordinary colour which is neither brown nor yellow nor olive green but a mixture of all three, and 'Buxton Blue', a slate blue; among the selfs, which have no face, I have had 'Primrose Dame', 'Maggie Mott', which is lavender mauve with a cream centre, and 'Jack-anapes' whose lower petals are bright yellow and whose upper petals are chocolate red; among those with elongated flowers I have had 'Huntercombe Purple' in intense violet and 'Moonlight' in palest yellow; and among those violas and violettas with very small flowers I have had 'Ardross Gem', violet blue with a gold centre, 'Malvena', creamy white, and 'Nellie Britten' (syn. 'Haslemere') a mauve pink which is the pick of the lot.

None has disappointed although one or two have mysteriously disappeared during the winter, not from cold I am sure. Still, it is a simple matter to take cuttings during the summer or autumn. They all dislike strong sunlight and dry soil but other than that are easy to please. An occasional spray for greenfly, a mid-season feed and cutting down in November is all they ask in return for a long display. I am not going to suggest any associations with other plants here because they will be incorporated into nearly all our summer schemes later on. For the old roses there is no finer underplanting.

During May yellow has been losing its supremacy. The daffodils are over and the forsythias are fading, and as these two potent groups take their leave a colourful contest has developed between the other hues. It has been up to the gardener to decide who should have the upper hand and I hope you will favour the deep reds, the violets, the clear pinks and the pure blues. It is they who will lead us into the heavy clarets and crimsons, the dark purples, magentas and damask whites of June. But we must not lose the sense of carnival and gaiety which comes from having, in quantity, representatives from all parts of the spectrum. Many outstanding plants with yellow, red and orange flowers are blooming now and they must all be welcomed.

I suspect laburnum walkways have been springing up all over the country following the spectacular exhibit at the 1984 Chelsea Flower Show. Of course the idea is not a new one, and indeed the exhibit was intended as a tribute to Lord Aberconway, whose garden at Bodnant in North Wales has boasted a laburnum walkway since the 1880s, but it must have inspired many gardeners to attempt a similar project for the first time. The impact is quite overwhelming, a tunnel of radiant yellow so brilliant and dazzling that you must shield your eyes when entering. If you do not have the space for a walkway, you could settle for one triumphant arch, composed of metal hoops for example, around which the laburnum stems would be woven and interlaced. I would underplant with the richest colours I could find – oranges, scarlets and blood reds (aquilegias, violas, irises and wallflowers). My choice of laburnum would be the form with the immensely long racemes, *L.* × *watereri* 'Vossii'.

Most of the more desirable species roses have yellow flowers and open in May, a good month before their more flamboyant cousins. *Rosa primula* is perhaps the most remarkable. It makes an upright shrub 6 feet tall, clothed in wonderful ferny foliage and small, single primrose flowers; but its unique feature is its fragrance which emanates not from its flowers but from its leaves. After a shower of rain the garden is enveloped in a heady cloud of incense and you are transported back to Turkestan, to a land of heat, of rocky desert and of prayer. *R.* × *cantabrigiensis* cannot compete in scent but is more beautiful in flower. The blooms are large, a clear pale yellow, and completely smother the ferny branches; and it grows altogether taller. *R. hugonis* is similar but less refined.

The modern shrub rose 'Frühlingsgold' is quite different to these small-flowered roses. Its stout arching branches are furnished with coarser leaves and its flowers are huge saucers of creamy yellow filled with golden stamens. They are ghostly and sweetly scented, superb above species paeonies like *P. emodi*, spires of lemon thermopsis and butter-yellow brooms.

In dry sunny spots the yellow asphodel, *Asphodeline lutea*, opens in May. Its spikes of scruffy flowers rise 3 feet from the ground, above a tuft of blue-green leaves. In the yellow borders of Brympton d'Evercy in Somerset the spikes stand alone against the rich Ham stone most effectively, but they are also good with blue ceanothus and ivory wallflowers. The white asphodel, *Asphodelus albus*, flowers a little later and is notable because its white stars emerge from brown calyces. Associate it with bronze foliage.

The first daylily, *Hemerocallis flava*, is out now. This remains one of the best varieties in spite of the fact that the market has been flooded with new forms, doubles and singles, reds, oranges, whites and pinks. Its small clear yellow trumpets are sweetly fragrant and blow in their dozens above the grassy leaves. It is happy in sun or shade, provided that the soil does not dry out. Daylilies are valuable ground-cover plants and, as I have mentioned before, especially useful for concealing the aftermath of early bulbs. Their foliage is pleasing enough to be a feature, either as an under-planting to small trees or as part of the backbone of a border. It is perfect with the white form of *Dicentra spectabilis*, *Geranium sylvaticum* 'Album' and variegated foliage.

Thermopsis mollis and the similar *T. caroliniana* ought to be far more widely grown. The flower spikes could easily be mistaken for those of yellow lupins and rise to a little over 2 feet, but they are altogether neater plants which do not make a large clump of foliage and they can therefore be trusted nearer the front of the border. They prefer a light soil and plenty of sunlight. Try them with blood-red wallflowers and violas.

In the warm side of the spectrum one of the most important groups of perennials are the globe flowers. They come in various tones of yellow and orange, loose balls of colour for moist positions in sun or shade, and their leaves are attractively divided. I consider the best yellows to be the creamy *Trollius* × *hybridus* (syn. *T.* × *cultorum*) 'Alabaster' and the pure lemon *T. europaeus* 'Superbus', and the best orange to be *T.* × *h.* 'Orange Princess'. I am not so keen on the more open flowers of *T. ledebourii*, even though they are filled with narrow petals and come in striking colours. Fine schemes are produced with just these various forms associated together but you might like to back them with golden elder, yellow-variegated dogwood and foaming stands of *Smilacina racemosa*.

Rosa moyesii has a special place in gardens because its colour is unique among roses. The flowers are a true red with no hint of yellow or crimson, small, flat and filled with dark stamens and when showering over white paeonies and iris and backed by a climber like 'Madame Alfred Carrière', there is nothing more spectacular. It makes a tall gaunt shrub and in late summer it enters the stage again with its vermilion hips. *R.m.* 'Geranium' is more compact, has larger hips and has flowers of sealing-wax red. Both are worth cultivating. 'Geranium' marks the corners of the Purple Border at Sissinghurst, giving relief from the more sombre hues.

At ground-level reds are provided by geums and heucheras, although both groups offer other colours as well. The geums number some of my favourite early summer perennials. On the whole I am not fond of the more violent hues – such as *G. borisii* with its open flowers of vivid orange – and always go for the pastel tones – such as the soft orange 'Georgenburg'. *G. rivale* gives us the most exciting colours and an exquisite shape to boot, with its rounded leaves, hairy stems and nodding flowers. 'Leonard's Variety' is a soft brick-red, 'Lionel Cox' is a pale limey-cream and Beth Chatto's seedling 'Coppertone' is pale apricot. All these plants are scarcely a foot in height and should live at the front of the border, in part shade, with violas and alchemilla, bronze heucheras and euphorbias in schemes of orange and yellow, deep red and brown.

We need delay our audience with the four royal families no longer. The arrival of June is the signal for the purple standards of the iris to unfurl and for the garden to submit to an Eastern occupation. I say purple standards because the old species, *I. germanica*, will usually be the first of the tall bearded forms to open. The younger, more dashing varieties grant their forebear his short moment of glory and then burst on to the stage themselves in their multicoloured finery, after which *I. germanica* is unable to compete. But for those few days he reigns supreme, standing upright among flights of white columbines and backed by the reddish-purple foliage of berberis and cherries.

The bearded hybrids are close on his heels and arrive in waves from now until early July. Colours range from the golden browns and whites of the Arabian Desert to the indigo and azure blue of the Caspian Sea, from the pinks and apricots of dancers' veils to the garnet reds and imperial blacks of sultans' robes. Sunny borders become tented encampments, strewn with silks, vibrant with colour and riotous with festive spirit; and gardens abandon themselves to a shameless opulence, enjoying a sophistication of colour, shape and texture which they have not experienced since the year began.

Choosing varieties from among the hundreds available is no small task. It is tempting to go for those with the most evocative names like 'Desert Song' and 'Persian Romance', but a surer method is to obtain a catalogue from Kelways (Langport, Somerset), visit their nursery or their stand at Chelsea and put searching questions to the nurserymen. Of the cooler colours I recommend 'Blue Smoke', a clear violet-blue, 'Eleanor's Pride', a soft powder-blue, 'Jane Phillips', a pale lavender-blue, 'Black Swan', a deep violet-black, 'Sable Knight', a dark purple-black, 'Cliffs of Dover', a creamy white, and 'The Citadel' in crisp snow-white; of the warmer colours 'Canary Bird', a strong lemon-yellow, 'Golden Planet' a bright golden-yellow, 'Rocket', a golden tan, 'Juliet', a coppery orange, and 'Red Rum', a mahogany red. But there are so many variations of colour and differences in the shape and poise of standards and falls that you will want to select varieties for yourself.

Irises have to be planted at the front of the border because they need the maximum amount of sunlight on their exposed rhizomes, and this poses problems. Their leaves may be fresh and dramatic early in the year but after flowering they soon become discoloured and unsightly. We cannot train anything much over them because this places their rhizomes in shade. The answer is to interplant with late-flowering bulbs or wispy perennials and, if you wish, reduce their foliage to 9 inches in height. Suitable bulbs are galtonias and acidantheras, and suitable perennials flax and *Gaura lindheimeri*.

In Jekyllian days we would have had long narrow iris beds as part of our early summer garden, and you may feel that this is a luxury you can still afford. If not, then you must incorporate your irises into your main borders, either in short groups down the middle or in stout clumps at the corners. With so many shades and tints of each hue available you can happily scheme in very narrow slices of the spectrum and confine each group to one dominant tone. Black, purple, violet and lavender irises in front of pale pink roses and silver artemisia; gold, lemon and cream irises with deep red paeonies and claret-leaved smoke bush. Alternatively, you can give the plants their freedom and conjure up this pagan carnival, letting apricot dance with rose, and lavender with silver pink, all among the rich crimsons, blacks and royal blues of the sultan's court.

The desert colours should have their own scheme elsewhere, for this is the only early summer opportunity we have of painting with brown. We were able to do so in March and April with the spice-coloured polyanthus and to some extent we can do so later with the heleniums but now is our main chance for an extensive coppery group. Plant bronze-yellow forms with orange browns and mahogany reds and set them against rather an austere background, perhaps a gravel path or a stone wall, so that we are not distracted from this image of desert sands by the lush greenery of other plants.

From further east come the paeonies to rival the irises in

magnificence. Quite different in character with their sumptuous bowls of fragrant petals, they nevertheless share with the irises an exotic appearance and confirm the gardener's June to be a month of untold luxury. In sun or part shade, in heavy or light soil they flower freely from the beginning of the month until mid-July, and even when out of flower their foliage is often of great value. The mahogany of their spring growth and the copper reds of their autumn leaves provide valuable foils for early and late flowers, and even in their dull-green summer foliage they are not to be despised.

The Chinese paeonies confine their colours to pinks, reds, whites and yellows but within those bounds they pass through every tint and shade. Once again, Kelways is the nursery to offer mouth-watering variety. Among the pinks there is 'Albert Crousse', shell pink with streaks of carmine, 'Auguste Dessert', a strong silvery rose, and 'Sarah Bernhardt', a delicious silver-pink; among the reds 'Félix Crousse', a bright rose-red, 'Inspecteur Lavergne', a clear crimson, 'Président Poincaré', a ruby crimson with a spicy scent, and the deep crimson 'M. Martin Cahusac'; among the whites 'Baroness Schroeder', pure white flushed with palest pink, 'Kelway's Supreme', a blush white, and 'Duchesse de Nemours', a pure white suffused with sulphur; and among the yellows the incomparable 'Laura Dessert', a sharp blend of lemon and cream.

The pink, rose and carmine colours complement the blues and violets of the irises well and their presence means that we now have quality plants from all parts of the spectrum. In other circumstances we might think twice about associating plants so different in shape and form as the paeony and the iris, but this is June and the carnival mood must be encouraged. The only points to bear in mind are that the paeony needs a rich diet of manure and compost around its crown, a feast that spells death to the frugal iris, and that if you plant the paeony and the iris side by side you are leaving yourself the difficult task of making a relatively large area interesting for the rest of the summer with little help from the main ingredients.

Wherever you grow generous groups of paeonies you are faced with this problem. Help is at hand among the clematis. Plant either the herbaceous sorts like *C.* × *durandii* or *C. recta* 'Purpurea' or the true climbers like *C. viticella* or *C. texensis*, which you cut hard back in early spring, on the shady side of your paeonies and let them scramble over them, concealing their leaves and bringing late colour. If this sounds too untidy you can grow tall half-hardy perennials like *Salvia uliginosa* and *S. guaranitica* or shrubby plants like *Fuchsia magellanica* 'Alba', which is invariably cut to the ground in winter in cold areas, in front of the paeonies to mask them. Unlike the irises, we do not have to worry about shading their crowns for the rest of the summer.

Because the pinks and reds of the paeonies far surpass those of the irises, it is to the paeonies that we turn when we want to compose a truly feminine scheme. Associated with soft violet or lavender-blue delphiniums, white poppies and peach-coloured daylilies, blush-white roses, salmon poppies and powder-blue irises, the silver-pink, cherry-red and ruby-crimson paeonies shimmer like cushions of satin. The white, cream and yellow varieties are equally splendid among other pale moonlight colours or among the deeper tones of plum-black iris or wine-blotched cistus.

Not all the caravan's colours are silky soft or velvet dark. There are garish notes too, brilliant and fiery, fierce and unruly, to threaten and challenge and make you hold your breath. Such notes are provided by the various forms of the oriental poppy, *Papaver orientale*. The most fleeting of the Eastern visitors, they are also perhaps the plants which most perfectly express the mood and character of June. Their flowers are huge and flamboyant and yet have a simplicity and purity of design which prevents them from ever appearing vulgar; the glistening texture of their petals and their dazzling colours combine with this immodest size to make plants which are the epitome of outlandish beauty. Their colour schemes could be nothing but eastern – rich flame-oranges and reds around a mysterious core of maroon black – and they bring heat and bravado to every plant group.

The most startling forms are 'Goliath' and 'Beauty of Livermere', glowing scarlet-reds, 'Marcus Perry', a vermilion red, and 'Lord Lambourne', an orange scarlet, and if your taste is for gentler tones there is 'Indian Chief' in maroon red, 'Mrs Perry' in salmon pink and 'Turkish Delight' in peach pink. There is also a very distinct white form with black blotches called simply, and rather unimaginatively, 'Black and White', which is a must for the white border.

Oriental poppies make a lot of growth – they form huge mounds of hairy leaves and their flower spikes often rise to 4 feet – and they need support to prevent them from sprawling. Fortunately their seed heads are attractive, so you are not forced to cut the plants down immediately after flowering (though you can do this with impunity), but if your poppies are in prominent positions you will have to behead them. Gertrude Jekyll recommends planting gypsophila behind them which quickly foams over their crowns and hides the gaps left by their absent leaves. A planting of asters or chrysanthemums in front is also effective, or, even better, of the blue mallow 'Primley Blue'.

The intense fire and brimstone of orange-scarlet poppies and large single yellow roses like 'Frühlingsgold' is a group worth having, fuelled with chrome irises and bronze foliage, but it is also profitable to use these fiery hues as contrasts with violet irises and delphiniums. Explosive partnerships are an important component of the June garden, shaking borders out of their customary harmonious and cosy environment and carrying them off into the exotic, multicoloured and often dangerous world of the nomadic tribes.

With the iris, the paeony and the poppy encamped in your garden, it is left to the rose to carry the Eastern theme up into shrub and tree, over wall and pillar. There is little doubt that if every gardener were asked to name the one flower which he most associated with the month of June, the answer would be the rose; and yet we would probably all be picturing a different plant. Some of us would be thinking of a squat 3 foot bush, clipped into a neat dome and adorned with oversize yet perfectly proportioned blooms of coral pink; others of us would be thinking of a rambling climber of monstrous growth, showering creamy white petals from the tops of apple trees; and still others will be thinking of tall arching shrubs smothered in quartered flowers of deepest crimson.

The rose is a plant of many guises and characters. Some come to us straight from the hillsides of Afghanistan and Western China, wild and untamed; some come to us via the scented gardens of the Empress Josephine at La Malmaison, dark and luxurious as Victorian ball dresses and many are still arriving, ever more sophisticated and disease resistant, from the expert nurserymen all over the world. Not all find favour with every gardener (in fact, nothing brings out garden snobbishness faster than a conversation about roses), but with such a huge choice of species and varieties there is a plant of the right habit and temperament for every situation and function in every garden.

For the second time I shall risk incurring your wrath and with a sweeping gesture dispense with two great categories of rose. The first category comprises the species roses. Some of these we have already considered earlier in this chapter and in the chapter on foliage plants and some we will consider later, but the vast majority will have to be omitted for reasons of economy. Few of them can compete with the shrub, climbing and rambling roses in terms of quality of bloom and most are suitable only for the wilder parts of the garden, not necessarily because they are vigorous and untidy but because they have a simple woodland character and appearance which is quite lost in the extravagance of the June borders. The second category I shall omit comprises the so-called bush roses. Under this heading come the hybrid teas, the floribundas and the polyanthas. With some exceptions these roses are far too 'ornamental' for the romantic garden; they have an air of artificiality about them which comes from the fact that all the nurserymen's efforts have been channelled towards the quality, size and abundance of bloom at the expense of character, shapeliness of bush and often even of scent. They have no personality, no natural manner of growth to enable them to blend gently with their neighbours, and in winter they look hideous. This is not to say that they have no place in the garden. Of course they have, but in a formal and obviously manmade setting, not in the tangled framework of the romantic garden.

Let us therefore confine ourselves to those shrub and climbing roses which by their lavish display of flowers, their penetrating scents and their carefree growth contribute further to our wayward theme. Imagine yourself in the walled gardens of Sissinghurst Castle or Mottisfont Abbey, where the National Trust house their collection of old roses, knee deep in petals and intoxicated by sweet perfume, before you a blurred vision of pinks and whites, magentas and crimsons. Or in Kiftsgate Court dreamily contemplating the ferocious white waterfall of the Kiftsgate rose tumbling down from a tall tree to be carried away in a striped torrent of 'Rosa Mundi'. Here you have the rose at its most seductive and these are the images which should haunt us as we consider the various varieties and draw up our lists, to add still more riches to our Eastern caravan.

Rosa rugosa is one of the most distinctive of shrub roses. It makes an upright suckering plant, about 5 feet tall, with fresh green leaves and an abundance of thorns. Flowering is early and continues spasmodically throughout the summer until the fat orange hips ripen in late August, and there is a second flush. The scent is overpowering, sweet and spicy. Vita Sackville-West thought the white form 'Alba', possessed the most far-reaching fragrance of any rose, and this is the form to grow in preference to *R. rugosa* itself. The white of those large cups is dazzling and sits far more comfortably among the fiery hips than do the flowers of the crimson forms.

Two other fine snow-whites are the semi-double 'Blanc Double de Coubert' and 'Schneezwerg', whose flowers are smaller and plentiful. The purity of colour of the white rugosas makes them eminently suitable for inclusion in white schemes, among silver-variegated foliage and clumps of white irises, and later, when their hips are out, among tall Japanese anemones.

The crimson-purple 'Roseraie de l'Hay' is delicious with violet-blue flowers and glaucous grey foliage but fights furiously with the clear bright pink of 'Sarah van Fleet'. 'Fru Dagmar Hastrup' in flesh pink is the easiest of all to accommodate among the pinks and whites of the other rose tribes, and its hips are crimson not orange. But the most surprising and one of the most desirable members of the group is 'Agnes', who seems to have focused her attention on the creamy stamens of the other rugosas and fashioned her petals accordingly. They are a remarkable milky yellow but, in my garden at least, are not produced in anything like the quantity of her relatives. She makes a perfect background for brown and yellow irises, a noble companion for *Geranium* 'Johnson's Blue' and, combined with 'Blanc Double de Coubert' a lovely centrepiece for a yellow and white scheme.

If the rugosas make a satin screen at the back of the border, the gallicas make a velvet cover for the front. They are bushy and compact, generally growing only to 3 feet, which tempts some people to grow them as hedges (not me). Alas they only flower once but their June display is bountiful, and the dark leaves and almost thornless stems are weighed down by quantities of richly coloured flowers, full petalled and sweetly fragrant. These tend to fade with age quite quickly so that every plant carries not one but a mixture of subtle tones. The darkest flowers are borne by 'Cardinal Richelieu', whose lilac-pink buds open to a rich damson-purple and whose petals are fully reflexed, 'Tuscany Superb', a deep crimson with a hint of magenta which fades to a crimson violet and which is highlighted by a boss of golden stamens, and 'Charles de Mills', which has exceptionally large and flat flowers of rich wine-crimson and a delicious scent. There are also many outstanding violet and pink varieties, among them 'Belle de Crécy', which opens a shocking pink but rapidly turns to violet grey and is powerfully fragrant, 'Belle Isis', a pure flesh-pink, 'Duchesse de Montebello', which has pale foliage and fully double flowers of blush pink, and 'Jenny Duval', a greyish violet flushed with magenta and purple. And, of course, there are the striped gallicas such as 'Camaieux' whose pale pink flowers are splashed with crimson purple, stains which fade to magenta and then to palest lilac, and the famous 'Rosa Mundi' (syn. 'Versicolor') whose light crimson flowers are streaked with blush white. A mixed planting of these dark and striped varieties looks like the aftermath of a great drinking bout with the linen tablecloths marked and soiled with spilt burgundy, claret and port wines.

With the front and middle rows of our borders given over entirely to gallicas, the effect would be far too heavy and full-bodied. We need more pale colours to relieve and enliven the crimsons and purples. So let us turn to the damask and the alba roses to provide them. Both have greyish-green foliage and bear soft clear flowers in pink or white. The damasks have a very graceful appearance and carry their blooms in loose clusters over their cut leaves. Almost all the best forms are pure pink. There is 'Celsiana', semi-double and pale pink with golden stamens, 'Ispahan', a lively pink, free flowering and very fragrant, and 'La Ville de Bruxelles' with huge flowers of rich pink and a lingering scent. But there is also a white variety of the highest quality which ought to have pride of place in every garden. It is 'Madame Hardy' with her flat quartered blooms and crumpled petals packed tightly around a light green eye. She mixes wonderfully with all the difficult crimson and magenta shades, a calming influence on a turbulent scene.

The albas include some of the most delicate of roses, exquisite in foliage and flower. Their leaves are greyer than those of the damasks and the colour of their perfectly formed blooms crisper and even more captivating. Their scent is also superb. 'Félicité Parmentier' has reflexed flowers of flesh pink and 'Koenigin von Danemarck' ('Queen of Denmark') has quartered flowers which open carmine and fade to clear pink, but the two marvels of the group are 'Céleste' with its pure shell-pink flowers and grey leaves and 'Maiden's Blush' with its warm blush-pink flowers and unforgettable fragrance. In cool schemes of whites, blues, violets and other clear pinks they are without equal.

So far shapeliness of shrub has gone hand in hand with quality of bloom but when we come to the Provence roses, *R.* × *centifolia*, we encounter a coarseness and untidiness of leaf and habit which is not easy to overlook. But in June they make amends with their drooping flowers which flood the garden with fragrance and bring new tones to our schemes. *R.* × *centifolia* itself certainly deserves inclusion for its globular sugary-pink flowers and cottage garden associations and so does the similarly coloured 'Chapeau de Napoléon' whose sprouting green buds suggest a relationship with the moss roses, but if you only have room for one pink Provence rose it should be 'Fantin Latour'. Of all the pink roses this is my favourite. In form it has none of the ungainliness of its cousins and its flowers are full-petalled, warm blush-pink and folded around a button eye.

Of the remaining centifolia varieties I am tempted by only three: the white 'Blanchefleur' with flat creamy-tinted pink flowers, light green foliage and a vigorous habit; the richly shaded 'Robert le Diable', with shapely flowers of a dusky cerise-purple; and 'Tour de Malakoff', a confection of magenta, violet and lavender purple.

Further deep and velvet colours are provided by the moss roses, which are really centifolias whose buds are clothed in fragrant mossy growth. Most are valuable only as curiosities but some possess flowers which are truly sumptuous. I am thinking of the rich crimson-purple of 'Capitaine Basroger' and 'William Lobb', the even darker 'Capitaine John Ingram' and the near black of 'Nuits de Young'. There are fine pinks and whites in the type itself, *R.* × *centifolia* 'Muscosa' and the white form, 'Muscosa Alba' ('Shailer's White Moss') and in the varieties 'Général Kléber', in soft pink, and 'Maréchal Davoust' in bright crimson-pink, but if your borders are bulging at the seams confine yourself to the dark varieties and keep to the damasks, albas and centifolias for your paler roses.

Most of the centifolia and moss roses grow to 4 or 5 feet tall, so they are very much second-row plants. Many of them benefit from support, and all enjoy regular pruning. I do not know how you like to grow your larger shrub roses, whether you like to leave them very much to their own devices, wrap their long shoots around a framework of wooden poles or arch them over metal hoops. All three methods are effective but you should be guided in every case by the desire to keep a well-balanced plant which is not congested with old and weak growth.

A characteristic of most of these old roses so far considered is that their flowering is brief, just a few weeks in late June and early July. Of course, this does not deter romantic gardeners for the anticipation of that sublime summer spectacle and the sweet memory of it afterwards are sufficient to see us happily through the year, but cool-headed gardeners may be a little concerned at filling their borders with sizeable shrubs which give such a short display. Fortunately, you need not turn away from the shrub roses to find your alternatives. There is a whole range of recurrent and perpetual flowering varieties, every bit as desirable as the gallicas, damasks, albas and centifolias among the scented ranks of the bourbons, the hybrid perpetuals and musks and the modern shrub roses to satisfy your needs. Naturally they excite romantic gardeners just as much, but our roaming spirit takes less account of such sensible concerns in its quest for colour and scent.

The Bourbon roses bring more silk into the June borders to strew among the damask and velvet. Their flowers are again full petalled and highly fragrant and as shrubs most are strong and vigorous, growing to 5 or 6 feet. There is one attractive white variety called 'Boule de Neige', which has dark leaves and sprays of creamy reflexed flowers; and some remarkable and eyecatching striped varieties in 'Variegata di Bologna', with blush-white petals splashed with crimson purple, 'Commandant Beaurepaire', a pink streaked with carmine and purple, and 'Honorine de Brabant', with pale pink petals stained with crimson and violet. My favourite varieties are among the pinks – 'La Reine Victoria' in intense rose-pink, 'Madame Pierre Oger' in flesh pink, tinged with rose (both these have flowers like balls of silk), 'Madame Isaac Pereire' in rosy magenta, and 'Souvenir de la Malmaison' in palest pink with huge quartered blooms.

For more dark crimsons and purples we must look to the hybrid perpetuals, which have the same fullness of flower as the bourbons and give good late displays in addition to their main June flowering. 'Baron Girod de l'Ain' has crimson petals edged in white, 'Empereur du Maroc' is the deepest maroon-crimson but has rather weak growth, and 'Souvenir du Docteur Jamain' is in my opinion the best dark rose in cultivation, its flowers being of the most intense damson-purple with a velvet texture and a magnificent fragrance. It does not enjoy hot sun. There are other first-rate shrubs among the violets and pinks. 'Reine des Violettes' is the most wonderful violet-purple with quartered blooms, greyish leaves and an elegant shape, 'Baronne Prévost' is pale rose, and 'Mrs John Laing' is a superb lilac-pink with a delicious scent. The other two varieties of outstanding form are the white 'Frau Karl Druschki', full petalled, flushed with lemon but alas no scent, and the striped 'Ferdinand Pichard', similar to 'Commandant Beau-repaire' but less vigorous and repeat flowering. With the exception of 'Empereur du Maroc' these are all second-row plants, growing to around 5 feet.

The most bountiful group of shrub roses are the hybrid musks. Of comparatively recent origin, they are especially useful to the scheming gardener because they are at their peak towards the middle of July, just as the other roses are tiring, and because they bring new colours to the rose borders, yellows, apricots and buffs which up to now have been almost absent among shrubs. I ought perhaps to have left these roses until the next chapter, but I include them here because they provide a pivot from which we can say farewell to the misty pinks and clouded purples and travel onward towards the golden yellows of high summer.

In appearance the hybrid musks are quite different to the old roses. They carry their flowers in great sprays like the floribundas and have dark glossy leaves like the hybrid teas, but they retain the old fullness of flower and overpowering fragrance which are so vital to our rich theme. They are all 5 or 6 feet tall. 'Buff Beauty' is one of the finest with a powerful tea scent and rich apricot-yellow blooms set off to perfection by the young red stems and bronze leaves; 'Cornelia' opens a bronze apricot and fades to a creamy pink and has a strong musk scent; and 'Moonlight' is a creamy yellow with golden stamens and mahogany stems. Of the pinks I would single out 'Felicia' which is a strong silver-pink and neater in shape than many, and 'Penelope' which has creamy pink flowers and a rich musk fragrance.

Before we leave the shrub roses and begin to explore the world of the climbers and ramblers, we must look at some of the varieties which do not fit comfortably into any of our previous categories, and which have been the product of this century. They come under the heading of Modern Shrub Roses in books and catalogues, but many have the luxurious blooms of the old shrubs. Many of the most desirable have been raised by David Austin

Roses of Albrighton but I want to mention just three other varieties which are of an equally high standard. The first is 'Zigeuner Knabe' (or 'Gypsy Boy') which flowers only once, in June, but is then smothered in bright crimson-purple flowers, semi-double and fragrant; the second is 'Nevada' which is more generous with its flowers and produces smaller crops through the summer after its main burst – the flowers are creamy white, more single than semi-double, and have golden stamens; and the third is 'Golden Wings', most generous of all, whose large, pure-yellow, almost single flowers are filled with amber stamens and appear all through the summer, making it a must for the yellow border. 'Nevada' and 'Golden Wings' are not in keeping with the character of the old full-petalled rose, so they should be grown in a different part of the garden, among blues and silvers or in much hotter schemes.

David Austin Roses aptly describe their new introductions as 'new roses in the old tradition' and they blend very happily with the ancient varieties. They have an old-fashioned appearance, powerful scents and freedom of flowering, attributes which promise to make them exceedingly popular. I must immediately confess that I grow none of them (I have not an inch of space to accommodate them at present) but I have admired them both at Chelsea and in other people's gardens. They seem to fall into two categories, 'bushes' and 'shrubs'. The bushes grow to around 3 feet and the 'shrubs' to 4 or 5 feet. Among the former I particularly like 'Chaucer' in rose pink which is scented of myrrh, 'Perdita' in rich pink and 'Wife of Bath' another rose pink, and among the latter the warm butter-yellow 'Graham Thomas' – a fitting tribute to this great rosarian, it seems to me – and 'The Reeve' another warm rose-pink. But it is obvious that I have many more to meet and that before long I shall be turfing out some of the older occupants of my borders to welcome them into the garden.

On the whole I prefer to keep the yellow- and buff-coloured roses away from my main rose groups. Their presence tends to destroy the feeling of Eastern luxury conjured up by all those violets and magentas, velvet crimsons and rich wine-reds, and so I build separate schemes around them comprising silver foliage, potentillas, daylilies and thalictrums, and let the darker colours have the upper hand in the rest of the garden. With the arrival of the old roses the garden should move away from that spirit of frivolity that we fostered at the beginning of the month and wallow in a heavier opulence – after all, the sultans are now here. Of course, if your crimson groups are very extensive you may want a touch of yellow here and there to refresh and relieve, but you will usually find that there are enough variations of colour among the dark roses, which are in any case supported by whites and pinks, to present a stimulating enough picture.

Providing that they are in the same colour range, herbaceous perennials can be freely introduced into the rose schemes. A lavish carpet of violas and pansies, pinks and campanulas, foaming bushes of catmint, and erect stands of astrantias, alliums and foxgloves contribute much to the old world mood of your velvet groups. Shrubs like philadelphus and cistus are also fitting companions, especially those with maroon-blotched flowers. It is not only the mixture of colours that we should bear in mind but also the blend of scents, and the fruity fragrance of the philadelphus and the pungent aroma of the cistus will complement attractively the more sophisticated perfumes around them.

It is not only the borders which have been engulfed by the rose. The whole garden drips with their scented petals; trees droop with the weight of great ramblers; posts and pillars froth with the tiny sprays of noisette climbers; and the house itself is imprisoned by webs of teas and bourbons who have abandoned life at ground-level to seek a greater glory nearer the sun. All these roses must now be introduced before our picture of the early summer garden is complete.

There are as many ways of using climbing and rambling roses as there are of using clematis. They can be employed as ground cover, as mantles for covering tree stumps and old sheds, as wall and roofing material for wooden arches, summerhouses and shady retreats, and as decoration for trees and large shrubs. They can be sited against walls and be allowed to weave themselves around windows and doorways, over drainpipes and under guttering, reclaiming with your approval everything manmade and converting it back to a tangle of leaf and flower. You should take care, however, that things do not get entirely out of hand. I have in my mind a picture of the little cottage at Borde Hill in Sussex so overgrown with climbing plants that it had to be abandoned, and of the notice outside explaining that the plants were so rare that no one had dared prune them.

But caution is, I fear, not one of the traits of the romantic gardener and I am sure that you too grow far too many roses and are as reluctant as I am to snip off branches which hold the promise of so much colour and scent. Among the ranks of the climbers and ramblers there are scores to tempt us, and no amount of pleading by anxious builders and decorators is going to hold us back. I shall not divide these roses into their various clans nor even separate climbers from ramblers, for their uses in the garden are very much the same. Two general points, however, should be borne in mind. Firstly, the majority of ramblers flower only once, during June and July, and you might therefore prefer to reserve the key positions around your garden for the climbers, many of which continue to provide quantities of colour well into the autumn. Secondly, climbers are on the whole better suited to wall cultivation than ramblers, which are far more susceptible to mildew.

Of course, some rambling roses make truly monstrous growth and can only be trusted either growing into tall trees or scrambling over unsightly buildings; they are not for timid gardeners and not for places where there is any chance that they might outgrow their welcome. In this category comes *R. brunonii* 'La Mortola', a superior but rather tender variety which hales from the Hanbury Garden on the Italian Riviera and has clusters of powerfully scented pure-white flowers and greyish downy foliage; *R. filipes* 'Kiftsgate' whose sweetly-scented white flowers are small but carried in tremendous sprays and followed by great bunches of red hips; *R. longicuspis*, the latest to flower, whose large panicles of creamy flowers are filled with yellow stamens and carry the un- mistakable scent of bananas (this rose shows its vigour from the moment it is planted and is thus a better choice than the Kiftsgate rose for those smothering jobs where speed is essential, but 'Kiftsgate' does eventually make the bigger plant); 'Bobbie James' and 'Wedding Day', both with fat trusses of creamy white blooms and light, glossy foliage, the former's flowers exhaling a sweet musk fragrance and the latter's smelling of oranges and emerging from buff-yellow buds; and the blush-pink 'Paul's Himalayan Musk' whose double blooms are suffused with lilac and shower down from the tops of trees, releasing their warm scent as they fall. All these will easily exceed 35 feet in height and extend as much across, and as backdrops to gardens of old roses are sensa- tional.

Most of the other ramblers are of more moderate size, growing to between 15 and 20 feet, and can thus be safely grouped with the climbers. The whites, pinks and crimsons remain the prime candidates for inclusion since they help to establish the mood of the late June garden and give us harmonious backgrounds for the old shrub roses. Among the whites I would select 'Aimée Vibert', whose pure, semi-double, yellow-stamened blooms, wonderfully scented, are set off to perfection by its dark glossy foliage; 'Madame Alfred Carrière', a well-known, highly fragrant, perpetual-flowering, almost disease-free rose whose large double blooms are flushed palest pink – a good climber for a north wall; the late-blooming rambler 'Sander's White', strongly scented with pure white semi-double blossom; the orange-scented rambler 'The Garland', which has bunches of flat, single, creamy white flowers coloured with a shot of salmon; and the bushy rambler 'Félicité et Perpétue', which buries itself in crimson-painted buds and tiny white rosettes.

There are many outstanding pinks such as the rambler 'Adelaide d'Orléans' with its clusters of small double blooms in a confection of rose and cream; the famous rambler 'Albertine' with its semi-double copper-pink flowers and penetrating scent; 'Cécile Brunner' with its diminutive double pink blooms (unfortunately these appear only once, at midsummer); 'Madame Grégoire Staechelin', another non-recurrent performer but with flesh-pink flowers and the most delicious scent imaginable; and my favourite, 'New Dawn', which has glossy foliage as a foil to its silver-pink, scented, double flowers.

Good quality crimson climbers are few and far between but there are two bewitching varieties, 'Étoile de Hollande', which is dark, tea-shaped and powerfully fragrant, and 'Guinée', a black-crimson velvet rose, similar to 'Souvenir du Docteur Jamain' and often as troublesome, which I grow beside the crimson-stained white clematis 'Miss Bateman', though they only just overlap in performance. Among the ramblers there are some decadent violets which combine well with the deep crimsons. 'Bleu Magenta', with large full-petalled blooms stained a rich purple but soon fading to violet grey, is only weakly scented and is perhaps overshadowed by 'Veilchenblau', whose clusters of semi-double flowers also fade from crimson to violet but have a central boss of golden stamens and are scented of apples – it is often recommended for shady positions.

For silver and bronze plant groups and for growing against grey and honey-coloured walls there is a fine selection of climbing and rambling roses in warmer tones. 'Albéric Barbier' is a rambler with pale, creamy yellow flowers scented of apples; 'Alister Stella

Gray' has flat quartered flowers of warm yellow, sweetly scented and carried in abundance throughout the summer, and this, together with 'Paul's Lemon Pillar', a once-flowering rose with luminous lemon blooms of remarkable quality, would always be my first choice among the yellow climbers; 'Golden Showers' is a popular climber with strong yellow, double flowers and so is 'Lawrence Johnston', named after the maker of Hidcote, whose blooms are large, bright and semi-double. In groups where the colour scheme is to be progressed towards apricot and orange we can look to 'Lady Hillingdon', a tea-scented climber of exceptional beauty, vigorous and perpetual, and with a bronze tinge to its leaves; to that old cottage garden favourite, 'Gloire de Dijon', whose flowers are golden buff and packed with petals; and to that unusual rambler 'Paul Transon', which has small, flat double flowers of coppery orange-salmon, scented of apples, and whose colour tones in surprisingly well with the warm red brick of Sissinghurst.

For those occasions when you want a really startling image you could plant one of those potent climbers such as 'Danse du Feu', which has spectacular clusters of double flowers in orange-scarlet, 'Parkdirektor Riggers', which is a blazing deep red, velvety and free-flowering, or 'Paul's Scarlet Climber', the most fiery rose of all with blooms of intense, electrifying scarlet. These are for bold gardeners only and should be used sparingly. Certainly I would not advise you to plant them against your perimeter fences or house walls, for if you do so you are immediately encouraging a rivalry between colours which might be hard to suppress, making it nearly impossible to achieve any gentle images within the garden. Furthermore, your background will be a constant distraction, leading the eye away from the foreground, destroying any sense of mystery and suspense that you might want to create, and making your garden seem much smaller than it is. Far better to keep the framework of the garden relatively mild and play fierce effects against it now and again.

Has it ever struck you as curious that the rose which is the very symbol of pagan beauty – wild, luxurious and drenched in scent – should also be the symbol of the English cottage garden and come to stand for an ideal of tranquillity and of a carefree life? So entangled is it in our history and our literature that it has become as comfortably resident here as the descendants of the Norman invaders (of which I am one). Now it is just as easy to bring out its

Englishness in colour schemes as it is to bring out its foreign character. I say this because I am worried that some gardeners may have felt rather ill at ease as we abandoned our natural reserve at the beginning of this chapter and embarked on an Eastern voyage, to collect silks and velvets, rugs and perfumes. The way to do it is to concentrate attention on the softer, paler colours rather than the dark shadowy tones, to focus on the clearer, glowing texture of petals instead of the heavy velvets, and above all to assemble around your roses plants which lighten the image, such as pastel blues, pale yellows and apricots, rather than contribute to the opulence, such as deep reds, dark blues and purples. Alternatively you can retain the richer shades but carry the mind not towards the East but back into the Victorian past – the wines and crimsons of the old roses belong as much to the nineteenth-century English drawing-room as they do to a sultan's carpeted palace – by collecting plenty of plants with old-fashioned colouring, such as dusky rose and pink, and old-fashioned associations, such as astrantias and dianthus, to mix with them.

Those of us who like our rose schemes to be outlandish and extravagant will still turn to gentle pastel effects from time to time, especially when using the soft-yellow and buff-flowered varieties, and we will explore some of these later. But as we review some of the other plants which bloom in June and early July, thoughts of heavy purple opulence remain uppermost in our minds.

It is difficult to think of these other midsummer plants except in a rose context, but there are other shrubs which are equally deserving of dominant positions. The deutzias, for instance, bring a special grace to the garden with their arching stems weighed down with pink and white blossom. Many of the finest, such as the greyish-leaved *D. chunii* and the upright white-flowered *D. setchuenensis corymbiflora*, do not open until July but many of the hybrids like 'Mont Rose' and 'Perle Rose', both in rosy pink, are foaming away in June. Their star-shaped flowers are held in dense corymbs and last for several weeks, and the shrubs grow to about 5 feet. In a sea of blue *Campanula persicifolia* and between jets of delphiniums they look marvellous.

They could also be incorporated into an old world scheme of pinks and whites, for which there would be no better underplanting than *Astrantia major*. There is much affection among gardeners for this ancient plant which is so restrained in colouring but sophisticated in design. The tiny florets are arranged like a pin-cushion upon a saucer of bracts, in a pattern of pink, green and greyish white, and the leaves are dark and deeply cut. In the variety 'Margery Fish' (syn. 'Shaggy') the flowers are larger and cleaner. In a pink setting these white astrantias are delightful and at Sissinghurst they are massed among martagon lilies beneath the rose 'Maytime' and the shell-pink *Escallonia* 'Edinensis'. You might also like to try the rose-pink astrantia, *A. maxima*, whose soft tints are useful in every pastel group, especially among pale blues. All these forms grow to 2 feet and are perfectly happy in shade.

No June garden would be complete without a good sprinkling of members of the genus *Dianthus*. The garden pinks have become as much a part of the gardener's summer as the rose, and deservedly for, like the rose, they combine richness of colouring with sweetness of scent. They also display in the same colour range as the old roses and make fine companions for them, while their glaucous blue foliage helps to bind front-line plantings of campanulas and violas. On the whole, I prefer to see them in silver schemes with artemisias, ballotas and stachys, ice-blue campanulas and blue-leaved, silver-pink roses such as 'Céleste' and 'Maiden's Blush', rather than in deeper groups of crimson roses and blood-red violas but there are some varieties of pink which are more suited to a warmer treatment.

A number of pinks are attractively laced and marbled which gives them a wonderfully old-fashioned appearence. Of these 'Dad's Favourite', with maroon lacing and central blotch on white semi-double flowers, 'Gran's Favourite', with mauve lacing, 'Laced Romeo', with deep red lacing, 'London Delight', with mauve lacing on pink flowers, and 'Prudence', with purple lacing on pink flowers, are irresistible. For a bizarre grouping try them in front of some of the striped and splashed shrub roses. Many of the deep crimson selfs are also worth having, in particular 'Desmond', 'Portrait' and 'Thomas', together with that gem 'Brympton Red', whose crimson is marbled with maroon. Isolated against silver and blue foliage they are very striking.

The white-flowered pinks can be happily introduced into silver and yellow schemes as well as pink ones. Those which have green eyes, such as the double 'White Ladies' and the single 'Charles Musgrave', are especially desirable; of the pure whites I would still always choose old 'Mrs Sinkins'. Imagine these growing with achilleas, thalictrums and phlomis, backed by a great fan of the pineapple-scented broom *Cytisus battandieri*, and the whole scheme stained with bloody pools of 'Desmond' and 'Portrait'.

Ramparts Nurseries have a comprehensive selection of pinks and their lists will encourage you to keep trying new varieties. To grow them successfully you need to choose sunny sites and to ensure that your soil is well-drained. If you take a little trouble over planting and dead-head the plants occasionally you will be rewarded with a long succession of flowers well into the summer.

The common foxglove, *Digitalis purpurea*, is at its best now and the pink and white forms can be allowed to seed themselves about in the wilder parts of the garden. The whites are quite ghostly in the woodland shadows among twisted branches and sun-starved shrubs. Unfortunately, they are biennials and too troublesome for the borders, having to be continually dug up and replaced and their ugly seedheads cut down. But there are two excellent perennial varieties which are easily raised from seed and which are far superior in colouring to their cousins. *D. grandiflora* is a creamy yellow and *D.* × *mertonensis* is a creamy rose and often compared to the colour of crushed strawberries. Both grow to 2 feet and thrive in semi-shade. The latter is very effective with violet-blue polemoniums, but stands out well against clear pink roses and geraniums.

I wonder if you know *Morina longifolia*, which is another plant that comes readily from seed. It looks like a fearsome thistle for most of the time for its leaves are arranged in a prickly rosette but in fact it is relatively harmless and surprises you in early July by producing an elegant spire, 3 feet tall, around which cling whorls of narrow hooded flowers in pink and white. It likes partial shade and looks well among astrantias which are just as intriguing in shape and reasonably close in colour.

I first met *Phuopsis stylosa* in Margery Fish's garden at East Lambrook Manor in Somerset, where it seemed to have crept into every sunny plant group. It looks like a dry-land version of pond weed, and is almost as invasive. Its near prostrate stems are clothed in narrow foliage and support light domes of bright pink flowers from June onwards. Perhaps it is too untidy for most people's borders in spite of its long flowering period but I find it a lively underplanting for pink roses, and at Highclere Castle in Hampshire there is a sensitive association with the old-fashioned heads of red valerian. I should add that some gardeners find its sweaty smell less than appealing.

More pink sunlovers are found among the ornamental onions. These are perfect companions for the old shrub roses, their violet-pink colours toning in with the crimsons and pinks, their lacy flowers contrasting with the silks and velvets and their bizarre shape and topheavy appearance contributing to the feeling that the June garden has lost its grip on reality. *Allium christophii* (syn. *A. albopilosum*) is the most graceful with its huge heads of shooting stars in metallic lilac-pink. Each bulb produces one head which it balances on a stout stem 18 inches high and the strap-like leaves gathered at the base begin to shrivel almost before the flowers are out. To give them a firmer background many gardeners grow them among the foliage of bearded irises. The seedheads are valuable as well as the flowers and would benefit from finding themselves part of an orange and brown scheme by July and August.

A. sphaerocephalum is often dismissed as unworthy, presumably because its flowerheads are much smaller than those of its cousins, but the reddish purple of its pear-shaped blooms is excellent among violet blues. It looks well, for example, beside its cousin *A. caeruleum* whose heads are round and deep. Both grow to 2 feet. The tallest allium, *A. giganteum*, opens in July having climbed to around 4 feet, but although its size is impressive its heads are so tight and perfectly round that they make the plant look quite artificial. Far preferable are the larger domes of *A. aflatunense*, which open at 3 feet, but this species together with the low-growing *A. karataviense* are usually over by the time the roses take the stage.

If you have room to squeeze one more large shrub into your pink and purple schemes, plant *Buddleia alternifolia*. Here is another untamed beauty, breezy and light-headed, which flings out its slender arms in all directions and shrouds itself in a lilac mist. The display is brief but memorable and is a useful antidote to heavy schemes. The flowers exhale a faint sweetness which occasionally catches you on the air but more frequently has to be sought out. This shrub is also effective among blues and greys, wine blacks and yellows and would make a marvellous pivot in the border leading you from shadowy tones towards clearer, sharper ones.

A border filled exclusively with campanulas would be quite a sight. All those bells ringing away in shades of violet, blue, lilac and white, church bells and hand bells, treble bells and tenor bells. We would want a generous planting of *C.* 'Burghaltii' with its imposing sized flowers of unusual colour – pale lilac-grey from maroon buds – and quantities of *C. persicifolia*, dangling with violet-blue flowers on the type (larger ones on 'Telham Beauty') and white flowers on 'Alba'. In the foreground we would have hummocks of *C. carpatica* in its various forms – pale blue in 'Blue Moonlight', deep blue in 'Isobel' and white in 'Bressingham White' – and the diminutive variety of *C. lactiflora* called, rather unfortunately, 'Pouffe'. And at the back there would be clouds of tall lactifloras in violet, lavender, white and, in the form 'Loddon Anna', pink swirling around spires of mauve-blue *C. latifolia* 'Gloaming'. There are many others we could add, especially from among the dwarf varieties, to turn this into an absorbing collection as well as an attractive feature.

Campanulas are good mixers not only among themselves. They combine well with the old roses from both the cooler and the warmer sides of the spectrum, and the pale, washy tones of many varieties manage to tame even the most savage magentas and carmines. They are particularly fine in smoky groups of greys and whites – massed in front of a gigantic *Rosa soulieana*, for example – and in partially shaded positions where their glowing hues are at their most intense.

Catmint, *Nepeta* × *faassenii*, is another obvious companion for roses, helping to blur schemes and soften the hard edges of paths. Commonplace it may be but that is no reason to banish it from your garden. Its brilliant leaf colour early in the year is superb among oranges and yellows, and now its clouds of lavender-blue flowers linger like an autumn mist beneath shrubs and tall perennials. The variety 'Six Hills Giant' is twice as large as *N.* × *faassenii* itself, growing to about 3 feet.

A similar role is served by *Salvia* × *superba* which also grows to 3 feet. Its spires of typical sage-like flowers are a blend of violet and reddish purple and demonstrate how well these two colours combine; if you cut them down after flowering a fresh set of spires will follow. 'East Friesland' is a shorter version. Other attractive shades are found in *S. haematodes*, a lavender blue, and its hybrid 'Indigo', an intense violet-blue which both reach 3 feet. Like catmint, all these sages need full sun to perform well, and make fine contrasts for yellow flowers. Against crimson-purple roses they hold their ground well.

The delphiniums provide jets of purple and blue to introduce into all our schemes. I do not intend to become side-tracked by the innumerable varieties on the market, for unless you are a delphinium enthusiast you will be content to grow your varieties from mixed Blackmore and Langdon seed and from seed of the Pacific Hybrids – pink shades from 'Astolat', whites from 'Galahad', pale blues from 'Camelaird', and deep blues from 'Black Knight'. Thus you are able to fill your borders at very little expense, and have fountains of colour from June until August. Plants can be grown in small groups or led in long, thin drifts through mounds of silver-pink paeonies and roses or behind cushions of yellow daylilies and potentillas. The advantage of drifts is that you can cut down the flower spikes without leaving large gaps, but I like Gertrude Jekyll's idea of leaving them alone and training late-flowering clematis up them, such as *C. viticella*.

Smaller and more graceful plants are found among the Belladonna Hybrids. These grow to about 3 or 4 feet and their funnel-shaped flowers are well spaced up the spikes, giving them a light and airy quality. They associate splendidly with gypsophila. 'Pink Sensation' is a soft rose and 'Lamartine' a good strong blue. For a really intense gentian blue, try the dwarf *D. tatsienense*. This also comes readily from seed, and a decent stretch of it will enliven the front of any bed, notably in rock gardens which by now are beginning to doze off. It must have good drainage and plenty of sun.

I have frequently mentioned cistus in my suggestions for plant associations and now is the moment to meet them face to face. They are without doubt some of the most exciting of summery shrubs. (I am biased of course, for any plant that carries wine-blotched flowers needs no further recommendation to enter my garden gates.) Their flowers are like crumpled taffeta, smooth and glistening, while you have only to smell their gummy leaves to be reminded of those hot and dusty Mediterranean roads along which you walked in search of seeds and cuttings. It would not matter if they gave only brief displays but, on the contrary, they bury themselves in petals during June and July. Naturally they have their faults. Most will not survive very bad winters and many grow rather leggy at the base, but since they are all easily struck from softwood cuttings and young plants grow fast and heartily neither of these factors weighs heavily against them.

The plain white-flowered varieties are rather boring, although I do grow *C.* × *corbariensis* which has crimson-tinged buds. The ones

to acquire are *C*. × *cyprius*, a 5-foot shrub with leaden leaves, *C.
ladanifer*, upright and taller, and *C*. × *verguinii*, lean and tricky.
All these have white flowers stained with crimson or chocolate.
There is also a fine maroon-blotched rose-pink cistus called
C. × *purpureus*. Do not grow them all side by side but scatter them
among your roses and irises, harmonizing their predominant
colours and highlighting their stains. Cistus will not tolerate poorly
drained soils; other than that their only requirement is for sun and
more sun so that they can sprawl and lounge and roast their
branches.

There are purple-blotched flowers among the philadelphus too,
but here the colour contrast is not as cleanly executed. The purple
comes in smudges rather than deep stains. 'Belle Etoile' is the
largest, at around 6 feet, and is suitable for the back of the border
or for wilder positions where its coarse foliage and unwieldy shape
can be ignored once flowering is over. Its single white flowers are
borne so profusely that they pull down the branches, and shrubs
look as if they are wreathed in Hawaiian garlands. The hybrid
'Sybille' is similar but is easier to accommodate for it only grows
to 4 feet. It is a perfect partner for the white rockets of *Verbascum
chaixii* 'Album', whose flowers also have wine-purple centres.

Of course, we do not really grow philadelphus for the colour of
their flowers. It is their delicious orange-flower scent wafting
through the garden that we want, mingling with the musk and tea
fragrance of the roses. The clear white-flowered varieties are therefore no less desirable than those whose flowers are tinged with
purple. The large, double-flowered 'Virginal', at 10 feet, is worth
obtaining if you have the space for it, as is the early, creamy, single-
flowered *P. coronarius*; otherwise there is the lower-growing
'Avalanche', with single flowers and a fitting name, and the dwarf
'Manteau d'Hermine', which is double and creamy.

Feathery heads of flower are always welcome because they
give us contrast in form and bring a touch of circus excitement
to our schemes. *Aruncus dioicus* (formerly *A. sylvester* and *Spiraea
aruncus*) has just such a character. Its effervescent plumes of
creamy white can reach 7 feet in height and are magnificent
among solid greens and whites or associated with misty mauves
and violets. Unfortunately, the display is all too brief, scarcely
more than a couple of weeks at the end of June, after which the
flowerheads rapidly deteriorate. On male plants, which have
superior plumes, they turn an unsightly brown, and on female

plants they become heavy with green seed pods. Still, these can be removed and their ferny leaves are pleasant enough to form a foliar bridge for later schemes. There is a good low-growing variety called 'Kneiffii', whose leaves are more finely cut.

I should not want to be without *Gillenia trifoliata*, whose flowering also coincides with the old roses. This is a very graceful and airy perennial, not often seen, which grows to about 4 feet and sends out flights of slim white flowers from its red calyces. It is the combination of red and white which equips it so well for pink groups. In addition, its lightness of form and diffused colour can be employed in the same way as that of gypsophila to bring momentary relief from very hot plant groups, such as a mass of scarlet lychnis. As with aruncus, most positions will suit it, in sun or shade.

It is time now to leave the pinks and purples, crimsons and whites which have dominated our thoughts for the last twenty pages and to investigate those plants which make their contributions on the other side of the spectrum. The warmer colours handed over supremacy at the end of the spring and although they are still abundant in the garden for most of June, by the end of the month they have been swamped and do not return to power until August. This continual change in emphasis ensures variety and enables the gardener to experiment with different moods and colour effects. As June has advanced we have slowly heaped on darker and heavier colours to succeed the lively ones, and by early June a crimson opulence rests on the borders. But we have remained true to our Eastern theme, having simply flung open the doors of the caravans and the covers of the tents to enjoy the dark riches inside. We have never abandoned our quest for silks and velvets and perfumes and all the other trappings which transport us to a pagan world.

We depend a great deal on the damask whites, glowing violets and silvery pinks to prevent our schemes from ever becoming oppressive or gloomy, but now and then we need a complete change. This we can bring about either by the gentle introduction of a pastel scheme of apricot, lemon, pale blue and cream or by a sudden fiery interlude of scarlet, orange and gold.

Fruity scents are very much a part of the midsummer garden, and one of the most remarkable is breathed by the Moroccan broom, *Cytisus battandieri*. Opening at the end of June, its cones of golden-yellow flowers possess a powerful pineapple fragrance which on hot days travels far. It is deliciously blended with the orange-flower scent of philadelphus and of a rose like 'The Garland'. Even if it had no fragrance we would still grow this broom for its rich contrast of bright yellow flowers against silver foliage. Its leaves are shaped like those of a laburnum and are silky smooth. It must be treated as a wall shrub in all but the mildest areas, and with a southerly or westerly aspect can easily exceed 12 feet in height. It is particularly valuable as a backcloth for silver and yellow schemes, but is also superb among roses, whether apricots like 'Lady Hillingdon' and 'Buff Beauty' or lemons like 'Albéric Barbier' and 'Paul's Lemon Pillar'. *Phlomis fruticosa* is also flowering now, you may recall, and might be used to pick up the image of dense yellow flowerheads against silver foliage further down the border; its mustard tones, however, are too disturbing for a very close association with the broom.

More mustard yellow is delivered by the tallest of the yarrows, *Achillea filipendulina*. This is a plant for the back of the sunny border where it will grow to 6 feet. Its large flat flowerheads contrast well with all the spires, bells and trumpets around them and, as every professional garden designer will tell you, enable you to trace horizontal lines through your plant groups. The ferny leaves are also attractive. 'Gold Plate' is a fine sturdy form, and much smaller, at around 3 feet, is 'Coronation Gold' with greyish-green foliage. For the front of the border there are gentler yellows, 'Moonshine' in sulphur and *A.* × *taygetea* in Devon cream. Both have beautiful foliage, grey and finely cut, and look delicious among whites and clear blues. These achilleas begin flowering in late June and go on into August, so they can be partnered with a number of different plants, including purple salvias, scarlet lychnis and violet delphiniums.

Also valuable for contrasts are the foxtail lilies. Their dense spikes of star-shaped flowers look like rockets and shoot up above their companions often to a height of 8 feet. Some species such as the short white *Eremurus himalaicus* and the giant pink *E. elwesii* flower quite early, around the end of May, but the two aristocrats, *E. stenophyllus* (syn. *E. bungei*) and *E. robustus*, delay their opening until the middle of June or later. *E. stenophyllus* reaches 4 feet and by the end of the month is a gentle blend of warm tones. As the upper flowers open a bright yellow, the lower flowers are fading to brown, and this together with the tuft of orange anthers inserted into each flower gives the whole column the appearance of being composed of golden honey. *E. robustus* is much taller, at around 7 feet, and its pale pink stars, which also fade to brown, are just the right soft and indecisive colour for use in mixed groups of pastels. All eremerus need full sun, good drainage, and some protection from extremes of cold – piles of grit or ashes heaped over their crowns in winter, for instance. Their leaves are strap-like and scruffy, and they will need to be concealed later by one of our old stalwarts such as gypsophila, *Aster divaricatus* or nasturtiums.

A number of daylilies are well under way by now. I would recommend especially the greenish primrose-yellow flowered variety called 'Whichford', the orange 'Burning Daylight', the crimson and gold 'Stafford', and, most delightful of all, the small flowered varieties whose petals have a bronze reverse like 'Golden Chimes' and the lemon yellow 'Corky'. These are all good front- or middle-row components of warm schemes and have a long flowering period. I am not so keen on the pink and salmon varieties because their colours are usually combined with strong yellows in the form of veins or flashes, but with the quantity of new varieties being introduced each year I am sure that there will soon be some purer shades to tempt me.

The continuity of flowering of the evening primroses is even more staggering than that of the daylilies. Some species maintain their display until early autumn, notably *Oenothera odorata* (syn *O. stricta*). Its flowers open pale lemon at dusk and by the next morning have faded to peach. The fruity sweetness of their scent is delicious and is quite distinct from other summer fragrances. Plants grow to 3 feet and enjoy full sun. *O. tetragona* is shorter, at around 18 inches, and has clusters of bright yellow cupped flowers which emerge from reddish buds. These are most brilliant in the variety 'Fireworks'. *O. tetragona* 'Glaber' is similar but has bronzy foliage. And the lowest growing species is *O. missouriensis*, which has prostrate stems, long narrow leaves, and huge cups of pure yellow. It is also powerfully and sweetly fragrant, and makes an important contribution to plantings on sunbaked soil. The red-budded varieties of evening primrose make good companions to the vermilions and scarlets – plants such as lychnis, astilbes, and crocosmias – while the cleaner and paler tones of *O. stricta* and *O. missouriensis* can be trusted among violets and blues as well. Try the latter with black-leaved ophiopogon.

Sisyrinchium striatum 'Variegatum' has been near the top of my Wants List for at least three years and although I must have visited scores of nurseries, I have never been offered it. Why it is so scarce I cannot say for you often see bold groups of it in public and National Trust gardens. Its clumps of pale iris-like leaves are striped with Devon cream and tone in wonderfully with the spires of straw-yellow flowers which open from mid-June until the end of July. Still, I am quite content with *S. striatum* itself, whose foliage is just plain greyish-green. The long arms of flowers are worth close inspection, for every bloom is marked with maroon on its reverse, encouraging you to try purplish-red associations. You might grow it beside *Iris chrysographes* 'Rubella' or against a claret-leaved shrub. In the Cotswolds it is often isolated outside the garden gates in front of the dry stone wall, cream against honey yellow, and it would be hard to improve on this.

The two yellow thalictrums, *T. flavum* and *T. speciosissimum*, open in June. Both have heads of lemon fluff supported on 5-foot stems and beautifully cut foliage like a maidenhair fern, but *T. speciosissimum* scores over its cousin because its leaves are glaucous blue instead of green. It is this combination of dainty heads and graceful foliage which makes these plants desirable rather than any special quality of flower. In green and yellow schemes, among variegated hostas, bamboos and golden grasses, *T. flavum* will provide an attractive contrast in form, while in blue and yellow schemes, among euphorbias, rues and blue grasses, *T. speciosissimum* stands supreme. But their purity of colour and misty image allows them to infiltrate most plant groups, even pinks and crimsons, and, as with other thalictrums, I find I never have enough of them.

I have already extolled the virtues of *Verbascum chaixii* 'Album' in white and purple schemes and especially as a partner to *Philadelphus* 'Sybille'. Its flowers are white with a purple eye and are densely packed up its 3-foot spikes. However, the majority of verbascums produce flowers in warmer tones and are useful members of midsummer pastel groups. *V. thapsiforme* (syn. *V. densiflorum*) is deep yellow, *V. × hybridum* 'Cotswold Queen' is buff (both these have purplish centres) and *V. × h.* 'Gainsborough' is creamy yellow. They all carry their flowers on thin spikes, 3 or 4 feet tall, above clumps of nondescript leaves; if these are cut down after flowering, new spikes will grow from lower leaf joints, and so a loose display is maintained for much of the summer. Unfortunately, plants are not very long-lived and you must ensure a population by taking root cuttings. There was an attractive

coppery scheme at the last Chelsea Show involving these verbascums supplemented with the bronze-red plumes of *Astilbe*
'Federsee', dusky-pink sprays of the biennial *Salvia sclarea turkestanica* and branches of copper beech. I like to set them behind
quite firm shapes as an antidote to their wild and untidy growth,
such as bronze heucheras and low-growing copper-red berberis.

Like lilies-of-the-valley, alstroemerias are plants which many
people consistently fail to establish in their gardens, while others
find them rampant and invasive and are forced to throw out
bucketfuls of roots every year. Until a couple of years ago I
belonged squarely in the former category. I planted dry roots and
I planted young pot-grown seedlings, and not a single one
survived. Then I tried sowing seed directly into their intended
site, so that roots would never be disturbed, and this was quite
successful. But the one foolproof method proved to be to dig up a
large clump of roots from a friend's garden, soil and all, during
August, after the leaves had withered, and dropping them gingerly
into the border. Obviously they did not realize they had been
moved and any dastardly plan they would have hatched to cheat
me was foiled.

A. aurantiaca is the commonest species. It grows to 3 feet and
covers itself in bright orange trumpets, which are speckled with
black, from the end of June until mid-July. The variety 'Moerheim
Orange' is deeper and 'Tawny Orange' tends towards bronze. A
long bed of orange alstroemerias is a luxuriant sight but their
stems die down quickly and need to be covered over with something. Nasturtiums will maintain the fiery scene. The Ligtu
Hybrids are a little taller than *A. aurantiaca* and give a range of
pastel colours from pink and salmon to peach and apricot. Like
their cousin they want a warm sheltered spot and good drainage.
Even more exotic is *A. pulchella* in deep red and green. It is
supposed to be very tender but it came through last winter, a
fairly mild one I will admit, without any protection in my garden.
I did not mean to expose it to the vagaries of the season; I just
forgot to cover it with bracken.

I have postponed meeting the honeysuckles until now because
most are at their best in June and July, but some, such as *Lonicera
tragophylla*, *L.* × *brownii* and *L.* × *tellmanniana*, began their display
in late May. A tangle of honeysuckle is one of the essentials of the
English garden. It is a link with our native hedgerows and with
our earliest cottage gardens, and a symbol of our scorn of formal

gardening and classical symmetry. The honeysuckle demands informal treatment, and is rarely successfully grown against a wall. Scrambling up trees, over stumps, along rough wooden fences and through trelliswork it is properly in its element, flinging its flowers and dripping its perfume and weaving its knotted cloak without fear of nipping secateurs.

The common honeysuckle, *L. periclymenum*, has two superior forms which will usually be chosen in preference to the type. 'Belgica' is the early Dutch honeysuckle and has reddish-purple and pale yellow flowers, powerfully and sweetly scented, from May until July with a late flush in September. 'Serotina', the late Dutch honeysuckle, is similar, a little more pinky, and flowers from July right into the autumn. Both are bushier and more floriferous than *L. periclymenum* itself. More yellow in colouring is *L. caprifolium*, the early cream honeysuckle, whose flowers are only occasionally flushed with pink. It also has attractive glaucous blue-green leaves, making it a truly magnificent plant for yellow associations. *L.* × *americana* is another yellow and reddish-purple flowered plant, extremely floriferous and fragrant, which is spectacular in June and July.

The purest coloured honeysuckles are unfortunately scentless. This should not dissuade you from planting them, but you may have to think of them as a different race of climbing plant so that you do not keep pushing your nose into the flowers and being disappointed. The two red varieties are *L. sempervirens*, which is semi-evergreen and has scarlet and yellow trumpets, and *L.* × *brownii*, which is less orange and has tighter heads. *L. sempervirens* flowers in June and July and needs some shelter from cold winds, while *L.* × *brownii* is totally hardy and regularly follows up its early summer display with a second burst late in the season. The best pure yellow varieties are *L. tragophylla*, which has huge heads of golden-yellow flowers and bluish-green foliage, and *L.* × *tellmanniana*, whose flowers are a rich amber.

All four varieties have a richness and depth of warm colour that singles them out from their neighbours, and they make excellent focal points to lead you from one part of the garden to another. The reds are best seen among greens or pure whites, such as roses and clematis, while the coppery yellows are delicious beside cream roses like 'Bobbie James' and 'Wedding Day'. None of these honeysuckles, however, will tolerate strong sunlight and they must be grown either in partial or complete shade.

It is likely that you will not be able to absorb many more strong hues into your garden without disturbing the heavy velvet and soft pastel schemes. The brightest yellows and oranges have been used only as highlights for and brief respites from our main colour groups, and so it is with the bright reds. The violas and aquilegias are giving us the odd touch of blood or flame, and a few roses and paeonies are glowing garnet and ruby above them. If you feel you have room for further red splashes then you might consider the astilbes and the lychnis.

I must confess that I do not grow many varieties of astilbe and cannot guide you smoothly through the ranks of the pink, magenta, orange and Ostrich Plume varieties. But the whites and reds I do grow – the superb dense plumes of 'White Gloria' above dark foliage, the bright white of 'Deutschland', and the deep red of 'Fanal', the best of the reds, whose young foliage and later plumes look so splendid beside the brilliant yellow of Bowles's golden sedge. In a different spot I might have backed this team with golden-variegated cornus. The trouble with astilbes is that they really want very moist conditions. Of course they seem quite happy in the ordinary border, in sun or shade and even on moderately dry soil, but you have only to see the luxuriant spectacle they make beside ponds and lakes, their feathery heads waving and reflecting in the water, to realize how pathetic your exiled specimens are. That is why I have never been tempted to grow them more extensively, although I do obtain much pleasure from the few I grow in solitary splendour.

The Maltese Cross, *Lychnis chalcedonica*, provides us with one of the wickedest reds of the year. Its tight flat heads are a shrieking scarlet, rise to 3 or 4 feet and threaten everything around them. Timid gardeners will isolate them among green, and indeed they do look particularly intense beside glossy foliage, but others may like to set them against other fierce hues. I have seen them successfully teamed with yellow achilleas – there is a vague similarity in the shape of their flowerheads – and they also look well in front of golden elder. *L.* × *arkwrightii* is an intense vermilion, more orange than red, with looser heads of flowers, and it only grows to 18 inches. It too is a fearsome character and needs to be sited with caution. Fortunately its foliage assists us greatly, for its leaves are a dusky metallic green with purple undersides and make a fine foil for the flowers. Capitalizing on this, an obvious partner is *Ligularia clivorum* 'Desdemona' whose leaves are similarly coloured but far larger, and you might back the group with a dusky purple shrub, such as *Corylus maxima* 'Purpurea'. If this sounds too tame, try introducing lemon-yellow evening primroses. Both these lychnis enjoy full sunshine.

The Summer's Height

The arrival of the old roses is for many people the climax of the gardening year. Nothing that precedes them and nothing that follows them can rival that luxurious blend of rich colour and sweet perfume, sensuous texture and wayward shape. But by mid-July most roses have exhausted themselves and unless, on those dark winter evenings when you leaf through catalogues and draw up lists, you have forced yourself to look beyond the intoxicating spectacle of the midsummer garden and have gathered a sufficient quantity of plants for the rest of the summer, your borders will look as if they are already preparing themselves for the slow decline towards autumn. There are still a good two months of full colour ahead of us and the chest of plant treasures must still be almost half full. The traditional herbaceous border is only now beginning to get under way and it is chiefly to the hardy herbaceous plants, supplemented by annuals and tender perennials, that we turn to fill our palette for high summer.

During July the mood of the garden changes once more. The freshness of the greens and the luminous purity of the pastels is exchanged for heavier and harder tones. The sun is becoming too strong for delicate schemes, early growth is already yellowing and in places the grass is turning brown. The dry, calm weather is enticing the whole family outdoors, a jug of iced lemonade sits permanently on the table, and croquet tournaments are being regularly and savagely fought. There is a feeling of stability permeating the borders, as the trusty old perennials take the stage and act out their parts with classic precision, often for months on end. It is a time of peace and prosperity, a time to sit back and enjoy the fullness of summer. But there is a real danger that this stable and tranquil scene may also seem smug and self-satisfied. There are many plants contributing colour which, although reliable and attractive, have none of the personality and charm of their June cousins. They perform well and receive plenty of applause, but they give us no surprises and never excite our gypsy spirit. It takes all the gardener's guile to ensure that such plants are countered with wilder forms and that our solid schemes are continually interrupted by fleeting and unexpected visions. Plant groups must never become static or predictable.

One tribe of plants which does much to lift rather flat schemes is clematis. I realize that I have given this noble group scant treatment up to now and it is time to make amends. Of the large-flowered hybrids many have been in flower for ages and many have now finished: blues like 'Lasurstern', with deep violet-blue sepals (not petals, we are told) around a boss of creamy stamens, 'Lady Northcliffe', with exquisite blooms of rich lavender-blue, and 'Mrs Cholmondeley', which has more open flowers flushed with lilac; purples like 'The President', with deep violet sepals highlighted by silvery stamens and undersides; carmine reds like 'Ville de Lyon', with relatively small overlapping sepals and cream stamens; and whites like 'Henryi', with a bronzy-yellow central boss, 'Marie Boisselet' (syn. 'Madame le Coultre') which is creamy white all over, and my favourite 'Miss Bateman', whose white sepals are striped with green and whose stamens are maroon purple. Some of them, such as 'Lasurstern', 'Ville de Lyon' and 'The President', will keep on producing flowers for another couple of months. All these are magnificent when grown up walls and pillars with other flowering climbers – the blues wandering among crimson roses, the deep purples filtering through white and yellow roses, and the whites meandering among vines and scarlet honeysuckles.

The same treatment suits the later flowering hybrids, most of which are just beginning to get into their stride by early July: blues like 'Perle d'Azur', with pale violet-blue sepals and cream stamens; purples like 'Gypsy Queen', dark and velvety and late to open; deep reds like 'Niobe', with velvet sepals and green stamens; and near whites like 'Huldine', small flowered and well poised, whose mauve-tinged flowers are best seen from below. But clematis can also be used out in the borders and it is these combinations with shrubs and perennials that are particularly worth exploring now. You have only to visit a garden such as John Treasure's at Tenbury Wells in Worcestershire to see all the possibilities. There clematis ramble through shrubs and over perennials, up trees and across bare ground, clothing and carpeting everything in their path. Meeting old friends in such refreshingly new surroundings is an eye-opening experience and makes you realize how un-imaginative most of us are in our use of plants. A willingness to experiment and a little artistic vision is all that is required. Close your eyes and picture these partnerships in Treasure's garden – wreaths of greyish lavender ('Beauty of Richmond') embracing a glaucous blue conifer; a veil of intense reddish-purple, dark and velvety ('Madame Grangé'), draped over the dusky grey of *Phlomis fruticosa*; and a cloud of ruby-red bells ('Gravetye Beauty') en-gulfing a mat of gentian blue *Anagallis linifolia*. I have already mentioned the superlative association of *Berberis temolaica* with the rich violet clematis 'Etoile Violette'.

Most clematis are suitable for this informal border treatment, but I would avoid those which are over-vigorous, particularly the rampageous species clematis, and those which you cannot cut down in early spring during your annual tidy-up, such as *C. alpina* and *C. macropetala* (which should not really be pruned at all). Varieties that flower in early summer can be reduced to their lowest sets of strong buds, and the late performers can be cut back completely, to a couple of feet above ground-level.

Either you can arrange matters so that the clematis flowers at the same time as its host and its companions or so that it succeeds them and enlivens an otherwise dreary scene. I have referred to the latter approach in the chapter on spring associations. For the present let us concentrate on the use of clematis as part of summer schemes, and as we look at some of the familiar shrubs and perennials of this season try to imagine how they could be trans-formed by a light mantle of foreign blossom.

Perhaps the most pleasing border clematis are the hybrids of *C. texensis* and *C. viticella*, for they have retained their rustic character and their simple, relatively small flowers blend happily with everything else. The two *texensis* hybrids I would choose are 'Etoile Rose' with its little nodding bells of cerise, edged in silvery pink, and 'Gravetye Beauty', whose bells are more open and are stained a rich ruby-red. Of the viticellas, which are essentially like dim-inutive versions of the large-flowered hybrids, I would have 'Etoile Violette', which has intense violet-purple sepals around cream stamens, 'Royal Velours', which is a rich crimson, the species itself, with loose nodding flowers of bright purple, and its marvellous wine-red form, 'Rubra'.

The clematis have brought us into the realms of purple and blue so let us remain here and consider some of the other plants which are performing in this part of the spectrum. About the middle of July *Buddleia davidii* opens its long racemes and all the world's butterflies descend on the garden for a Bacchic orgy. For this reason alone I would grow buddleias. The presence of wildlife gives an added dimension to the enjoyment of a garden which should not be underestimated. Striped hoverflies and electric-blue dragonflies journeying through the borders, young flycatchers learning acrobatics from the safe launch-pads of croquet hoops, and a small family of hedgehogs, forced out into daylight by hunger or thirst, hurrying across the open lawn are entertaining sights, bringing welcome distraction from gardening chores and animating the scene.

Of course, buddleias have their drawbacks. They are attractive for a very short time and when their display is over they just sit there, a great mass of indifferent foliage. But they need not occupy too much space, and if they are hard pruned in March and plants are discarded before they become too rough and woody at the base, they do make handsome fountains of growth, contrasting in form with their neighbours. Some of the best colours are offered by 'Black Knight', a deep violet, 'Royal Red', a strong reddish-purple, and 'Ile de France', a bright violet.

A few buddleias do have good foliage and where paler flowers are needed these forms should be sought. The most impressive is perhaps *B. fallowiana* 'Alba' whose leaves are grey and whose flowers are cream with an orange eye. For silver and white schemes it is superb (also among deep reds like cotinus), towering 7 feet above its companions and shooting its racemes like streamers across them from July until October. You could have it beside the powder-blue *Ceanothus* 'Gloire de Versailles' as well, with stands of brilliant orange turk's cap lilies in front to set the group alight. Another fine plant is *B.* × 'Lochinch', a hybrid between *B. fallowiana* and *B. davidii*. Its leaves are grey-green and its dense panicles of flowers lilac blue; it is a fine partner for *Solanum crispum*, both being quite grey in impact. This would be another opportunity to weave in a deep violet clematis.

There are two other buddleias deserving of attention which are quite distinct from their more flamboyant relatives. The first, *B. crispa*, is best treated as a wall shrub and in a sunny spot will grow to 10 feet. Its felted leaves are much whiter than those of *B. fallowiana* 'Alba', and its flowers are lilac and borne in short dense spikes. A scheme of grey and pink suits this shrub to perfection, comprising dianthus and dorycnium, ballotas and stachys, silver-pink cistus and artemisias. The sweet honey scent of the buddleia will also blend well with the sweet musk fragrance of a rose like 'Felicia'. The second, *B.* × *weyeriana* 'Golden Glow', is for pastel schemes. In its green foliage and rounded flowerheads it resembles the May-flowering *B. globosa*, from which it is descended, but its panicles are much looser and more elongated, and its colouring is much softer, almost a honey orange. I have made a happy marriage with *Abutilon* 'Kentish Belle' which has shuttlecocks of red and orange all summer and autumn.

All the lavenders flower in July, the violet blue 'Munstead', the intense violet 'Hidcote', the white 'Alba' (one of the last to open), the dwarf white 'Nana Alba', and the washy pink 'Loddon Pink' (so good in front of dark purple perilla). No garden can do without them. As formal edgings to beds of roses, as front-line border plants, lounging between stachys and purple violas, and as solitary specimens, basking in the sun and flopping over paths, they are always harmonious, and their scent is, with box and cistus, one of the most evocative of high summer. It is never difficult to find partners for them, but one of the most memorable I have seen was at Hidcote where clumps of deep violet lavender grow with creamy yellow santolina beside a formal pool, the colours being taken up by the shadows on the water and the sulphur bowls of the water-lilies floating on it.

Against sunny walls the lilac blue flowers of *Solanum crispum* unite to form huge clouds of blossom, heavy with rain. Try associating them with the maroon-black leaves of *Vitis vinifera* 'Purpurea' or the complicated blooms of passionflowers. Solanums make very large, vigorous, semi-evergreen climbers and their potato-like flowers are reflexed around a bright orange-yellow pip. The hardiest and most floriferous variety is called 'Glasnevin' and maintains its display right through the autumn. There is also a breathtakingly beautiful white-flowered form, *S. jasminoides* 'Album', which is not as hardy as its cousins. In cold winters plants are always cut to the ground and frequently killed, but when spared severe frost will reach 15 feet in height and as much across, providing you with a dramatic ingredient for yellow or orange schemes.

At ground-level the best shadowy foils are offered by the monkshoods, which arrive in July to replace the flagging delphiniums. The finest forms are descended from *Aconitum napellus*: 'Bicolor' has branching spikes of flowers in white and violet blue; 'Bressingham Spire' is sturdy and upright with flowers of intense violet-blue; and 'Spark's Variety' has branching spikes in pure dark violet-blue. All the flowers are hooded and look, on the inky-coloured varieties anyway, so sinister that you are not in the least surprised to learn that their roots contain such powerful poison that even wolves must fear for their lives. Fortunately, wolves are not one of the more troublesome pests in my corner of the British Isles, but I grow monkshoods all the same. They enjoy plenty of moisture but will thrive on any fertile soil, in sun or part shade, growing to around 3 feet tall. They are striking behind grey foliage and among very hot colours, such as those of lilies and crocosmias; you might also try them with deep red monardas.

Diffuse forms are indispensable for highlighting firmer and more solid shapes as well as for providing soft contrasts, and we must seek out such plants for every season. For high summer the most aristocratic is *Thalictrum delavayi* (often sold as *T. dipterocarpum*), whose panicles of flowers are loose and airy rather than resembling the powder puffs of its cousins; when they are in flower the effect is of a lilac mist advancing from the back of the border. Each flower is filled with cream stamens which cause the heads to shimmer when seen from a distance and the leaves are fresh and finely cut. Plants grow to 5 feet and will need staking but they are worth the trouble for there is no better background for dark monkshoods. The white form, 'Album', is also attractive as is 'Hewitt's Double', whose flowers are lilac and fully double. Thalictrums grow in sun or part shade and will flower from July until September.

I wonder if you grow *Verbena bonariensis*, that curious South American perennial. I first saw it in a Hampshire garden, perfectly silhouetted against a grey flint wall, its dense corymbs of bright lavender-purple flowers quite the most eye-catching performers in the border. It is very much a back-row plant, since it grows to 5 feet, but although you should plant densely around it, do not hide too much of its growth because half its attraction lies in its gaunt, scantily leaved stems, thick and dark; it is this skeletal appearance which distinguishes it from all the other plants which are dressed in their full summer apparel and gives us exactly the sort of midsummer surprise that keeps us entertained. Unfortunately, it is a short-lived plant and not very hardy so you must keep raising seeds; it flowers in its first year.

True blues are becoming scarce now. Among shrubs there are some summer-flowering ceanothus worth having. 'Gloire de Versailles' is the best known and it is deservedly popular for it carries its panicles of powder-blue flowers on and off from July until well into the autumn; but there are deeper colours available from the evergreen 'Autumnal Blue', which is dark, floriferous and exceedingly hardy, the deciduous 'Topaz', which is a rich light indigo, and 'Indigo', which is an even deeper indigo but less vigorous.

At ground-level the strongest blues come from the sea hollies. Their thistle heads are quite electric and make every colour scheme sit up, whether it is a group of pinks, greys and whites or a group of oranges, browns and yellows. *Eryngium tripartitum* forms a low hummock of rounded leaves from which emerge a mass of stems, sprawling and twisted, and a burst of small, intense blue flower-heads. *E.* × *oliverianum* is more upright and grows to around 3 feet, although it will need support. It makes more of an impact because its heads are much larger and because its stems become just as blue as the flowers and calyces. The real gem of the tribe opens slightly later than its cousins and is called *E. variifolium*. It grows to 18 inches, has leaves veined in white and tiny thistle heads of greyish blue. All sea hollies enjoy full sun and are particularly effective beside gravel paths, into which they will seed themselves like fury.

Indigofera gerardiana (now *I. heterantha* it seems) is an indispensable shrub, blooming throughout high summer and autumn and bringing a light ferny delicacy to all those heavy schemes. In hard winters it may be cut to the ground but it always resurfaces with vigour in the spring, sending up stout stems clothed with fine pinnate foliage. In gardens undisturbed by penetrating frost it may attain 12 feet; elsewhere it usually grows to between 3 and 6 feet, and appreciates a dry soil and plenty of sunshine. Its pea-shaped flowers are rose pink and are held in short racemes. *I. potaninii* is similar but has flowers in clear pale pink; needless to say it is equally desirable. I have seen both species superbly associated with meandering clematis – *I. gerardiana* with the intriguing double rose-lilac *C. viticella elegans plena*, and *I. potaninii* with the silvery rose 'Etoile Rose'. Certainly they should have companions which are sympathetic to their old-world colouring. Mine are grown among silver foliage with diascias and *Penstemon* 'Evelyn'.

I would not want to be without the shrubby mallow, *Lavatera olbia* 'Rosea', either. Many gardeners despise it, perhaps because of its 'difficult' colour or simply because everyone else has got one, but few shrubs give such a spectacular display for such a long time. It likes a warm sunny position where it will grow at a phenomenal rate to around 7 feet. This vigour soon exhausts it and it dies young, so it is a good idea to take some summer cuttings every few years; if it survives the winter, it should be pruned hard. Its greyish-green leaves suggest cool treatment among silvers and whites, but the huge rosy-pink mallow flowers associate wonderfully with violet blues. I have found an ideal pink companion to be the deep sugary pink aster 'Harrington's Pink', whose colour exactly matches the blotches at the base of the lavatera's flowers.

So many of high summer's star performers are less than fully hardy and must be continually propagated or protected. Cuttings have to be taken in late summer or early autumn, overwintered in cold frames or unheated greenhouses, potted up in early spring and planted out in early summer. Or the plants themselves must be covered over with straw or bracken for the winter, or lifted and stored, or transferred to a cold frame. All this sounds a frightful chore but it soon becomes part of the annual routine which you do as a matter of course, just as you mow the lawn or prune the roses. The secret is not to attempt any Jekyllian feats and only grow those numbers of plants with which you can reasonably cope; the work then never looks daunting and you do it without a second thought. Naturally labour-conscious gardeners would never think of growing any half-hardy plants but then they have been missing the juiciest morsels all through the year.

The diascias hail from South Africa and are quite new to cultivation. They all have simple open flowers, lipped like nemesias, in warm shades of pink which blend well with most colours, making them marvellous subjects for the edge of the border or for the rock garden. They need full sun and good drainage. *D. cordata* is almost prostrate and makes loose mats of growth from which rise gentle sprays of salmon-pink flowers 6 inches high; the hybrid 'Ruby Field' is similar but slightly larger, and is far more floriferous. Both will survive our normal winters unprotected but may succumb in severe ones. *D. rigescens* is much more tender and cuttings should be taken every year in case of accidents. This is the most handsome of the diascias, its stout stems rising to over a foot in height and tightly packed with blooms. The best partner I have seen with it is that unusual creeping mallow, *Sphaeralcea munroana*, with its dishes of brightest salmon-pink. The team was in a garden in Staffordshire and grew at the edge of a raised bed made of old railway sleepers, the mallow trailing under the diascia and dripping down the dark brown oak.

Powis Castle makes good use of diascias and has a long border of them beneath one of its mellow brick walls. They are invaluable plants for maintaining colour and interest, in flower from June until October, and *D. rigescens* in particular is a fine ingredient for summer bedding schemes. They look especially well beside glaucous blue foliage.

The musk mallow, *Malva moschata*, also flowers non-stop throughout the summer and autumn. Its flowers are carried on 3-foot spikes which emerge from tight hummocks of leaves; they are rosy pink in the type and white in *M.m* 'Alba'. Plants seed themselves everywhere and can be a nuisance for they are often not easy to extract. They are useful for incorporation in spring schemes since they occupy so little space early on but bulge out over a sizeable area when in flower, creating very pleasing effects. It is also rewarding to grow them near their close relatives, such as lavateras, hollyhocks and sidalceas, for a summer harmony of mallow flowers. The most exciting and most vigorous musk mallow is the 'Primley Blue' with flowers in a wonderful shade of slate blue, but it is not easy to obtain.

Penstemons give such bountiful displays from June until October that they can justly claim to be the most important short perennials of high summer. They bear their tubular flowers up their stems in the manner of foxgloves and usually attain between 2 and 3 feet in height. Most of the common garden forms are hybrids of *P. campanulatus*, *P. hartwegii* or *P. cobaea* (many are listed under *P.* × *gloxinioides*) and there is a colour for every scheme. 'Evelyn' is bright rose-pink, 'Apple Blossom' is pale silvery-pink, and 'Garnet' is rich deep-crimson; 'Schoenholzeri' (my favourite) is a real blood-red; 'Gentianoides' is lavender, 'Heavenly Blue' is pale blue and 'Sour Grapes' is bluish wine-purple.

Plants have survived the winter outdoors in Wales but as a rule I lift a few of each kind in November and transfer them to the cold frame, and take plenty of cuttings in the summer. All penstemons enjoy full sun. There is no end to the combinations you can devise, using plants either singly or in groups. The deep reds can be tried with yellow roses, the blues among pink mallows and the pinks with violet-blue caryopteris. You might also try to find other funnel-shaped flowers with which to plant them – phygelius, for example, or *Nicotiana langsdorffii*.

Pale shimmering pinks are always welcome, but especially so in high summer. Such tones are offered by the clones and hybrids of *Sidalcea malviflora*, another mallow whose small open flowers cling to stems 3 or 4 feet tall. 'Elsie Heugh', 'Sussex Beauty' and 'Loveliness' are among the softest and clearest pinks, while 'Rose Queen' and 'William Smith' give us shades of rose and magenta. They should be used at the front of the border as little plumes of pink, relieving rich groups of carmines and purples or highlighting cool groups of blues and violets. The silvery pinks are fine for pastel schemes, among salmons and corals, lilacs and lavenders, buffs and apricots, if you are still composing these for July and August. Like all mallows, sidalceas enjoy full sun.

White gains in importance as the summer advances, slowly emerging from mixed colour groups where its effect is muffled to shine out pure and brilliant in the heat of August, a time when we are most receptive to its fresh, cool nature. If you are planning a white border or a white garden this is the season in which to arrange its ice-cool climax. In July most of the whites are found among the ranks of the roses, cistus, and philadelphus and later the buddleias, with an occasional tangle of clematis or solanum to interrupt the flow. Such plants could be partnered with many different colours from pinks and purples to creams and yellows, but as we approach August you might like to think seriously of using white either on its own or with only the clearest and coldest of companions, so that you can enjoy at least one scheme which is in total and refreshing contrast to the mood of the season.

Apart from the shrubs and climbers, most of the white new-comers are annuals and we shall postpone meeting them until later in the chapter. But there are two groups of white-flowered perennials which open in July and which contribute much to the mood of the border. The first group comprises the gypsophilas. As low background plants against which to play the firm shapes of eryngiums and kniphofias, *Hosta sieboldiana* 'Elegans' and varie-gated *Iris pallida*, they are as valuable as artemisias, but perhaps their most important role is in smothering and concealing all those areas left bare by departed spring bulbs; as they set about this task they will lay a ribbon of mist at the front of the border from which other ghostly shapes may rise – lilies, for example, in white, red or blazing orange. The double form of gypsophila, 'Bristol Fairy', is on the whole preferable to the ordinary *G. paniculata* and grows to 3 feet; but for the front of the border choose the dwarf doubles, 'Plena Compacta' in white and 'Rosy Veil' in shell pink. The single-flowered *G. paniculata* finishes much earlier than the doubles and as the heads turn brown we can copy Gertrude Jekyll and train orange nasturtiums over them.

The most evocative white perennials, however, are the lilies. It is surprising how many gardeners still consider them to be trouble-some connoisseur's plants, forgetting that they have been grown in the wild tangle of cottage gardens for centuries. They love the company of other plants and are ideal occupants of the mixed border, especially useful for grouping around spring-flowering shrubs to provide late interest and for interplanting with plants such as bearded iris which share their dislike of fresh manure. Among dwarf shrubs and low-growing perennials – gypsophilas and artemisias can hardly be improved upon – they can properly display their statuesque shape.

The lily that we most associate with the cottage garden is the Madonna lily, *Lilium candidum*. Its spikes of silky white trumpets grow to over 3 feet tall and the flowers open in early July to coincide with many of the old shrub roses; the combination of silk and velvet, white and wine-crimson, and honey-thick and rich-rose fragrance is worth striving to obtain. Unusually this lily produces a tuft of fresh green leaves at its base and because this needs plenty of sunlight you should not drown your plants in very tall foliage. *Lilium regale* opens slightly later in July, in time to join the yellow and buff hybrid musk roses, and its bulbs positively enjoy being kept in the shade. It is much the same height as *L. candidum* but its trumpets are far more colourful, the reflexed petals being shaded rose-purple on the outside and its throat golden-yellow. It associates attractively with pink flowers and in a corner devoted to greens and luminous whites it will appear almost gaudy.

A third white lily which must be included is *L. martagon* 'Album'. Many people find the colouring of the species itself washy and unsatisfactory (it is a dull purplish-pink), but no such criticism can be levelled at 'Album'. Every stem hangs with quantities of pure white blooms so reflexed that they are exactly like turks' turbans, though in dappled shade they look like the lanterns of midnight revellers. Alas, this lily has no scent.

The two essentials for successful lily cultivation are good drainage and virus-free stock. In heavy soils it is worthwhile putting down a layer of gravel or broken crocks underneath the bulbs and incorporating some with sand at planting time to ensure that no rotting occurs. As for lily virus there are no sound preventatives other than continually spraying your plants with insecticide. You must just keep an eye open for misshapen stems and poorly developed buds and pull out and burn any affected plants without delay. If your lilies are scattered about the garden in mixed plantings they are clearly much more likely to escape disease than if they are planted in large concentrated groups.

Closely related to the lilies is that Himalayan marvel, *Cardiocrinum giganteum*. This is certainly a plant to make you stand back in amazement for its sturdy stems can be up to 10 feet tall and at their July peak can be studded with twenty huge trumpet flowers in glistening white. It should be grown around the corner of a path so that you come across it without warning, in as near to woodland conditions as you can manage – dappled shade, acid soil, moist and rich. Alas, after flowering old bulbs die off so you must continually raise new plants from offsets or seed (the latter is a very lengthy process). Bulbs need to be planted extremely shallowly.

If you have entirely abandoned your garden to the pinks and purples of midsummer you will want to redress the balance in July by admitting quantities of yellow, orange and red. An increase in temperature in your borders reflects the mood of an advancing summer, and as leaves turn brown or yellow they will contribute to the flavour of your schemes instead of detracting from them. By early August there will probably be an equal distribution of warm and cool colours such as we enjoyed in early June, and it will not be until August is well under way that the tables are turned and the yellows and oranges assume control. We must continue to seek out plants to interrupt and enliven our classic compositions of herbaceous perennials, which are as English as toast and marmalade, and to inject the occasional intruder, something bizarre or intriguing, something evocative of dry Mediterranean maquis or lush tropical forests, anything which can transport us to dreamier climes.

The Mount Etna broom, *Genista aetnensis*, fits squarely into this category and is a must for the romantic gardener. In its light billowing shape and informal beauty it belongs more to flighty June than to middle-aged July but in colour and impact it has the full flavour of August and points the way forward to a garden of potent images. No other plant so closely resembles a fountain of molten gold and if you allow it to shower down on to plants which might serve as foam – creamy santolinas are ideal – the liquid picture is complete. Alternatively, you can concentrate on its heat by assembling fiery tones around it, such as scarlet lychnis, orange lilies or strong-hued roses, and turn the fountain into a volcano. It might eventually grow to a height of 15 feet so you can imagine the spectacle it makes. Like all brooms it wants full sun and poor sandy soil.

I hope hypericums are not too common for you. The ordinary rose of Sharon, *H. calycinum*, is rather boring and is useful only as a dwarf evergreen weed-smotherer, but the 5-foot *H*. 'Hidcote' is well worth growing. Its large saucer-shaped flowers are golden yellow and appear from July until October. The temptation is to grow hypericums in poor shady positions because they are so tolerant, but you will be doing 'Hidcote' a disservice if you banish it to an unfavourable spot. It repays generous treatment and in a sunny, well-cultivated border among lemon, cream and apricot roses with perhaps a plume of violet thalictrum it will not disappoint.

The best variety for fruits is *H*. × *inodorum* 'Elstead'; these are bright red and follow the clusters of small yellow flowers in late summer. There are always flowers remaining on the shrubs when the fruits appear and the combination is eye-catching; it can be intensified by grouping golden foliage or other bright-yellow flowered plants near by.

To prepare us for the wave of composites which will sweep across the garden during August there are three forerunners. Each begins its display around midsummer and continues without pause until the autumn. There are many varieties of *Anthemis tinctoria* in various shades of yellow but it is advisable to select a lemon-yellow form like 'E. C. Buxton' or a creamy form like 'Wargrave Variety' for there are plenty of other composites providing stronger tones. Compared to some daisies, the flowers of anthemis are small but they are carried in profusion and supplemented by magnificent ferny foliage. Plants grow to around 3 feet and require full sun. The slightly silvery foliage suggests associations among greys and whites and among rich blues such as salvias and delphiniums, ceanothus and clematis.

Of all the daisies my favourite is that form of *Chrysanthemum frutescens* called 'Jamaica Primrose'. Like anthemis, its flowers have a rich golden centre and soft clear-yellow petals but they are considerably larger, and carried on very stout stems. It makes a solid floriferous bush, 3 feet tall, and should be given a prominent position in the summer border. At Powis Castle it is beautifully partnered with the slatey mallow 'Primley Blue' in a striking juxtaposition of light and shade. The one drawback to this plant is that it is not hardy inland, and cuttings have to be taken and overwintered in the greenhouse; but this is small effort for such a lavish display.

The third yellow composite in flower now is *Coreopsis verticillata* 'Grandiflora'. It is slightly shorter than its cousins but much daintier, with fine misty foliage and narrow stems. The flowers, however, are rich and golden, often untidily formed, and disproportionately large, so plants must be sited with care. They are particularly striking against broad green foliage, particularly if this is edged in yellow such as on *Hosta fortunei* 'Aureomarginata'.

Gardeners searching for new themes to introduce into the summer garden might now turn towards the tropics for inspiration. Fabulous and exotic plants have long been used by public gardens as part of their summer bedding displays, and these are often successful at conjuring up the flavour of the tropics for those who have chosen not to spend their summer holidays abroad. An English August is not so far removed from an African August, we think, as we set down our picnic-basket beneath the lush cannas and towering cordylines. But the parks departments' displays rely heavily on annuals and tender perennials, and the amateur gardener cannot hope to emulate them except on a very small scale. We must look rather to the exotic-looking hardy perennials and shrubs to provide the nucleus for our tropical schemes, which we can then supplement with a few carefully chosen bedding plants.

One group of plants which has a decidedly exotic feel about it is the genus *Kniphofia*. Some of these pokers open quite early in the year, and invariably look quite out of place in borders filled with paeonies, roses and iris, but in high summer and autumn their curious flowerheads combine well with agapanthus, phormiums, hemerocallis and yuccas to give us striking images of sun-baked terrain, alive with scuttling beetles, basking lizards and grazing gazelle. I find the single-coloured varieties far more attractive than the common bicolours, the familiar red hot pokers, and far more useful for they come in a range of hues encompassing white, yellow, orange and red. Among the tall forms, which grow to around 4 feet, I would select 'Wrexham Buttercup' in clear lemon-yellow and 'Yellow Hammer' which is warmer and richer; among the shorter forms, which grow to 3 feet, I would have 'Bees Lemon' in pure pale-yellow, honey-yellow 'Sunningdale Yellow' and 'Gold Else' in lime yellow, 'Ada' in rich orange-yellow and 'Fiery Fred' in brilliant orange, 'Modesta' in coral white, 'Green Jade' in pale green, and 'Little Maid' in cream, which is indispensable.

It is advisable to take precautions against very cold winters by wrapping your kniphofias in an overcoat of bracken or straw and tying their leaves together so that water cannot lodge and freeze in their crowns. But in most winters they are unscathed, even without protection. They are plants for well-drained sunny positions. Blue and white agapanthus are particularly good companions for yellow and orange pokers for their round heads of bell-shaped flowers provide just the right exotic yet contrasting foil for the fiery torches shining above them.

The plume poppy, *Macleaya cordata*, fits well into exotic or conventional plant groups, and its colours harmonize with warm and cool tones. Its foliage is almost more important than its flowerheads for its leaves are huge and lobed, greyish-green above and white below and they are splendid against the ghostly grey stems that support them. The stands grow to over 6 feet and are topped in summer by great panicles of creamy white flowers. Equally attractive is the bronze *M. microcarpa* and its variety 'Coral Plume' whose heads are a true coral, more orange than pink, and associate magnificently with the burnt oranges of daylilies and the salmons and apricots of late astilbes.

Macleayas should not be relegated to the back of the border; the stands are quite handsome enough to serve as specimens among smaller plants or as tall surprises to break the tiered effect of a border. *M. cordata* is a superb candidate for silver and white schemes where it can rise from a bed of gypsophila and artemisia, but you might also associate it with fluffy violet thalictrums and billowing blue ceanothus to achieve the same nebulous image with the bonus of colour. Macleayas will tolerate some shade but it is in full sun that they develop their whitest hue.

Ferocious orange and scarlet hues will provide the core of our fiery tropical theme. Now, in this hottest of months, is the moment to assemble the most dangerous and potent colours and mass them with the most exotic foliage we can find – purple-leafed *Heuchera micrantha* 'Palace Purple', brown phormiums and copper grasses, glaucous blue *Melianthus major*, giant *Kniphofia northiae* with its green serrated leaves (alas, mine succumbed in the winter of 1984), sharp-leafed yuccas, fatsias, paulownias, catalpas (these last two pruned to the ground each spring) and stag's horn sumach, whose deep red cones are now looking at their best. Stands of macleayas will punctuate the scheme, a grey-green backdrop for the burning torches of kniphofias and the great trumpets of hemerocallis. To the group we will also add lilies and, most dramatically, cannas.

It is a pity that that reliable newcomer *Lilium* 'Enchantment' with its spires of huge, reflexed star-shaped orange flowers has now finished its display, but it is succeeded by an equally magnificent lily, *L. croceum*. This produces an abundant supply of upright fiery chalices during July and will perform as well in part shade as in sun. It grows 3 feet tall and, like all stem-rooting lilies, needs to be planted deeply. Its August replacement could be the scented *L. henryi* which enjoys the same conditions. This is a golden-orange turk's cap lily whose stems often exceed 7 feet in height.

For yellow lilies I would look to the July-flowering Nankeen lily, *L.* × *testaceum*, which has large trumpets in a delicious shade of creamy apricot-yellow and a strong sweet fragrance. It is sun-loving and will grow to around 4 feet. And I would look to the yellow form of the tiger lily, *L. tigrinum flaviflorum*, whose soft yellow turk's caps are spotted with maroon. It looks extremely well with its common orange cousin, *L. tigrinum*.

The most startling tropical highlights will come from the cannas. Not only will their flower spikes ignite the scheme but their lush foliage, broad and exotic, will convey precisely the right mood. In some varieties the leaves are purple. I would select the apricot-flowered, purple-leafed 'Wyoming', the honey-yellow, green-leafed 'King Midas', the scarlet, purple-leafed 'Le Roi Humbert' and the scarlet, green-leafed 'La Bohème', though all of them are extremely hard to find nowadays. All grow to 4 feet. Of course cannas are not at all hardy and tubers must be lifted and stored just like dahlias. They require full sun and rich fare.

If there is just one new plant that I can persuade you to acquire let it be *Cosmos atrosanguineus*. Imagine a small single-flowered dahlia, deep maroon-red in colour and scented of bitter chocolate, and you will have a fair impression of cosmos. It starts into growth so late that you always think it has perished in the winter but once it surfaces it makes rapid progress, quickly attaining a height of 3 feet and beginning to flower in early July, after which it never flags and produces blooms continually until the autumn. It is hardy in the warmest areas but elsewhere plants can either be lifted and stored like dahlias and cannas or transplanted to the cold frame for the winter. You may find it difficult to obtain stock but once you have a plant you can increase it by early summer cuttings. Its use as a dark, shadowy ingredient is legion but I have found a companion *par excellence* to be the annual hibiscus 'Sunny Day' (what an appalling name), whose creamy yellow dishes are stained maroon-crimson at the base.

Rather a different scent is released by the bergamots, a mixture of aniseed and lemon, but this comes from the leaves and not the flowers. *Monarda didyma* 'Cambridge Scarlet' remains the finest red; it is not really scarlet, more a strong true red, and its flowers are held in a scruffy mophead 3 feet above the ground. Huge groups of monardas are a wonderful sight in July, their rich colour compensating for any lack of inspiration in their shape, but I like to use small groups to provide eye-catching interest in dormant parts of the border, for among greens they are highly effective. They also look well with purple salvias.

'Croftway Pink' is a good bright rose-pink variety, splendid with blues and whites, and 'Beauty of Cobham', which is softer and paler and easier to place, is an excellent partner for deep purples such as *Aconitum napellus* 'Spark's Variety'. All monardas enjoy a moist soil in full sun.

At the front of the border the various red forms of penstemon are blooming away, and these can be supplemented with two other groups of plants with funnel-shaped flowers, *Phygelius* and *Zauschneria*. *P. aequalis* bears its long narrow trumpets in a delicate shade of rosy red from July onwards and makes an attractive hummock 2 feet tall for sunny, well-drained borders. There is a new and highly desirable form with greenish-yellow flowers called 'Yellow Trumpet'. *P. capensis* is rather larger and is usually seen as a wall shrub although it can also be grown in a sheltered border. Its trumpets are scarlet and are most effective in early autumn beside leaves which are turning orange and rust.

Zauschnerias are less hardy than phygelius but they do come through most winters with a little protection. They make a mass of slender tubular flowers of brilliant scarlet from early August until October, and look well when teamed with brown trifoliums and copper grasses. The form of *Z. californica* called 'Glasnevin' is the one to seek out. *Z. cana* is also splendid with its narrow silver leaves, and is an essential ingredient for grey summer schemes. They enjoy the same conditions as phygelius, plenty of sun and perfect drainage.

Supplementing all these shrubs and perennials, from the end of June until the first frosts, is an army of annual plants in every conceivable shape and colour. I do not propose to cover more than a handful of these summer visitors in any detail, but I do want to spend some time extolling the virtues of admitting annuals into our borders and indicating some of the ways in which they can be used. I can sense, however, that some readers are starting to lose patience. At the beginning of the book I distinguished modern gardening from Jekyllian gardening by saying that the former has to rely for its effects on more permanent and less labour-intensive devices, whereas the latter could drastically change its images month by month by constantly removing, replacing and adding regardless of any outside considerations. Subsequently I have been encouraging you to raise biennials from seed, to grow a comprehensive range of half-hardy perennials and to take batches of cuttings all through the year. Is there not an inherent contradiction? Well, perhaps. But we are all keen gardeners, prepared to devote a little time to and to take a little trouble over our seasonal pictures, and I am not after all persuading you to undertake any major operations. Our biennials, annuals and tender perennials are simply exciting additions to our permanent schemes and we are restricting them to manageable numbers. For example, I limit myself to half a dozen varieties of annual each year; you might be able to cope with ten or with just two. Your summer schemes would not suffer unduly if you grew none, whereas Gertrude Jekyll's summer border would have disintegrated if the annuals were extracted. That is the difference.

The joy of annuals is that they give you the opportunity of experimenting with entirely new colour combinations every year at very little expense, and they provide material with which you can substantially alter the appearance and impact of your more permanent plant compositions. What is more, they enable you to pursue quite ambitious bathtub projects involving large numbers of plants and inspire you to attempt the most daring colour schemes – since you begin every year with a clean slate, there is nothing to lose.

Either you can reserve small beds, stone troughs or terracotta pots for the exclusive use of annuals and their summer companions or you can set aside areas for them near the front of your mixed borders in between perennials and shrubs. Earlier in the year these sites could have been occupied by spring bedding in the form of wallflowers and forget-me-nots, tulips and hyacinths; at the end of May these plants are removed and the soil is prepared for the new occupants which take up residence as soon as all danger of frost is past, usually in the first week of June.

Deciding which annuals to grow is an occupation for those long winter evenings. Wearied by a dozen seed catalogues, you can doze off in front of a roaring fire and dream of wandering drunkenly through a field of scented white tobacco flowers, or of climbing up a gigantic golden sunflower, taller even than the local church steeple, and discovering beyond a magic land carpeted entirely with mignonettes and snapdragons and quaking grasses. I must just sound two warning notes. The first is that seed catalogues are intended to beguile and enchant and make intricate seem straight, and their descriptions and illustrations can be misleading, particularly about colour. The second is that many annuals have passed through the hands of demented hybridists and have surfaced in grotesque forms, with monstrous heads or extra limbs and with every drop of natural grace and simplicity drained from them.

But there are many which live up to our expectations and are always rewarding to grow. Among the warm colours there are lemon and orange marigolds, gold and crimson antirrhinums, and flame nasturtiums which trail or climb and have leaves in glaucous blue or marked in cream, there are primrose and peach dimorphothecas (dwarf plants with large brown-eyed daisies), crimson- and scarlet-splashed mimulus, blood-red adonis (tiny flowers with black faces and feathery foliage), brilliant red verbenas and scarlet salvias; among the cool colours there are pale blue and rich indigo lobelias, powder-blue and violet ageratums, electric-blue *Salvia patens* and deep violet *S. farinacea* 'Victoria', bright blue, mauve and lavender echiums, cornflower-blue *Nigella* 'Miss Jekyll', deep purple, dark-leaved heliotropes with their cherry pie fragrance, sugary pink, spidery cleomes, floppy-flowered petunias in salmon pink, intense purple, wine-red, white and clear yellow, snow-white lavateras, white, bronze-leaved dwarf begonias, and green and white tobacco flowers (including that aristocrat among annuals *Nicotiana sylvestris* with its clusters of long, trumpet-shaped flowers, scented and white, which hang from 5-foot spires). For additional fragrance there are old-fashioned mignonettes in yellowish brown, pink and purple stocks and scrambling sweet peas; and for coloured foliage there is the lacy silver *Pyrethrum ptarmicaeflorum* (syn. *Achillea ptarmiciflora*), plum-black perillas, bronze-red and green ricinus with their tropical leaves, tall, dark purplish-brown atriplex and no end of coloured variants among the ranks of *Coleus blumei*.

Some of these annuals are quite independent and do not need partners to make an impact. I am thinking of Monet's gravel path at Giverny which he transformed with nasturtiums into a blurred vision of burning orange and smouldering red so that the pleasure of reaching the cool of the house was intensified. But usually we will want to combine several varieties of plant in every scheme. Annuals do not need to be partnered with other annuals; there are all those tender perennials, which you have nurtured through the winter, requiring accommodation – cannas, silver- and golden-leaved helichrysums, fiery venidio-arctotis, azure-blue *Convulvulus mauritanicus* with its prostrate habit and saucer-shaped flowers, silver *Senecio vira-vira* (syn. *S. leucostachys*) and succulent blue-leaved echeverias with their curious pointed flowers of bright orange tipped with yellow – as well as all those houseplants in need of a summer vacation outdoors – pelargoniums, variegated abutilons and sky-blue *Plumbago capensis*.

Troughs and pots are especially satisfying to plant up because there are more verticals to play with and plants can be made to hang precariously or cascade luxuriantly over the edges. Schemes must obviously be sympathetic to the colour and size of the containers used, but let me make some suggestions: salmon-red pelargoniums, silver helichrysum and deep blue lobelias; dark purple petunias, yellow-leaved helichrysum and fluffy violet ageratums; green tasselled amaranthus, heliotrope 'Marine' and green-funnelled *Nicotiana langsdorffii*; and orange pelargoniums, white bronze-leaved begonias and ice-blue convolvulus. The general rule is to have one tall ingredient, one mid-height ingredient and one trailer, but of course it is another rule to be twisted into knots.

Annual schemes elsewhere in the garden can either be fused with neighbouring plantings, as in the border where they become an integral part of the whole composition, or they can be independent, as in formal beds by the house or informal corners of a dormant shrubbery. You might like to design the latter according to the standard principles of parks department bedding, namely to think in terms of carpet plants, dot plants and edging plants. The carpet plants provide the meat of the scheme and cover the largest area, and there is usually one variety involved (two at the most). The dot plants are the highlights; they are taller than the carpet plants and can be arranged literally as dots through the scheme or in small groups. In colour they may harmonize or contrast with the carpet. The edging plants are an optional extra and should be omitted if you are using two different carpet plants; they may be the same height, shorter or taller than the carpet and usually take their colour cue from the dot plants.

It may sound absurd to adhere to such precise directions but in fact it is a highly instructive exercise for those of us who are more accustomed to pursuing vague ideas by the processes of trial and error. The techniques used by the parks departments have after all been tried and tested over decades, and although you may not think many of the resulting floral displays particularly beautiful or worth emulating, the faults are invariably in the colours chosen not in the schemes' construction. Some head gardeners are less skilled as artists than others.

Let me give you some examples of annual schemes which I have seen in various parks and private gardens or which I have devised myself: a rich carpet of purple and red verbenas (possibly 'Hidcote' and 'Lawrence Johnston') studded with silver pyrethrum; clumps of the orange ball-flowered, tender perennial *Streptosolen jamesonii* rising out of a sea of gentian-blue *Salvia patens* with a narrow shoreline of apricot *Mimulus aurantiacus* (syn. *M. glutinosus*); golden *Canna* 'King Midas' surrounded by a mass of *Nicotiana* 'Lime Green' and edged with yellow *Helichrysum petiolatum* 'Limelight'; violet-blue *Ageratum* 'Blue Heaven' as a carpet around deep violet *Salvia farinacea* 'Victoria', enclosed by a strip of *Pyrethrum*

ptarmicaeflorum; white petunias and scarlet salvias (bury your prejudice) swirling around plumes of white *Lavatera* 'Mont Blanc'.

July has now slipped into August and our thirst for rich, hot
schemes must be fully satisfied. Gone now is every vestige of youth
from the garden, and in its parched middle age the strongest and
most brilliant colours proclaim their dominance, basking in the
glare of a cruel sun and revelling in the embrace of smouldering
foliage. Most hot-coloured plants will blend admirably into two
summertime themes, the tropical jungle and, a new concept for
late summer, the daisy chain. Composites tend to swamp the
warm side of the spectrum from the end of July onwards and
unless they are marshalled into some sort of coherent pattern they
can easily make borders seem rather messy. A very satisfactory
way of arranging them is to weave a thread of daisies through the
second or third row of the border, allowing them occasionally to
drift back or spill forwards into the front row; this establishes a
unity and harmony for your late schemes and still gives you the
opportunity to play contrasting shapes against the daisy flowers
and to set more substantial forms beside them to balance their
dreary and rather skimpy foliage.

Undoubtedly the most valuable group of warm-coloured
composites is the genus *Helenium*. Many of these plants begin their
display in July and peter out towards the end of August – the
dwarf, compact 'Crimson Beauty' in reddish brown, the 3-foot
'Golden Youth', the coppery-orange 'Coppelia', and the 4-foot
'Moerheim Beauty' in bronze red, for example – although many
return with a second wave in September; others delay flowering
until August is well underway and last throughout September –
such as the 5-foot 'Bruno' in mahogany red and the 4-foot 'But-
terpat' in rich yellow – so there are always varieties in bloom. The
daisies are relatively small and are held on branching stems over
indifferent foliage; and the petals are arranged around a prominent
central knob which is often a rich brown.

Bronze and coppery purple foliage is the best foil for heleniums,
and if you can distribute your plants around mounds of cotinus,
berberis and heucheras and between clumps of *Atriplex hortensis*
'Rubra' you will be well rewarded. For the deeper reds and oranges
you might like to introduce some glowing golden foliage, and some
creamy highlights in the form of *Artemisia lactiflora*, that 6-foot
perennial with feathery plumes of blossom, macleayas and cimicifugas. All heleniums want plenty of sun.

I would not give the perennial members of the genera *Helianthus* or *Heliopsis* the time of day, but there is one more group of composites that ought to be welcomed into the late-summer border. The rudbeckias are, in the main, black-eyed, yellow-flowered daisies which when massed in the garden conjure up all the golden warmth and brassy cheek of a field of annual sunflowers in the midst of a Tuscan landscape. Their petals are long and narrow, not short and broad as in heleniums, so they complement them well. I would quite happily confine myself to one form, *R. fulgida* 'Goldsturm', if short of space, but *R. maxima* is distinctive with its huge black knobs and glaucous green foliage; it is a foot or so taller than 'Goldsturm' at 4 feet.

In silvery parts of the garden, nestling beneath senecios and phlomis, *Helichrysum* 'Sulphur Light' is now in bloom. It is like a yellow version of anaphalis, having narrow leaves clothed in white felt and fluffy flowers which open pure sulphur and fade to mustard. It is in fact an admirable companion for anaphalis at the front of the border, and enjoys the same well-drained sunny conditions. This is a first-rate plant, interesting over a long period and never difficult to place. Try it in front of *Caryopteris* × *clandonensis*. Whatever you do, do not confuse it with its relative *H. angustifolium*, which reeks of the worst Indian restaurant; they do not resemble each other in the least, of course, but if you are ordering from a catalogue the light may play tricks.

A comprehensive range of oranges, yellows and reds is offered by the crocosmias during August and September. The most familiar member of the clan is the common montbretia, *C.* × *crocosmiiflora*, with its broad grassy leaves and nodding flowers in flame orange. It is certainly one of the commonest perennials in cultivation and older gardeners have become so accustomed to seeing it in unopposed glory that they are invariably incredulous when they learn that other colour forms of crocosmia have been in existence for decades. In recent years there have been still further advances and there are now so many desirable varieties that it is hard to make a choice between them. I can recommend 'Emily McKenzie' with her large flowers of deep burnt-orange stained in red, the delicate apricot-yellow 'Citronella' (sometimes called 'Honey Angel' or is this variety distinct?), 'Jackanapes', some of whose petals are orange red and some yellow, soft orange 'Lady Hamilton' with apricot markings, and, best of all, 'Solfatare' whose apricot-yellow flowers are complemented by light bronze foliage.

Bolder and more muscular hybrids have been raised by Alan
Bloom at Bressingham. They are a foot or two taller than their
cousins, and their stout physique and branching sprays of flowers
indicate their close relationship with *C. masonorum*, that brilliant
orange crocosmia whose upright blooms are packed along the tips
of its undulating stems, and *Curtonus paniculatus*, a striking 4-foot
perennial with broad leaves and sprays of orange-scarlet blooms.
Both species are themselves worth growing – *C. masonorum* is particularly effective in front of giant yellow yarrow, *Achillea filipendulina*, as in John Treasure's garden, and you might try *Curtonus paniculatus* in front of the powder-blue ceanothus 'Gloire de
Versailles' or close to *Rosa moyesii* whose orange flagon-shaped hips
are now ripening. But the new hybrids are especially welcome
because they introduce pure scarlet into the ranks of yellow and
orange. I think 'Lucifer' and 'Emberglow' are the most spectacular, and provide just the right climactic moments for summer
schemes. They would certainly have featured in Gertrude Jekyll's
garden as part of the blazing core of her summer border, had they
been available then. 'Lucifer' is the clearest and most glistening of
the reds (it is taller than 'Emberglow' and flowers earlier) and
would be magnificent among white flowers or against silver variegated foliage, such as a fountain of *Miscanthus sinensis* 'Variegatus'.
Could you imagine a more sensational full-stop for a silvery
border?

The tall, broad-leaved crocosmias have a decidedly tropical
appearance and slot happily into our exotic schemes of giant
foliage and curious flowers, while the daintier forms can be
employed in more conventional groups in front of heleniums and
beneath roses. You find old montbretia in all sorts of shady corners
on the meanest of soils but few of its cousins are as accommodating,
so that it is as well to think of them as a family of sun lovers, which
prefer a moist rather than a dry soil. Most forms are quite hardy
but I always ensure that I have a few corms of the rarest varieties
in the cold frame, and cover the remaining clumps outside with a
layer of bracken; in warmer areas this would be quite unnecessary.

The first wave of chrysanthemums arrives around the middle of
August, bringing us an early taste of autumn and sending a shiver
of expectation down our spines. The desire to extend the joys of
autumn is deeply ingrained in the romantic gardener and with a
bit of luck and a great deal of guile we can just about pull it off.
You need to assemble a quantity of chrysanthemums and arrange

them around shrubs which ripen their berries and hips early or whose leaves take on early tints – examples are *Rosa moyesii*, *R. glauca*, *R. rugosa*, *R. villosa*, *Viburnum opulus*, cotoneasters and *Rhus typhina* – the group can be supplemented by other plants with autumn connotations, mainly frontrunners of late-flowering genera, such as early colchicums and asters, and by plants which have flowers or leaves in the autumnal shades of brown, copper, crimson and gold, such as heleniums, hemerocallis, berberis, cotinus and hypericums. Slight seasonal deceptions like this are usually very entertaining and are extremely satisfying to engineer; more dramatic deceptions, such as the conjuring up of tulips for a late summer RHS show, are rather sinister and, if practised in the garden, can be deeply disturbing.

There are a number of desirable chrysanthemums about, among which I would choose the bronze-orange 'Virginia' and the bronze-yellow 'Sheila' (these look well together and are both between 3 and 4 feet tall), the soft butter-yellow 'Golden Anemone', the deeper yellow 'Yellow Starlet', the lemon-white 'Wendy', the bright crimson, yellow-centred 'Belle' (this matches *Hemerocallis* 'Stafford' perfectly) and the soft mauve 'Grandchild' (a delightful shade, ideal against deep purple). Apart from 'Virginia' and 'Sheila' they are all around 2 feet tall. I saw a stunning association at Powis Castle where a rusty orange-yellow chrysanthemum ('Moira' perhaps) was grouped with the maroon-red leaves of *Sedum maximum* 'Atropurpureum'; the sedum's flowers had not yet opened so I could not tell how pleasantly the rosy-pink stars would mingle with the orange blooms.

Chrysanthemums, like the other composites, must be regarded as essentially background plants. They provide some delicious colours and some scruffy, old-world flavours for the late summer border but for highlights we must look elsewhere. One plant that enters the scene with a flourish and instantly catches our attention is *Lilium henryi*. It is an exact contemporary of the early chrysanthemums, opening in the latter half of August. Its turk's caps are flushed a warm shade of apricot-orange and dangle from arching brown stems which often grow to 7 feet. This lily is therefore a back-row ingredient, superb when peering through bronze atriplex or dripping on to purple salvias and ideal for tropical groups. It enjoys heavy soil and partial shade, and requires deep planting.

Another eye-catching plant is the Scottish flame flower, *Tropaeolum speciosum*, that slender climber which in many of our great gardens has the unique privilege of being allowed to use the ancient and much cherished yew hedges as its host. There are few more apposite associations in the August garden than this marriage of flame flower and yew, the fresh-green lobed leaves strung on threads across a heavy green backcloth and the tiny spurred flowers of brilliant scarlet like drops of blood seeping from the heart of the hedge.

This tropaeolum is often tricky to establish for it needs cool conditions, a shady aspect and a peaty soil to give of its best. In the warmer south its progress is slower and more cautious than in the north where it is much more likely to romp away, but it is worth persevering. I recall seeing a photograph of this plant teamed with the 'Goldheart' ivy which I thought was a first-rate partnership, so do not feel you need first plant yew. It dies back to a rhizome in winter.

There are several hardy fuchsias in flower now that must not be overlooked. They have none of the flamboyance of their tender cousins (some of which, such as the dark-leaved, scarlet-trumpeted 'Gartenmeister Bonstedt', I hope you are growing in tubs near your tropical schemes) but are nevertheless extremely valuable in the late border, their pendant, floating flowers contrasting with all around them. The large-flowered forms, like 'Madame Cornelissen' which is bright red with white skirts and the incomparable 'Mrs Popple' which is deep red with purple skirts, only grow to 3 feet and can be interplanted with early-flowering plants such as oriental poppies near the front of the border; while the small-flowered forms, like the red and purple 'Riccartonii' and the flesh-pink *F. magellanica molinae* (syn. *F.m.* 'Alba' – a misleading name) which is so perfect among violets and blues, sometimes reach 5 feet if spared by a mild winter and must be sited further back. You might consider leading a clematis – perhaps the imperial purple *C.* × *jackmanii* – into these tall forms to prolong the display and help to conceal the dreary foliage. It has to be said that none of these fuchsias looks very appetizing until late summer so early diversions close by – in the form of foliage plants, spring bulbs and perhaps a June-flowering shrub rose – are a good idea. They are all quite happy in shade.

If you have some moist sunny spots in need of summer colour you ought to look to the lobelias to fill them. The most familiar varieties are the scarlet *L. cardinalis* and the purple-leaved *L. fulgens* which luxuriate beside many a pond and stream, but there are also some fine hybrids available among which 'Dark Crusader', with purplish leaves and deep red flowers, and 'Queen Victoria', with brilliant red flowers, are outstanding. All these plants grow to around 3 feet and bloom in August and September. Take care when placing them next to oranges and yellows for there is a hint of carmine lurking in the red which can be disturbing; against green-leaved irises and hemerocallis or purple-leaved ligularias, whose flowers are held high, peace will prevail. The truest red lobelia is *L. tupa* which flowers in July and bears its hooded flowers on 5-foot spikes, but if you can locate it in a nursery, you are a better detective than me.

Traditional cottage garden groups have been alternating with strange and exotic groups throughout the year, ensuring that in between our voyages to wild and pagan regions we can rest in familiar and homely surroundings. In late summer, after excursions among lush jungles of cannas and fiery curtonus or through a maze of bleeding yew hedges, there is no more welcoming and comforting picture than an avenue of hollyhocks glowing in the sunshine. What English garden can do without them? Their great spires of saucer-shaped flowers are the symbol of the cottager's summer and they are as much a part of our gardening history as honeysuckles and roses. Do not depend on the seed catalogues for a supply of plants for their single- and double-flowered forms are invariably far too brilliant. Instead knock on cottage doors in the autumn and beg seed from their pastel-coloured varieties, and ensure that among those apricot, lemon, cream and rose shades there is an ample quantity of deep dark reds. Of course hollyhocks are plagued by that dreaded rust disease and many gardeners treat them as biennials; but for me that is too much of a palaver and I leave my plants in peace from year to year. If you grow your plants at the back of the border their pock-marked leaves can be easily concealed. They want full sun and will flower from July until the autumn. Associate them with other mallows if possible.

Our craving for cool white remains acute throughout the summer and fortunately there are plenty of plants through which it can maintain a strong presence. *Abelia* × *grandiflora* is one of the most valuable late-flowering shrubs but it is not reliably hardy in cold parts of the country. It makes a neat arching plant, 4 feet tall, and is smothered with white tubular flowers from late July until late September. These emerge from coppery-pink buds and the whole plant has a pinky appearance. Against a south-facing wall it could be associated with rich pink crinums and silver-leaved, pink-flowered *Dorycnium hirsutum*, and backed by a white climber like *Solanum jasminoides* 'Album'.

More spectacular flowers are provided by the eucryphias. Their large white dishes are filled with a shock of yellow anthers, tipped with red in *E.* × *nymansensis* 'Nymansay'. This wonderful shrub flowers in August and early September and makes a great column of leathery leaves and white blooms 20 feet high, given time. The form *E.* × *intermedia* 'Rostrevor' flowers for longer but the blooms are slightly smaller. Both these evergreens succeed their deciduous cousin, *E. glutinosa*, which begins its display in July and is perhaps the pick of the bunch. Not only are its pure-white flowers warmed by crimson anthers but its glossy leaves turn to brown and deep red in the autumn, providing a second spectacle. All eucryphias need shelter from cold winds and some shade from the burning sun of high summer, and they perform best on a moist lime-free soil. Their flowers are very similar to those of the hypericums and it is amusing to plant the two together; the rich yellow of *H.* 'Hidcote', partnered perhaps with some white Japanese anemones, would admirably highlight the warm centres of the eucryphias' blooms.

I include the shrubby hibiscus *H. syriacus* here because my favourite is, predictably, the clone called 'Redheart' whose large white cups are blotched maroon-red at their base. I suggest growing it in a sea of chocolate-scented *Cosmos atrosanguineus* as part of a larger white scheme, with in the background a long drift of tall, dark red hollyhocks to pick up the mallow shape and carry off the deep colour into the white distance. Of course there are other attractive colour forms in the pure white 'Snowdrift', the rose-pink 'Woodbridge', the pale pink 'Hamabo' and the violet-blue 'Blue Bird', but for me none compares with 'Redheart'. Certainly you should avoid the double-flowered forms which look like scrumpled pieces of tissue paper and have lost all their simple charm. Hibiscus require shelter and full sun but the only disadvantage of fulfilling their needs by giving them a prominent position on a precious south wall is that they are so boring for much of the year. Their leaves appear painfully late in the spring and even when fully clothed shrubs look drab and coarse. The solution is to back them with something that is stunning early on, such as a spring-flowering clematis teamed up with a summer-flowering rose.

An essential ingredient of the romantic garden is the common jasmine, *Jasminum officinale*, which opens during high summer. It must be allowed to grow in tangles, over a fence or pergola or cascading down an old brick wall or hanging from a dead tree in a piece of wild woodland. Its fragrance is so powerful and sickly sweet that I am surprised people grow it so close to the house; drifting across the garden in tantalizing wafts, coming from an unknown source, hidden by a thicket of shrubs, it becomes a thing of mystery and magic and its perfume excites the senses rather than suffocating them. The variety 'Affine' has larger white flowers, heavily suffused with pink, and in mild districts it is semi-evergreen like its parent.

The tall bottle-brushes of the various cimicifugas are important as contrasting shapes to all the daisies of summer and autumn, and can be grown either in groves through the border or as sentinels at the end of a colour scheme. A succession of flowers can be had from July until October with careful planning. The first to open is *C. racemosa* with pure white flowers on long racemes and elegantly divided leaves; in August comes *C.r. cordifolia* with creamier flowers and broader foliage; and in late September *C. simplex*, with its undulating racemes which arch over at a height of 4 feet (it has a fine purple-budded form in 'Elstead Variety'); and *C.s ramosa* which has the tallest white brushes of all. This last has a purple-leaved variant called 'Atropurpurea', which is the greatest of treasures. The combination of purple and white is magnificent and can be emphasized by a sympathetic planting of *Aster lateriflorus* 'Horizontalis' and some deep purple foliage such as *Euphorbia amygdaloides* 'Purpurea' and *Ajuga reptens* 'Atropurpurea'. Most cimicifugas grow to around 5 feet in height and are at their best in semi-shade. They are especially good with Japanese anemones and late monkshoods.

Galtonia candicans is one of the few hardy bulbs that flower in late summer and it is hard to see how we could manage without it. Like cimicifugas it is superb for ribbon planting since it occupies so little space earlier in the year; interwoven with paeonies or oriental poppies it will remain inconspicuous until its neighbours have completed their display and then rise up from the ground, throwing out its broad strap-like leaves and pushing up its tall flower spikes. When in bloom, during August and September, it is one of the more imposing border perennials for its spikes will attain 4 feet before they begin to drip with white bells. It associates well with the smaller bells of agapanthus – the deeper the blue the better – and with the funnel-shaped penstemons in all their many colour forms, but it is more likely that you will use it to enliven schemes of spring-flowering shrubs which are now dormant with a cool infusion of white. Galtonias enjoy a rich soil and plenty of sunshine.

Let us return for a moment to our tropical theme and consider the yuccas. No hardy plant looks more exotic than these fearsome creatures and yet they hail from nowhere more fantastic than North America. The two aristocrats are *Y. filamentosa* and *Y. flaccida* which both grow to around 5 feet tall. The latter has narrower foliage and more generously branched flower spikes, but both decorate themselves with creamy bells and both protect themselves with needle-tipped leaves. Gertrude Jekyll recognized their value as foliage plants and used them extensively. As anchors at the ends of borders and as specimens on terraces they have few rivals, but you must take care that you site them where they cannot stab you. The one growing near the stone seat in my garden has provoked many a blood-curdling scream. Full sun, shelter and a well-drained soil is the recipe for success. Try them with orange daylilies, yellow kniphofias and blue agapanthus.

Clear pink can easily seem out of place among the mature tones of late summer and to preserve its innocence you are usually obliged to surround it with silver and white. Stronger pinks, especially those tinged with rose, take their place more naturally among the powdery purples and sunburnt foliage which are beginning to take control of the formerly cool reaches of the border, and there is even a pink-flowered shrub which can be safely grown there.

T. pentandra is a maritime plant which lends itself well to cultivation inland as long as it receives full sunlight. It flowers in August and September and the combination of feathery green leaves and rosy-mauve racemes creates a delightfully misty background for firm shapes such as galtonias and purple-leaved atriplex and the prickly spikes of acanthus. Alternatively, the theme of mist can be taken up by clumps of cimicifugas and asters with the occasional ghostly figure of a yucca silhouetted against them. This tamarisk grows to 15 feet and will need to be pruned in the spring to keep it shapely.

In August the heralds of the late anemones arrive in the form of *A. hupehensis* and *A. tomentosa*. I must bury my prejudice against pink and yellow juxtapositions in order to admit these plants into the border but I like to accommodate them for, with the asters and the chrysanthemums, they set the mood for the early autumn garden. *A. hupehensis* is bright pink with golden stamens and *A. tomentosa* is a softer pink, has more attractively lobed foliage, and grows almost twice as tall, around 4 feet. In an odd way these rather crude colour combinations are exactly appropriate to the season and indicate the culmination of the maturing process of summer and the approach of autumnal decadence, but those with weak hearts will stay their hand a little longer and await the arrival of the pure whites and pink-flushed whites of the Japanese hybrids.

In the baking hot places at the foot of your south-facing walls the huge pink and white trumpets of *Crinum × powellii* should now be in evidence, smiling condescendingly at all those commonplace composites in the main border. The lily-like blooms are sweetly fragrant and are supported on sturdy stems 4 feet high above the thick strap-like leaves. The colour is rose pink in the common form, white in 'Album', pale pink in 'Haarlemense' and deep pink in 'Krelagei' (these forms are now very scarce), and they are superb when surrounded by short blue and white agapanthus. They are reliably hardy even in cold areas if given a thick winter overcoat of bracken or straw but they can also be successfully grown in pots and taken under cover during the coldest months. They enjoy a rich soil.

I can postpone the dreaded moment no longer when I must come face to face with phlox, the species which is for many gardeners the mainstay of the August garden. As the providers of large masses of colour they are, I confess, unparalleled and you would have to be a very self-confident gardener to orchestrate a colourful late-summer border without them, but as individuals they are smug and characterless for all their showy display and I would never give them a prominent position. Certainly an entire border of them such as you often see in larger gardens is chronically dull. One of their saving graces is that they are tolerant of shade and can be used to brighten up gloomy areas where there is little else in bloom; another is that many are beautifully scented, a quiet delicate scent that invariably catches you unawares.

The tall cylindrical heads of *P. maculata* are less often seen than the dumpy mounds of *P. paniculata* but they are a welcome relief from the advancing columns of their cousin. I think the best form is the fragrant lilac-pink 'Alpha' which grows to 3 feet. Of course there are far and away more varieties among the ranks of *P. paniculata* – pinks like the pale 'Balmoral' and the clear carmine-eyed 'Eva Cullum', and whites like 'Fujiyama' and 'White Admiral'. I hesitate to recommend any of the other brighter colour forms because I am unfamiliar with them and do not really think that phlox can carry off too much make-up; they are background plants not frontrunners. They like plenty of food and water during the growing season and need frequent splitting and dividing. Beware of the fiendish eelworm which feasts on these plants.

The knotweeds are providing some interesting pink flowers now and will continue their display right through the autumn. The smallest, and to me the most appealing, is *Polygonum vacciniifolium*, a prostrate creeping perennial which is like a slim miniature version of the spring-flowering bistort. Its tiny bottle-brushes are pale pink and borne in their thousands over the tight mats of foliage which are so congested with dead leaves that they always look coppery brown. It cascades down a stone wall in my garden, in full sun but with its roots tucked into the cool crevices between the stones; in such a position it becomes quite rampant. *P. affine* and its clone 'Donald Lowndes' are taller at about a foot, and their brushes are a deep reddish-pink. They make fine edging plants in sun or shade, combined with variegated grasses, pink and white phlox, and their 4-foot cousin *P. amplexicaule* 'Atrosanguineum', whose short spikes are crimson pink. A distinct member of the group is *P. campanulatum* which has loose heads of bells instead of bottle-brushes in pale pink. It seems to be rather neglected at present and deserves a revival of interest among gardeners. Like other polygonums it prefers a moist soil.

I enjoy seeing the Himalayan honeysuckle, *Leycesteria formosa*, in August dripping with long wine-purple bracts. These are studded with narrow white flowers in the summer and are later replaced by black berries. The leaves are coarse and unattractive but when they fall in the autumn (at least most of them fall; the stragglers have to be tugged) the shrub once again comes into its own, for the upright green stems are a valuable addition to the bare winter garden. It grows to 6 feet in height and looks well rising above lavender-blue asters, violet monkshoods and greyish-purple *Salvia officinalis* 'Purpurascens'. Leycesteria is another of those un-expected plants which excite curiosity and ensure variety in the garden and for these reasons alone it is worth a place. It is perfectly happy in semi-shade.

Some plants attract the attention of the romantic gardener

simply by their evocative names. We would grow them whatever they looked like just for the pleasure of rolling those foreign syllables over our tongues. Many of the old shrub roses come into this category – names like 'Robert le Diable', 'Variegata di Bologna' and 'Empereur du Maroc' – but there are many Latin names just as dreamy – *Paeonia mlokosewitschii, Euonymus cornutus quinquecornutus* and *Watsonia beatricis*. Let those meddling taxonomists dare change them. To this list of sacred names I would add *Perovskia atriplicifolia*.

Perowskia comes to us from dusty Afghanistan and it is not too fanciful to suggest that there is more than a trace of the scents of its dry homeland in its aromatic leaves. It makes a 3-foot haze of silver-white stems and grey-green serrated foliage and in August and September is topped by narrow plumes of violet-blue blossom. Gertrude Jekyll liked to grow it beside the large sedums but I prefer it among greys or outlined against deep purples. You could also use it to tone down some of the potent yellow groups which abound at this time of year. 'Blue Spire' is a superior form which has so far eluded me. I have been sold it twice but each time it was its parent flying false colours. It performs best on well-drained soil in full sun, and needs to be hard pruned in the spring.

The purplish spikes of *Acanthus spinosus* combine well with both leycesteria and perowskia. Here is another plant that perfectly epitomizes the mood of the season, lending its support to our exotic late-summer schemes and yet blending in colour with all the traditional border ingredients. The imposing flower spikes are 4 feet tall, clothed in mauve-purple blooms, and protected by sharp spines; but the foliage is just as valuable as the flowers for the arching leaves are huge, dark and deeply dissected. The acanthus therefore merits an important position, either in isolation against grey stone or in a gravel walk – to which it is well suited for it enjoys full sun, starved soil and good drainage – or in company out in the border in front of silvery or silver-variegated shrubs. The variety *spinosissimus* has even more deeply cut foliage and quite a grey appearance and is worth attempting in very hot positions. I can see no advantage in growing *A. mollis latifolius*, the form most commonly seen, which is seldom generous with its flowers, although its leaves are just as magnificent as those of *A. spinosus*. Once established, acanthus are quite indestructible, so you must make sure that you site it correctly at the outset; one of my plants was mistaken for a weed by an unwitting jobbing gardener but responded to the attacks of spade and poison by growing as if it had been serenaded by Pavarotti.

The first asters get under way during August, providing more daisy flowers for a garden already knee deep in them. Like chrysanthemums they are scruffy as individuals but delightful when massed in the border, sweeping through the lines of rose-pink perennials and grey-leaved shrubs, swelling at the foot of purplish shrubs like *Rosa glauca* and pushing out towards the front of the border between pillars of yellow *Kniphofia* 'Brimstone'. The lavender *A. acris* needs such lavish treatment to disguise its faults and so do the early forms of *A. amellus* like the 2-foot violet-purple 'King George' and the shorter 'Violet Queen'.

Some asters have sufficient quality to withstand closer scrutiny and can be assembled in more prominent positions: *A.* x *frikartii* 'Mönch', for example, which is arguably the most beautiful member of the genus and would be gravely offended if relegated to a supporting role. At Sissinghurst it is assembled in a place of honour beneath some *Prunus sargentii* and in September the combination of lavender-blue flowers and coloured foliage is breathtaking. This aster remains in beauty throughout August and September and although it grows to 3 feet in height never requires staking. For a dwarf edging plant at this time of year it would be hard to improve on *A. thomsonii* 'Nanus'. It only grows 18 inches tall and its soft violet-blue flowers are set off perfectly by greyish-green leaves. I have some in front of a hummock of reddish-purple *Berberis thunbergii* 'Atropurpurea'. All these asters enjoy a sunny site, regular feeding and as little disturbance as possible.

We must have giants leaping out at us from the shadows to keep our senses alert after all those smooth undulating border schemes, and one such plant which begins its display towards the end of August is *Eupatorium purpureum*. This is an 8-foot perennial with upright stems, tinged with purple, pointed leaves and large fluffy heads of rose-purple flowers. I first encountered it at Hidcote where it thrives among hydrangeas in the woodland garden. The purplish-leaved *H. aspera* (syn. *H. villosa*) makes one of the best companions for it but I have seen it among white forms as well where it stood out bravely. It seems to enjoy a rich, moist soil and will continue to perform right through the autumn.

Let us return to ground-level and consider two more purple carpeters before we leave to explore the blues. The sea lavender, *Limonium latifolium*, is, like gypsophila, one of those indispensable front-line perennials which erupt from small clumps into a cloud of blossom which drifts over neighbouring plants that have finished flowering. It is not quite as adaptable as gypsophila though, for it is much smaller at only a foot in height. Its leaves are broad, dark and evergreen and the flowers are lavender-blue in the type and rich violet-blue in 'Violetta'. It likes full sun and good drainage, and so is admirably suited to schemes of grey foliage where it will foam between steel-blue grasses and crimson penstemons.

The various colour forms of *Osteospermum jucundum* (formerly *Dimorphotheca jacunda*), *O. sinuata*, *O. barbariae* and *O. ecklonis* give us mats of large daisies from June until the first frosts. The commonest, *O.e.* 'Prostrata', is a real gem with snow-white petals, purple on their reverse, set around a disk of deep purple, glistening with spots of orange and blue. It is only 9 inches tall and associates well with dark shrub roses earlier in the summer and with yellow and orange composites later on. To appreciate its beauty fully it should perhaps be grown among other whites. There are plenty of variations on the pink and purple theme among the other varieties but my favourite is the deep claret 'Nairobi Purple' which has a blackish reverse to the petals. I have never seen the soft yellow and brown 'Buttermilk' but I have just ordered it on the strength of its description in a catalogue. It is apparently taller than the others, at around 2 feet. Unfortunately, none of these plants is really hardy; cuttings taken in early autumn root readily.

True blue remains scarce in late summer and enters schemes usually by means of annuals such as lobelias and salvias. Violas like 'Ullswater' and 'Azure Blue' are also providing patches of colour again after their July rest when they were clipped and fed, and they will now flower right into the winter. The summer-flowering ceanothus are still in bloom. Besides these, there are some newcomers. They do not arrive in coachloads but there are sufficient numbers with which to make some long cool stretches of blue from which you can quench your thirst after a feast of tawny oranges and yellows. Most of these new arrivals are shrubs and everyone's favourite is surely *Caryopteris* × *clandonensis*. It is without doubt among the most valuable shrubs for the mixed border, and makes a 5-foot mound of grey-green leaves decorated throughout August and September with fluffy clusters of mid-blue flowers. It wants full sun and an occasional spraying against capsid bugs which so disfigure the foliage. Apart from that it is easily pleased and roots quickly from cuttings so that you can introduce plants to different parts of the garden. You need to be a clairvoyant to distinguish between all the named forms on the market but 'Kew Blue' is a genuinely deeper and richer blue and worth acquiring. Among pinks, caryopteris are superb, lounging among rosy asters and penstemons and backed by lavatera or pale pink fuchsia, but they team up well with rust chrysanthemums and yellow crocosmias, and, of course, with greys and whites.

Clearer and purer blue comes from *Ceratostigma willmottianum*, a 3-foot shrub whose brilliant flowers resemble those of phlox. It is best grown in a sheltered south-facing border where it will flower from August onwards. The leaves assume crimson tints in the autumn which combine effectively with the blooms.

Those people with large woodland gardens can rely heavily on hydrangeas for rich blue tones. Others, including myself, may be reluctant to devote too much space to these plants which are so coarse and drab for the greater part of the year. Naturally whenever I see sky-blue hortensias like 'Générale Vicomtesse de Vibraye' or 'Niedersachsen', lacecaps like 'Blue Wave', or varieties of *H. serrata* like 'Bluebird' glowing so gloriously in the acid shade of northern gardens, I am filled with regrets that I have not filled a border with them, introduced the white plumes of *H. paniculata* 'Grandiflora' into their midst, and woven right through the scheme a fiery rope of orange tiger lilies. But I have not, and there it is.

The ordinary hyssop, *Hyssopus officinalis*, is a much underrated shrub which covers itself with short deep-blue spikes in late August, and is a marvellous partner for pale pink *Polygonum vaccinifolium*. Plants are easily raised from seed and will flower in their first year; this is the best way of acquiring them for the shrubs are only 2 feet tall and you need several together to make an impact. Hyssop gives body to low groups, for plants are virtually evergreen and are densely clothed in small dark leaves. It is best grown in full sun but seems to be reasonably happy in semi-shade. There are white and pink forms around, though I have not managed to find the latter.

I conclude the chapter with the aristocrat of blue-flowered perennials, the agapanthus. More and more gardeners are beginning to grow them, admiring their stately bearing and their long-lasting quality, and the lists of varieties offered by nurserymen are starting to become long and confusing. Forms vary in height from 2 to 4 feet but most have thick strap-like leaves and support their umbels of bell-shaped flowers on stout stems. Hardy species like *A. campanulatus* and garden forms like the Headbourne Hybrids can be grown from seed but you must take pot luck over the resulting colours. Discerning gardeners will acquire named clones – the pale blue 'Luly', the white 'Alice Gloucester' or the deep blue 'Isis' and 'Bressingham Blue', which are around 3 feet tall, and the intense 'Midnight Blue', which is only 2 feet tall. Blue agapanthus are good in all colour groups, combining well with yellow daylilies and creamy yuccas, orange kniphofias and scarlet crocosmias, annual schemes of silver pyrethrum and salmon-pink petunias, and even of lime-green tobacco flowers and wine-red cosmos. They are also splendid in tubs.

The
Brittle Violin of Frost

The shadows are now lengthening across the lawn and the nights are becoming cooler; soon the swallows will be gathering on telegraph wires, assuring each other that the return journey to Africa will seem shorter than the outward journey; and the first leaves are being shaken off the trees by winds which are gaining in strength. For the gardener these portents are not in the least depressing; on the contrary, they herald the approach of the greatest annual spectacle of all, the spontaneous combustion of the deciduous trees and shrubs.

The months of September and October are very much a preparation for this last dramatic turn. Individual trees and individual leaves take on early tints, orange and scarlet fruits and berries ripen, and quantities of summer flowers transform themselves into dry brown seedheads. Naturally we shall want to intensify this autumnal mood in our gardens by allowing the tawny oranges, coppery yellows and burning reds to sweep across the borders, swallowing up the remnants of summer schemes and reflecting on the ground the events that will shortly take place in the branches above.

There is, however, another side to the autumn garden. Because the sun is lower in the sky, the light is now softer and the atmosphere damper and cooler, conditions which favour those luminous colours from the cold side of the spectrum. Many pink- and blue-flowered plants seem to have been waiting for this change and now enter the scene, rivalling and even outnumbering those newcomers from the warm side of the spectrum who might consider the season to be rightfully theirs. Some come in muffled and smoky tones and are easy to blend with their opposite numbers; others are so clear and sharp that they seem quite at odds with the spirit of the season and it is not until the fires of autumn have died away that we realize that they have been preparing us for the livery of winter.

Almost all the new arrivals are herbaceous perennials or bulbs. Among pinks one of the most striking is *Chelone obliqua*, which opens in September and lasts for two months. Its flowers, which resemble the swollen blooms of snapdragons, are held in a cluster at the top of stout 2-foot stems, and are afforded a lively background by the bright green leaves. Its shades of shocking pink and carmine can either be flattered by soft pink chrysanthemums and deep blue monkshoods or by the tall spires of white cimicifugas and a silver mat of *Stachys lanata*. Chelones thrive in sun or semi-shade but in the more shadowy positions I would prefer to see the rare white form, 'Alba', than the flaring pink.

Few people seem to think of including flowering grasses in their late schemes, but some are as colourful as the more conventional flowers. *Pennisetum orientale* and *P. villosum* produce long fluffy inflorescences, aptly compared by Graham Stuart Thomas to hairy caterpillars, which contrast well with the daisy shapes of asters and chrysanthemums. The purplish-pink flowered *P. orientale* also harmonizes attractively with the flat heads of *Sedum* 'Autumn Joy', and at Sissinghurst I saw the creamy white *P. villosum* effectively teamed with the rose-pink chrysanthemum 'Anastasia' and great blue bushes of *Caryopteris × clandonensis*. In very cold areas these species may not be fully hardy. Since grasses resent disturbance in the autumn they should not be lifted and transferred to a coldframe but must be protected in the open with cloches or bracken. Pennisetums require full sun but seem to be tolerant of most soils.

The pouched flowers of *Physostegia virginiana* are not dissimilar to those of chelone, except that they are grouped on much taller spikes. The common name for this perennial is the obedient plant because you can adjust the flowerheads to point in any direction; it is thus an ideal plant for those who would prove their dominance over nature or those who, like me, cannot suppress their childish love of simple games. The finest variety of physostegia is 'Vivid', a strong rose-pink that usually lasts from late August until October. It is only a foot in height and looks well beside low-growing polygonums and silver foliage. Its cousins are taller, at around 3 feet, and require support. 'Rose Bouquet' and the white 'Summer Snow' are very attractive and have a slightly earlier season finishing in September.

One of the first signs that the garden is entering a new phase is the sudden eruption into flower of scores of small bulbs. With a few notable exceptions, bulbs have played no part in our border schemes since the spring but from now on we shall be increasingly dependent on them. They start to appear at the end of the summer, swell in numbers throughout the autumn months, confidently carry us through the winter and early spring, and depart in triumphant style in April and May. With a little forethought you can have streams of colour for almost every frosty day, cheering you up when you are at your lowest ebb. A few of the early bulbs are entirely autumnal in flavour but many have familiar springtime relatives and their appearance at this time of year reassures us of the seasonal cycle and encourages us to look forward to the delights of a future spring and not to dwell on the glories of a lost summer.

Cyclamen hederifolium (formerly *C. neapolitanum*) now carpets woodland floors in a confection of pink and white. Against a background of crisp brown leaves, with the massive trunks of beech and oak driven through their midst, the fragile flowers find their ideal setting and the effect is of a cloud of butterflies briefly alighting to feed and drink. It is no use attempting to organize the colours of cyclamen as we did with daffodils for there are countless variations and if you grow your plants from seed, the only affordable means of obtaining large numbers, you will not be able to predict precise shades anyway. The pure white form, however, will come true, enabling you to concentrate the lightest individuals in the darkest places.

There is as much variety in the ivy-shaped foliage, patterned and pencilled in silver and grey-green, as in the flowers, so that on their mattress of fallen leaves plants command attention long after the floral display is over. Cyclamen are tolerant of heavy shade and very dry soil during their summer dormancy; thus you need not throw up your hands in despair at the prospect of dealing with a dark, unpromising site but can leap up in your bath (providing you have drawn the curtains) and rejoice that you have a sanctuary suitable for a thousand butterflies.

Quite different in effect are the spidery lily-shaped flowers of *Nerine bowdenii*, which carry the exotic notes of high summer into the autumn garden. Like crinums, nerines require a hot position at the base of a south-facing wall, and bulbs should be planted shallowly so that they are thoroughly baked. The species and its superior form 'Fenwick's Variety' are perfectly hardy but the colour variants, of which there are now many, are best treated as greenhouse plants. The blooms are arranged in a dome at the top of 2-foot stems and the startling cerise pink of the hardy forms associates well with *Ceanothus* 'Autumnal Blue' and pale blue penstemons. Plants will flower until November.

The most versatile autumn-flowering bulbs are the colchicums and autumn crocuses which start to arrive in late August. They come in every shade of pink, purple and white and provide us with the means of laying down mats of colour on grass as well as on soil. The colchicums produce sheaves of flowers like great goblets and these appear without the accompaniment of foliage, hence their common name of naked ladies. Many gardeners find this lapse of decorum offensive and endeavour to conceal the indiscretion by clothing the ground with a thick layer of peri-winkles or ivy, through which the colchicums emerge, or by con-fining them to rough turf. The results are invariably pleasing but personally I enjoy seeing them in exposed isolation and bulbs do seem to perform better in open positions on uncluttered soil.

C. autumnale is the commonest species in gardens. Its flowers are a bright lilac-pink and there is an excellent pure white form, 'Album'. These are the most suitable colchicums for naturalizing in grass. For the more exciting colours we must plunder the ranks of *C. speciosum* whose flowers are larger and supported on sturdier stems. The type is reddish purple but you should also obtain the rich rose-pink 'Conquest' and the deep pink 'Atro-rubens', and stir in some of the huge white blooms of 'Album' for good measure. There is also a double-flowered variety in amethyst purple called 'Waterlily'. All these can be supplemented by the fascinating *C. agrippinum* and its rare cousin *C. variegatum* whose lilac-pink flowers are chequered like fritillaries.

Most of the colchicums fall into that 'difficult' colour band between pink and purple. Caution tells us to keep them close to silver foliage and blues like caryopteris and catmint, but remember that colour is not as plentiful as it was and forceful partnerships are coming into favour once again. Try them near some strong violet-blue asters and some clear yellow chrysanthemums. The trouble with colchicums is that they produce such a quantity of foliage in the spring which then dies away in summer leaving gaping holes in the border. It is thus a good idea to grow something substantial in front of them such as bergenias or stachys and keep the bulbs in narrow drifts if you wish to grow them in the main border; alternatively grow them in a part of the garden which is not under such close scrutiny, such as a piece of shrubbery or woodland where they can rub shoulders with cyclamen.

Autumn crocuses are easier to accommodate, producing their tufts of white-veined leaves at the same time as the flowers in the usual crocus manner, and having their colour range among the violets and blues. The first varieties to appear, in September, are *C. speciosus* (confusing, is it not? See *Colchicum speciosum* above) and its offspring. The flowers of the type are a glowing lavender-blue, veined with violet, and they combine well with the yellows of sternbergia and zephyranthes. The cultivars 'Oxonian', 'Aitchisonii' and 'Albus' have larger blooms in deep violet-blue, lavender blue and white respectively. Other desirable forms include the October-flowering *C. medius*, which has lilac-purple petals, an orange-scarlet style and yellow anthers (a striking combination) and *C. laevigatus* 'Fontenayi', whose lilac petals are usually veined in purple and are arranged around an orange style.

Autumn crocuses and colchicums make attractive carpets for the late-flowering roses which are making an important contribution to our present schemes. The hybrid musk roses and the rugosas are among the most reliable and floriferous but you can expect good autumn displays from many old favourites as diverse as 'Baron Girod de l'Ain', 'Madame Isaac Pereire', 'Comte de Chambord', 'The Fairy', 'New Dawn', 'Zéphirine Drouhin', 'Reine des Violettes', 'Ferdinand Pichard', 'Nevada', 'Iceberg', 'Mermaid', 'Golden Wings' and 'Gloire de Dijon'. It is indeed a treat to have an abundance of roses in flower again but although in quality of bloom many surpass their June displays, do not expect to recapture the Eastern feasts of early summer. The garden has aged since then, the settings have changed and the company is different.

We rely heavily on purplish flowers to bring colour to the autumn border, and to two genera in particular, *Aconitum* and *Aster*. The monkshoods give us firm upright shapes to set beside kniphofias and cimicifugas or interrupt a low line of golden coreopsis, bronze-orange chrysanthemums and crimson penstemons; the asters give us hazier forms which linger among the browns of dying perennials like wisps of wood smoke from a smouldering bonfire.

A. carmichaelii (sometimes confused with *A. fischeri*) is the species of monkshood to acquire for late displays. It grows 4 feet tall, has deeply cut foliage which is respectable throughout the summer, and in September and October produces its typically hooded flowers in a soft shade of lavender blue. Deeper violet-blues come from the varieties 'Arendsii' and the taller 'Kelmscott'. Like their summer-flowering relatives they are plants for a retentive soil, in sun or shade.

By contrast there are dozens of asters from which to make a choice. There are floppy varieties like the white-flowered, black-stemmed *A. divaricatus* which Gertrude Jekyll allowed to collapse over her bergenias (it was called *A. corymbosus* in her day), and the lavender *A. acris* (*A. sedifolius*) 'Nanus' and *A. canus* which spill over stone paths in a foaming tangle. There is the superb, late-flowering *A. lateriflorus* 'Horizontalis' which grows up in bulging tiers of coppery-purple foliage studded with small white flowers, each with a reddish-purple centre. I have underplanted my group with dark purple ajugas. And then there are the two great species, *A. novae-angliae* and *A. novi-belgii*, which have sired so many desirable offspring, in all shades of violet, purple, pink and white.

From *A. novae-angliae* come 'Alma Potschke' and 'September Ruby', both a dazzling rose-pink and around 4 feet tall, and the incomparable 'Harrington's Pink', 3 feet tall and a unique shade of strong sugary pink without a trace of violet. From *A. novi-belgii* come the deep violet-blue 'Eventide' and the lavender blue 'Marie Ballard', 3 feet and 2 feet tall respectively, the soft violet-blue 'Audrey' and the white 'Snowsprite', both around a foot tall, and the dwarf 'Lady in Blue', which is almost identical in colour to 'Audrey'.

Varieties of *A. novi-belgii* are often badly affected by mildew – 'Eventide' is the worst offender in my garden – and need to be sprayed regularly with a fungicide; frequent division in spring is also a sound policy. I like Gertrude Jekyll's idea of growing asters in a bed of grey foliage, comprising stachys, phlomis and white-flowered pinks; the scheme is warmed by pale yellow marigolds and snapdragons and some golden foliage. This would make a cool respite from all the coppers and bronzes, and provide a welcome September lull before the volcano erupts and we are showered with flaming particles.

An autumn-flowering edging plant that is often overlooked is *Liriope muscari*. It has dark grassy leaves and erect spikes of deep violet flowers which scarcely reach a foot in height. It is also evergreen and can therefore be given some structural role to play at the front of the border in between more fleeting perennials or annuals. A pale background shows off the rather sombre tones to their best advantage – my group is in front of that glaucous blue conifer called 'Boulevard' – and you may like to associate your plants with their close relative, the black-leaved *Ophiopogon planiscapus* 'Nigrescens', to make an evil, spidery team. Liriopes also look well in front of the orange spikes of *Kniphofia galpinii*. There are white and variegated forms in existence but they are not commonly offered by nurseries; considering liriopes are such useful plants, thriving in sun or shade, it is surprising that the trade has not taken more interest in them.

I ought perhaps to have included *Origanum laevigatum* in the last chapter for it is well under way by the end of August. But as the competition dwindles it really comes into its own and throughout September and October its clouds of tiny violet flowers dance on their wiry 18-inch stems to much applause. The leaves of this origanum are glaucous blue and are a magnificent foil for the flowers; in a grey border plants stand out well. A clump also contrasts pleasantly with short rusty chrysanthemums like 'Imp' and 'Tiara'. It wants full sun.

True blue is a far less comfortable occupant of the autumn garden than violet, lavender and purple. Its crispness and clarity challenge all the tired and burnished tones around it, so that if you are planning to introduce rich blue into your borders you would do well to concentrate it in one or two places, rather than to scatter it carelessly throughout all your schemes.

Apart from hydrangeas and ceratostigmas, the main contributors of blue among shrubs are the ceanothus. Those that are flowering now are either summer performers with an extended season, like 'Gloire de Versailles', or spring performers indulging in a second curtain call, like 'Delight' or 'A. T. Johnson'. But one hybrid stands out from its genus as being the late bloomer par excellence. This is 'Autumnal Blue', one of the hardiest of evergreen ceanothus, which makes its entry in late summer and produces its rich blue flowers in profusion throughout the autumn months. Try it in a pool of yellow sternbergias with a tangle of *Clematis tangutica* and the creamy plumes of pampas grass nearby.

At ground-level the most dazzling blues come from the gentians. *G. asclepiadea* is usually past its best by September but it will still be contributing colour. This is a gentian for everybody, for it is not as particular about soil as its cousins and will thrive even on chalk. Its dark inky trumpets and willowy leaves are borne on thin arching stems which will need support if you grow your plants in prominent positions; in less tidy places it may be allowed to sprawl, perhaps in the company of silver-leafed deadnettles like 'White Nancy' or 'Beacon Silver'. It likes a deep soil in shade.

Those gardeners who do not have acid soils can spare themselves much anguish by not contemplating the glowing ranks of gentians which are denied to them. Floods of deep blue *G. sino-ornata* which submerge the woodland floor of gardens like Sheffield Park in Sussex must remain as far out of reach as a plantation of banana trees, yellow with fruit and shimmering with swarms of metallic hummingbirds. Of course you can grow a solitary banana tree indoors in a pot (until it gets too big), and so you can fill a stone trough or raised bed with peaty soil and leafmould and float a dozen gentians in it, but for me the difference between the inspiring vision and the humble result is too enormous to encourage me to undertake the project.

Pure laundry white is as arresting and as rare as pure blue. Many of the white-flowered plants of autumn are either shaded cream or ivory or have yellow centres which raise their temperature and enable them to harmonize better with the tawny tones which predominate. The most sumptuous white flowers are those of *Magnolia grandiflora*. This magnificent shrub began its display in July but its September and October performance is generally its most bountiful. The type has been superseded by three superlative clones, 'Exmouth', whose polished leaves have a pronounced coppery suede underside, 'Ferruginea', an erect, compact form also with glossy and felted foliage, and 'Goliath', which has shorter leaves and extra large blooms. The combination of cream and copper strikes exactly the right autumnal chord, and brings the full flavour of the season right up to the house walls – for magnolias need that sunny south wall to encourage them to excel.

Even with these new clones you must still wait some years before your plants deign to flower. But you can sustain yourself by thinking of that morning when you will be able to throw open your bedroom window, reach out to a great bowl of creamy waxy petals, and drink a long draught of lemon scent.

Another plant with gloriously fragrant flowers is *Acidanthera murielae* (properly called *Gladiolus callianthus* it seems). It is a bulbous perennial with erect rushy leaves and 3-foot stems topped with snow-white flowers in September and October. The petals are pointed and there is a deep purple blotch at their base. Unfortunately it is not at all hardy and you can either plant out the corms in late spring – in a sunny and well-drained position – and lift them after flowering, or you can treat plants as greenhouse subjects and set them outside in pots for the summer and autumn. They are well worth a little trouble for the sweet scent carries far, and at this time of year you are likely to be in need of stimulating tonics.

The tiny everlasting daisies of *Anaphalis triplinervis* and its taller cousin *A. yedoensis* are very much in evidence now, their ivory shades beautifully highlighted by their silvery foliage. In *A. triplinervis* the leaves are completely grey but in *A. yedoensis* they are green above and white below. Both plants are essential ingredients for white borders, harmonizing attractively with blue rues and grasses and forming neat edging strips for all sorts of summer and autumn flowers from lilies to anemones. They are striking in front of purple-leaved smoke bushes and among yellow composites, for their flowers do have tiny yellow eyes. They are as happy in semi-shade as in sun and prefer a retentive to a dry soil. They can thus occupy places in your white border which other silver plants would not tolerate.

The tall Japanese anemones are some of the most typical components of the September and October border, associating well with chrysanthemums and asters, late roses and rusty foliage, and if you can afford the space to let them run free, you will be rewarded with tumbling layers of pink and white blooms, each with a golden yellow centre, for weeks on end. The large-flowered 'White Queen' and that splendid variety 'Honorine Jobert', whose satin-white petals are reflected in the darkest green foliage, may wander, as at Sissinghurst, between white rugosa roses and silver artemisias, the whites and greens relieved by orange hips and yellow stamens; and the rose-pink *A.* × *hybrida*, the paler 'Queen Charlotte' and the deep pink 'Prinz Heinrich' may elbow their way through wine-purple 'Souvenir du Docteur Jamain' and crimson 'Baron Girod de l'Ain', side-step a mat of rosy colchicums and arrive at the corner of the border to peer into a terracotta pot of scented acidantheras.

A graceful companion for the pink anemones is the seldom seen

Gaura lindheimeri, whose flights of slim, half-formed white flowers depart from bright pink buds. Plants grow to 4 feet in height but are not at all sturdy and need to be staked. They seem to thrive in a poor, well-drained soil in full sun, and were it not for their tendency to collapse they would be first-class subjects for growing between the cracks of paving. I find they are easily raised from cuttings so that once you find a source for your first plant you can dot plants over the garden.

What do you feel about admitting pampas grasses into the garden? I know that they have now become a suburban cliché and that owners of modern bungalows cannot expect to obtain a realistic price for their dwellings unless there is a pampas grass in regal isolation in the middle of the front lawn. But in other settings they can look quite sensational. I once visited a nursery in Cheshire where, at the back of one of their trial fields, in front of a thick belt of deciduous woodland there grew two or three lines of these plants, perhaps 300 yards in length. The lines were some distance from the road so that seen from the car window they were a swaying, feathery blur against a copper background. There was nothing suburban about that effect. Of course, only the largest gardens could imitate the scale of this scheme but if you placed your grasses near your boundary hedge – ideally beech or hornbeam – in a whirlwind of dry brown leaves, you would create a highly effective autumnal accent and, with luck, conjure up the spirit of the South American plains complete with horses, gauchos and flying bolas.

There are many inferior forms of pampas grass on the market with scruffy grey plumes and a weak constitution so it is important to buy a named variety. 'Monstrosa' and 'Sunningdale Silver' are excellent tall forms, at around 10 feet high, with beautifully creamy and fluffy heads, and for schemes on the smallest scale there is the 5-foot 'Pumila', the golden-variegated 'Gold Band' and the new silver-variegated 'Silver Comet'. The botanical name for pampas grass is *Cortaderia selloana*.

To supplement these creamy whites there are now plenty of sharp yellows. Their acid tones enliven groups of golden composites and bronze foliage through the autumn and remain a stimulant throughout the winter months as well, complementing the pinks and purples. *Clematis tangutica* heads this category and provides colour until October. Its yellow lanterns began to appear in August but by September are joined by the fluffy seedheads, and it is this association of yellow sepals and balls of silvery silk which gives the plant its Eastern flavour and earns it a favourable site in the romantic garden. *C. orientalis* is very similar but, in most forms, has more finely cut foliage, smaller flowers and sepals as thick as lemon peel; it is more particular about its site, which has to be sunny, and is not as hardy in its youth. In most cases therefore *C. tangutica* is the more desirable species. It looks particularly striking when grown up a wall with Virginia creeper, *Parthenocissus quinquefolia*, whose leaves have now turned a rich scarlet; but it is also effective scrambling over a dark green yew or a group of conifers and in winter its seedheads will imprison the trees in a web of white.

The only quality *C. tangutica* cannot offer is scent. For that we must turn to the primrose-yellow *C. rehderiana* which has much the same flowering season. Its tiny bells are borne in panicles among the nettle-shaped leaves and have a penetrating and wonderfully fruity scent of cowslips. The pale flowers need a dark background to show them off, perhaps *Vitis vinifera* 'Purpurea'. A rather different scent, heavy and sickly sweet, is emitted by *C. flammula*. Its flowers closely resemble those of our native traveller's joy, *C. vitalba*, but are smaller and whiter, and its foliage is decidedly superior. But it is for its fragrance that we grow it and plants half hidden in the dappled shade of trees make more of a magical contribution to the autumn garden than those grown in the glare of publicity.

Mahonia lomariifolia and its hardy hybrid 'Lionel Fortescue' have their flowering season in the autumn and are in full swing when their relatives, like *M. media* and *M. japonica*, are just starting to get under way. *M. lomariifolia* is without doubt the aristocrat of the genus. It has the finest pinnate leaves of all and extremely long racemes of bright yellow bells which grow in an erect position, but alas it is not very hardy and gardeners in cold areas must settle for 'Lionel Fortescue' which is almost identical. From October until December the flowers are borne in quantity, and when underplanted with sternbergias and outlined against other evergreens a group makes a very firm and substantial scheme to contrast with the fading colours around them. I have mine in a shady, sheltered spot near the yellow-splashed ivy 'Goldheart'. These autumn mahonias are faintly scented but we must wait until *M. japonica* is at its peak of performance before we can really wallow in lily-of-the-valley fragrance.

An unusual yellow-flowered perennial that opens in September is *Kirengeshoma palmata*. It makes a 3-foot mound of broad maple-like leaves which are attractive throughout the summer, and its pendant flowers are shaped exactly like shuttlecocks with black rounded bases and long pale petals. Black stems contribute further to this exquisite colour combination. Black-leaved ophiopogon could be grouped beneath it to emphasize these qualities. Kirengeshomas like cool semi-shade. At Wisley they are grown among various coloured chrysanthemums, but I think their delicate and perfectly executed blooms need more refined treatment and I prefer to see them either with fine-leaved foliage plants or with simple glistening white flowers such as Japanese anemones.

Gardeners eager to balance their mats of violet and rose-pink crocuses and colchicums with mats of warmer colours can turn to two dwarf bulbs, *Sternbergia lutea* and *Zephyranthes candida*. Both have cup-shaped flowers in the crocus manner. In *S. lutea* (the variety to obtain is *S.l. angustifolia*) they are the brightest yellow and are supported by fresh green strap-like leaves, but in *Z. candida* they are the palest cream and the leaves are narrow and grassy. Both species want a hot dry position and perform best after a baking summer. If the cream of zephyranthes is blended with the white of crocuses and the yellow of sternbergias with the white of colchicums, sizeable pools of warm colour can be established in which to reflect the blue of ceanothus, the purple of hebes or the orange-scarlet of *Phygelius capensis*; adventurous gardeners might even admit a stretch of shocking pink nerines into their midst.

A second wave of chrysanthemums gathers momentum in late September and sweeps over the garden in October and November, bringing ridges and troughs of late colour for all parts of the border. The orange, yellow and red shades provide the meat for every warm colour group and associate well with the dying tones of the herbage around them; even the untidy shape of their flowers suits the late border's unkempt appearance. There are many good varieties available but I would single out, from among the short pompom sorts, the coppery-orange 'Imp', the bronze-yellow 'Tiara', and the deep red 'Brightness', and from the tall 5-foot sorts, 'Ruby Mound' in rich crimson. 'Brightness' is especially good in front of *Cotinus coggygria* 'Royal Purple' whose leaves are now turning a very similar shade of red.

The pink and white shades of chrysanthemums serve with the asters, anemones and monkshoods as the mainstays of cool colour groups and here also there are some outstanding varieties. There is the 2-foot pompom 'Anastasia' in rosy pink, the old favourite, the late-flowering 'Emperor of China', whose silver-pink blooms are flattered by crimson-tinged buds and leaves, and the single-flowered 'Wedding Day' whose white daisies are distinguished by having a green rather than a yellow centre.

It is a pity that there are so few dazzling oranges among autumn perennials to set against the clear blues and smoky violets and to echo the tints of the turning leaves. But in this season of flame and smoke there are at least the blazing torches of kniphofias to kindle fires in the border and to ignite the lower branches of the trees above them. The most exotic is 'C. M. Prichard' (*K. rooperi*) with its huge fat pokers, 5 feet high, glowing in the typical red-hot style of orange-scarlet and bright yellow. The most attractive and useful is *K. galpinii*, a very slender species with grassy foliage and wiry stems, whose thin pokers are a rich orange and grow to less than 3 feet. If you surround your plants with the smouldering oranges and crimsons of chrysanthemums and heleniums and build up to the group in the Jekyllian manner through cream, lemon and golden yellows (apart from all the chrysanthemums there are yellow kniphofias like 'Brimstone', 'Gold Else' and 'Little Maid' still in flower) you can intensify the feeling of heat and the sense that you have reached the heart of the fire.

If you have resisted the temptation to pull out the seedlings of *Physalis franchetii* which have been detracting from the picture of weed-free neatness you have been striving to achieve through the summer, these might now be adding to your fiery scheme with their bright orange-red Chinese lanterns. Margery Fish had the idea of letting them grow through tangled carpets of blue-flowered periwinkle which I have copied in my garden. The lanterns, which are held on 2-foot stems, begin to turn colour in September and remain attractive for several months. Plants thrive in the poorest soil in sunny or shady sites.

A remarkable perennial, still far too seldom grown, is the kaffir lily, *Schizostylis coccinea*. Sparkling red is not a common colour in September and October and yet it harmonizes so well with all the autumn tones that any plant bearing this colour should be pounced upon. The large star-shaped blooms of the type and its superior form 'Major' are not really a scarlet but a deep true red lightened by a satin sheen, and they associate marvellously with tawny orange chrysanthemums and copper foliage. There are many other colour forms including the deep pink 'Professor Barnard' and the pale pink 'Mrs Hegarty' but my favourite is the

November-flowering 'Viscountess Byng', a pure glistening pink which cries out for the company of silver foliage – try it with *Pyrethrum ptarmicaeflorum* (*Achillea ptarmiciflora*) and deep violet *Salvia farinacea* 'Victoria'.

I have found all these varieties perfectly hardy in Wales, though they do have the protection of a south-facing wall and a winter covering of bracken when I remember. They dislike very dry soil and many people grow them at the edge of ponds, where their rushy leaves seem quite at home and their 2-foot spikes of flowers lean out over the water and make silky reflections.

In many gardens the only autumn-flowering perennial is *Sedum spectabile* 'Autumn Joy' and what dull places they are. Of course we could not do without those sturdy clumps of fleshy leaves and stems and those flat heads of dark red flowers, for the plants are interesting and respectable the year round. But they give me no thrill of excitement, except when the flowers tremble with butter-flies and bees, and I confess that I rather grudge them space. You will tell me that their solid form gives just the right support to wispy perennials like gauras and physostegias, that their horizontal lines contrast effectively with upright monkshoods and cimicifugas, and that their deep red colour combines wonderfully with fluffy white pennisetums and powdery blue caryopteris, and I cannot argue with you. It is just that they are rather too smug and spotless for the romantic garden, a goody-two-shoes concentrating on her lessons in the rough and tumble of the classroom.

It is impossible to predict exactly when in October or November the first sparks from the maples or the spindle trees will land on dry combustible material and cause the autumn fires to grow and spread through garden and woodland. Some years the fires break out sporadically and remain dim, stifled by prolonged rainfall or severe frosts, but every now and then they are nurtured by still, warm weather and fanned by gentle breezes and the result is a spectacular blaze which takes weeks to die down.

It is almost as difficult to forecast the exact colours that indi-vidual trees and shrubs will turn. There is tremendous variation within a given species and many plants, such as fothergillas, parro-tias and nyssas, assume different tints in shade to those they assume in sunlight. Furthermore, the temperature and weather play a great part in influencing the activity within the plant cells; a warm spell seems to encourage the yellows and oranges to make an appea-rance, while a cold spell favours the crimsons and scarlets.

But all this uncertainty only heightens the feeling of suspense and the gardener, sublime with anticipation, spends every October day looking up into branches for early signs and clues about the display to come. Of course, the uncertainty also means that we cannot plan precise colour schemes in the way that we have been doing since the spring, and that we must leave much more to chance. Fortunately, because the vast majority of deciduous trees and shrubs take on warm tones of red, orange, brown or yellow, juxtapositions are invariably harmonious, and unexpected tints just add more fuel to the fiery scene. This does not mean that we should attempt no special colour effects, for we usually know the approximate colours that leaves will turn and, as long as we are prepared for some discrepancy between what we expect and what we are given, we can at least set yellowish colours against reddish colours and orangey colours against coppery colours. We can also choose and grow together the more reliable autumn performers and concentrate in certain areas of the garden those which regularly produce the most startling colours or the most muted.

It has to be said that people with less than park-sized gardens cannot afford to devote much space to large plants whose only contribution is a fleeting display of scarlet in early November. As always we must be ruthless in our selection of material, favouring those trees and shrubs which also flower or fruit well or have interesting foliage during the spring and summer. Often we need only supply autumnal highlights in the form of a small group of enkianthus or a tall solitary liquidambar and we can reach outside the garden for our backdrop, perhaps a neighbour's copper beech or a distant belt of woodland. Occasionally we must take the plunge and recklessly plant a stand of maples or a group of honey locusts, cursing our foolish deed for much of the year but rejoicing at our wisdom in the autumn, as we sit in a shower of crimson or gold, muttering half-remembered lines from Keats.

Let me then draw your attention to some of the more striking trees and shrubs and suggest some associations, leaving you to puzzle out how on earth you are to accommodate them in your pocket-handkerchief of a garden. Among those which take on strong red tints I would single out the ordinary *Acer japonicum*, whose beautifully lobed leaves turn crimson-scarlet, and *A. palmatum* 'Heptalobum Osakazuki', which has deeply dissected foliage in brilliant flame-scarlet; *Liquidambar styraciflua* is another tree with maple-like leaves that becomes a pyramid of blood crimson in the autumn (the clone 'Lane Roberts' is even deeper and apparently more reliable); *Stewartia sinensis* has rather dull oval leaves but these turn a rich mahogany-crimson, and in addition the tree bears scented white, cup-shaped flowers in high summer and has interesting flaking bark; many of the dogwoods turn red, such as *Cornus florida* which becomes cherry scarlet, *C. kousa* which becomes bronze crimson and *C. mas* which becomes purplish red; *Disanthus cercidifolius* is a fascinating shrub with smooth, round glaucous leaves which start to turn crimson in late summer and increase in beauty through the autumn; *Enkianthus perulatus* is a medium-sized shrub which becomes a mound of dazzling scarlet and bears clusters of pendant, cup-shaped white flowers in the spring; the oak-leaved hydrangea, *H. quercifolia*, is an attractive feature all year, bears cones of white flowers in August and turns a dark bronze-crimson; and *Viburnum plicatum* 'Lanarth' smothers itself in white flowers in late spring and becomes a mound of blood red in the autumn.

Flame orange is brought to us by the sugar maple, *Acer saccharum*, and its more manageable fastigiate cultivar 'Temple's Upright'; a number of sorbuses turn a glowing orange including *S. americana*, a small tree which carries heavy bunches of red fruits, and *S. commixta*, which has extremely fine foliage, an upright habit, and magnificent flame tints; *Prunus sargentii* always turns bright orange and crimson very early in the season and many other cherries take on flame or coppery orange tints including *P. yedoensis* and *P.* 'Shirofugen'; *Cotinus coggygria* becomes a billowing orange-scarlet in the autumn, as well as giving us its smoky inflorescences in early summer, and the colouring is even more brilliant in the variety 'Flame'; *Enkianthus campanulatus* turns orange and scarlet and has clusters of sulphur yellow flowers in the spring; early flowers are also borne by *Fothergilla major* in the form of short creamy-white bottle-brushes as a bonus to its fiery autumn tints; but the two most startling orange-scarlets are *Parrotia persica*, a small tree which bears intriguing blood-crimson flowers in spring, and *Nyssa sylvatica*, a larger tree which has, I am afraid, very little to distinguish it other than its autumn colours which are quite unparalleled, and which in spite of having a thousand flamboyant rivals, always steals the show at Sheffield Park.

For yellow we can look to the common field maple, *Acer campestre*, to *A. pensylvanicum*, which has marvellously patterned bark as well as dazzling autumn foliage, and to *A. palmatum* 'Senkaki', another small tree with eye-catching branches and deeply cut leaves which change to clear yellow; the paper birch, *Betula papyrifera*, offers flaking white bark in addition to its glowing yellow leaves and in *B. lutea* the paper bark is golden brown; the maidenhair tree, *Ginkgo biloba*, commands attention throughout the year with its unique, lettuce-green, fan-shaped foliage but this turns a vivid yellow in the autumn bringing it right to the fore; the honey locust, *Gleditsia triacanthos*, would also earn a place because of its everyday foliage, which is pinnate and feathery, even if it did not turn a warm yellow in the autumn – the slow-growing, upright 'Elegantissima' is my favourite form, although the larger 'Sunburst' whose young leaves are also yellow seems more popular; and what of the aristocratic tulip tree, *Liriodendron tulipifera*, which not only has bright autumn foliage and unusual, smooth lobed leaves but flowers to boot, which are lime-yellow, tulip-shaped and produced at midsummer?

So a corner given over to autumn colour need not be such a sacrifice; if the ingredients are carefully chosen they will keep us gently entertained in other seasons as well and by introducing masses of spring bulbs into the soil and using our autumn shrubs as hosts for summer-flowering roses, honeysuckles, jasmines or clematis we can even orchestrate a few high notes. Furthermore, a number of herbaceous perennials which we would want to include in the garden for the sake of their flowers or general foliage effect also have striking autumn tints and could be assembled here – plants such as paeonies flame with orange and red at this time of year (their bright crimson springtime foliage associates marvellously with early bulbs), and bergenias assume deep red stains and blotches now, and would provide an evergreen anchor for the group and a bloody foil for snowdrops and winter aconites later on.

The colour combinations of these autumn schemes should be as fiery as possible, lighting the November skies with vivid hues. This is the last great spectacle of the year and it must be a memorable one, so I would urge you to select ingredients which are likely to produce the strongest contrasts in colour with their neighbours: we are aiming for the most exciting display to compensate for the briefness of its duration. Picture a flaming column of crimson-scarlet liquidambar burning its passage through orange-scarlet enkianthus and fothergilla to roar at a wall of golden-yellow maples; or a bonfire of parrotia outlined against the russets of far-off oaks and beeches and fuelled by the scarlet of dogwoods and the yellow of witch-hazels; or a stately maidenhair tree, gleaming with molten gold, guarding its side of a path against the incursions of an ancient Irish yew, black-green and dusty, waving long ruby tentacles of that sumptuous vine, *Vitis coignetiae*.

Gardeners with acid soil have the greatest scope for creating sensational autumn colour effects for many woodland plants which produce the finest tints will not grow in alkaline conditions and of those that will, a further number refuse to colour well in their alien homes. I should have stressed this earlier, I know, for I will have encouraged some readers to attempt impossible feats. Those who garden on limy soil should strike out stewartia, disanthus, enkianthus, fothergilla and nyssa from their lists and turn for support towards the cotoneasters, particularly the scarlet *C. horizontalis*, the berberis, particularly the orange *B. thunbergii*, and the euonymus, notably *E. alatus* which becomes a subdued yellow and crimson in shade but a flaring orange-scarlet in sunlight.

Leaf colour may be the inspiration for our late autumn groups but it need not be the only ingredient. October- and November-flowering perennials, shrubs and bulbs can all be included and, most importantly, so can the various shrubs and small trees which are now laden with fruits and berries. Again we have to exercise restraint in our selection of material for these berrying plants usually occupy sizeable areas of soil (many must be grown in small groups to ensure good fruit crops) and although displays are more reliable and predictable than those of leaf colour, the birds generally consume much of the produce as soon as the first frosts have softened the fruits.

Some of the best scarlet fruits are produced by the cotoneasters, the familiar herringbone-shaped *C. horizontalis*, the prostrate *C. dammeri*, the tall arching 'Cornubia' which is so lavish with its great bunches of fruits, and 'John Waterer' whose berries drip from long ascending branches; numerous female hollies give us bountiful crops including *Ilex* × *altaclarensis* 'Camelliifolia', which makes a pyramid of large dark leaves and purplish stems, the silver-variegated *I. aquifolium* 'Argenteomarginata', the bright green 'Pyramidalis', and the huge-leaved *I. latifolia*; pyracanthas can be rather overpowering, so heavy are their crops of berries, and no exceptions are *P. atalantioides* and the compact hybrid 'Watereri' which bury themselves in brilliant red fruits, but they are invaluable evergreen screening plants, especially for north walls; red-hipped roses include the greyish-purple *R. glauca*, the rugosa 'Fru Dagmar Hastrup' and the scented-leaved *R. villosa*, whose fruits are crimson and plump like apples; *Skimmia japonica* is a small evergreen shrub that produces clusters of fruit after its white flowers, though both sexes are required to achieve a display; *Viburnum opulus* and its short form 'Compactum' have almost translucent scarlet berries that dangle in clusters in addition to their golden-yellow autumn foliage; and among small trees we can turn to *Sorbus americana*, whose fruits are bright scarlet, *S. aria*, the whitebeam, with blood-red fruits, *S. sargentiana*, another scarlet-fruited tree which displays very late in the season, and to the small crab apple, *Malus* 'Crittenden', whose generous crops of scarlet fruits last well.

Brilliant orange fruits are also borne by a number of sorbuses including the mountain ash, *S. aucuparia*, and its upright form 'Fastigiata' (the splendid combinations of fiery leaves and berries are unequalled by any other plant, and if you give way to the temptation of devising a small plantation of mixed varieties, you will have a bonfire worthy of the season); the thorns make attractive gnarled trees usually laden with berries, and one of the finest orange-fruited varieties is *Crataegus × lavallei*, whose deep green leaves are held long after other deciduous trees have shed theirs; cotoneasters with flame-orange berries include *C. franchetii sternianus*, which has silver undersides to its leaves, and the semi-evergreen *C. salicifolius* 'Autumn Fire'; startling orange pyracanthas include *P. coccinea* 'Lalandei', which is vigorous and always sumptuous, and the yellowish orange 'Waterer's Orange'; but my favourite orange-berried plant is *Hippophae rhamnoides*, a large shrub with silver willowy leaves (picture the colour combination) which remains little known in spite of being a British native – the females bear the fruit but they need a male near by.

Yellow berries can also be had in quantity. *Sorbus* 'Joseph Rock' has amber-yellow fruits which seem less appealing to the birds than the scarlet ones of its cousins, and those produced by the variety of *S. aucuparia* called 'Xanthocarpa' are a similarly warm shade of golden tan; there is a crab apple called 'Golden Hornet' with glowing yellow fruits that makes a fine feature; there are two large cotoneasters, 'Exburiensis' and 'Rothschildianus', which are particularly noted for their apricot-yellow berries; *Ilex aquifolium* 'Bacciflava' is a yellow-berried holly and so is 'Pyramidalis Fructuluteo'; *Pyracantha atalantioides* 'Aurea' and *P.*

crenatoserrata 'Knap Hill Lemon' are both rich yellow-fruiting forms; and the guelder rose, *Viburnum opulus*, has a superb golden-yellow-fruited variant called 'Xanthocarpum'.

All these warm-coloured berries can be muddled up together as supports and underplantings to foliage groups, and the different notes of red, orange and yellow will echo the fiery tones above them. In isolation against an appropriately coppery background, berried plants are often as effective as autumn foliage plants – they are certainly longer lasting – and they can also look well in the border among perennials that are still in flower. But it is in those fiery foliage groups that they are at their best, pushing through the burning leaves, the different shapes and colours of their fruits contrasting with each other, orange flagons beside tomato-coloured balls and golden apples above heaps of scarlet cherries, all joining in the fray with ropes of crimson vines and webs of clematis seedheads.

Not all berried plants are fit for this bonfire. Some are too curious or ornamental to be lost in the flames while others display colours which would be at odds with the spirit of the schemes. The euonymus, for example, produce the most beautiful and fascinating fruits which demand close scrutiny and which are far better sited in a quiet area where there are no distractions. The common spindle, *E. europaeus*, is itself worthy of planting for its winged carmine pink seed capsules and its brilliant orange berries (a furious colour clash, of course) but a more generously fruiting form has been selected called 'Red Cascade' and an unusual white form, 'Albus', whose orange berries are shielded by ivory wings. The species *E. sachalinensis* has larger fruits and makes a pleasing border shrub, and for a small feature there is *E. cornutus* and its variety *quinquecornutus* whose fruits carry horns. Euonymus are more reliable if they are grown in small groups.

Company is essential for callicarpas to achieve pollination. The variety to grow is *C. bodinieri giraldii*, a medium-sized shrub with arresting violet berries that appear after its unremarkable lilac flowers. It is a plant that never fails to cause comment, and it is ideally sited among silver foliage and late asters or in front of grey stone walls. Another strangely coloured fruit is offered by *Clerodendrum trichotomum fargesii*, an appropriately tortuous name for such a bizarre performer. Clerodendrum is a large sun-loving shrub with coarse foliage, unpleasantly scented when bruised, but which produces fragrant white flowers just like a jasmine in late summer. These are contained in deep carmine-red calyces which persist after the flowers have fallen and the dazzling turquoise berries are formed and displayed.

As the leaves of deciduous plants start to fall in quantity and most of the orange and scarlet berries are devoured by the birds, the skeleton of the garden is gradually exposed. This is the moment of truth for the romantic gardener. Have we been able to take that objective look at the structure of our gardens? Have we planned for these bleak winter months by carefully siting evergreen trees, shrubs and perennials? Or, with the vanishing of the leaves and flowers, have our borders lost all their dignity and coherence? Our minds drugged by fleeting colours and scents, did we lose our strength of purpose and instead of planting those sentinel pines or those anchoring boxes as we promised ourselves last winter, did we succumb to the charms of that new variety of flowering cherry we saw at Chelsea or to yet more of Graham Thomas's blowsy shrub roses?

Well, at least it looks like winter in our gardens and we can scoff at our neighbours whose borders are so cosy and snug in their warm layers of heathers and conifers (they looked identical at midsummer incidentally) that the naked beauty of the season is never experienced. But winter does last a long time and staring out at a scene of total desolation can become depressing. We should therefore make some effort to achieve that ideal balance between bare branches and solid evergreen shapes, even if it means the sacrifice of some choice flowering subjects. Not only do evergreens maintain the framework of the garden and furnish it during the empty months but they also give us shelter and privacy. They screen us from unsightly objects and prying eyes the year round and they protect us from the worst of the late autumn and winter gales. They have therefore a very important practical role to play as well as an aesthetic role, particularly along the boundary lines of the garden. Here we may plant formal hedges of yew or holly or we may construct informal groups of trees and shrubs, drawing on that large fund of material which includes holm oaks, pines, spruces, firs, junipers, cedars, wellingtonias, arbutus, aucubas, berberis, camellias, rhododendrons, boxes, mahonias, elaeagnus, cotoneasters, stranvaesias, pieris, escallonias, eucalyptus, pyracanthas, senecios, lauristinus (*Viburnum tinus*), false cypresses, cryptomerias, cupressus, thuyas and hemlocks. Our intention should not be to devise dense impenetrable barriers of foliage, for this has the adverse result of causing a good deal of wind turbulence, but rather to link our evergreens with deciduous species so that we have a more natural screen through which the wind is gently filtered and reduced in strength.

Many of these same large plants can be used at the back of our mixed borders forming the larger links in a chain of evergreen foliage that binds together the entire composition. The smaller links could be provided by cistus, osmanthus, olearias, sarcococcas, skimmias, euonymus, daphnes, pittosporums, fatsias and choisyas and by evergreen perennials like hellebores, *Iris foetidissima*, euphorbias, tellimas, heucheras, heathers, bergenias, liriopes, yuccas, periwinkles, sisyrinchiums, London pride, phormiums, libertias, bamboos, grasses and kniphofias. Even against walls we can have winter greenery from shrubs and climbers like ceanothus, carpenterias, garryas, eucryphias, ivies and *Clematis armandii*.

These then are the plants that will give the winter garden some substance and once they are safely installed we can begin our search for coloured and scented highlights. But before we investigate the flowering plants let us remain for a moment among the deciduous trees and shrubs to wander briefly among the stems of willows, brambles and dogwoods, the trunks of cherries and birches and beneath the branches of maples. Since the gardener's palette is by no means overflowing with flowers between mid-November and mid-March, to obtain good patches of bright colour we have to look in some less obvious places.

There is nothing startling about the trunks of cherry trees but their smooth rich mahogany is a warm welcoming colour that is attractive to come across on your occasional expeditions into the winter garden. The trunks of *Prunus serrula* and *P. sargentii* are especially luxurious. The strawberry tree, *Arbutus unedo*, has deep orange-brown stems and bark that is always in tatters, an intriguing characteristic shared by the paperbark maple, *Acer griseum*, whose rust-coloured covering flakes and curls to reveal the pale tan young wood beneath. Other trees have patterned trunks, blotched in white and green like the snake bark maple, *Acer pensylvanicum*, and the London plane, *Platanus × acerifolia* (syn. *P. × hispanica*) or lined in apricot and buff like *Betula ermanii*.

More dramatic are the ghostly trunks of the silver birch, *B. pendula*, and the whiter *B. jacquemontii*, which looks as if it has just been given a coat of emulsion paint. Against evergreen shrubs they stand out marvellously and make an eyecatching incident for the distant reaches of the garden. Two brambles, *Rubus cock-burnianus* and *R. thibetanus* also have whitewashed stems. The former is too tall and vigorous for anywhere but the wild garden but the latter, which grows to around 5 feet, is more easily controlled and its patterned ferny leaves are a valuable addition to the summer border, a shimmering foil for a low-growing shrub rose, for example, with pink, white or crimson flowers. The violet willow, *Salix daphnoides*, has a white bloom to its purple stems as does the smaller *S. irrorata*. These look well in association with their brigher relatives or behind the plum-black dogwood *Cornus alba* 'Kesselringii' and the black catkins of *S. melanostachys* which arrive in early spring.

If you have to limit yourself to just a handful of shrubs with colourful stems then clearly you must make your choice from among the most dazzling red and yellow varieties. In the depths of winter you will yearn for the brightest and most cheerful spectacle and nothing is surer to raise your spirits than the sight of a mixed plantation of scarlet, orange, gold and lime-green willows and dogwoods illuminated by the morning sun. *S. alba* 'Britzensis' is a glowing orange-scarlet and 'Vitellina' a brilliant golden-yellow and these may be fronted by the crimson-scarlet Westonbirt dogwood, *Cornus alba* 'Sibirica' and the bright olive-yellow *C. stolonifera* 'Flaviramea'. Near by we could grow the coral bark maple, *Acer palmatum* 'Senkaki', whose young shoots are reddish pink, the yellow birch, *B. lutea*, and the fabulous maple, *A. pensylvanicum* 'Erythrocladum', whose stems and branches are painted scarlet and white. A few strands of leycesteria and kerria with their upright green stems would provide contrast and support for the group.

It is essential that all these trees and shrubs grown for the beauty of their stems and trunks should be sited in positions which escape the long arms of winter shadows, at least for most of the day. The difference in impact between plants in sunlight and plants in shade is huge and in this season when there are so many muted tones we must not waste any chances for a sudden blaze of colour. This does not mean that we should give them positions where they will be bathed in sunshine all the year; the foliage of most of the willows and dogwoods is far too pedestrian for such royal treatment. Rather they could be screened in summer by groups of deciduous plants and their whereabouts revealed only in winter when the curtain in front of them drops. Their bright winter colours will not suffer at all from being seen through a thin web of branches. In order to display their finest livery the willows and dogwoods must of course be coppiced annually or biennially, an operation which is carried out in early April.

Very few of winter's flowers can equal the brilliance of these coloured stems, but what they lack in intensity they more than make up for in shape, poise and, more often than not, in fragrance. These qualities cannot properly be appreciated at a distance, and if you are the sort of gardener who barricades yourself indoors as soon as the weather turns really cold and will not be tempted outside again until spring is on your doorstep, these plants are not for you. Hardier gardeners, however, who take as much interest in the treasures of this season as of any other and who are prepared to make the occasional sortie into the winter garden, will be generously rewarded and, even if they find it too cold to linger outdoors for long, can return with armfuls of delicate and scented blooms which they can study and sniff at their leisure in the warmth of their sitting-rooms. Newcomers make an appearance in our borders during every winter month and if you are constantly aware of this regeneration, your sense of loss over the few deaths that the season also brings is greatly reduced. Hibernating gardeners, on the other hand, who can only see the blackened shapes of olearias and pittosporums from behind their double-glazed windows will only sink further into depression and, with a painful groan, tunnel back under a mound of rugs, teeth chattering.

Many people choose to devote a corner of their garden entirely to winter-flowering plants. This is usually very close to the house, either beside the front door or near the front gates, somewhere easily accessible and where there is much human traffic. Certainly there should be flowers here which can be enjoyed in winter but such precious areas need to appear welcoming in other seasons as well, so I would not tip the scales too much in winter's favour. My main objection to a winter corner, however, is that it presents an unnaturally bountiful picture in a season that is so careful and measured in its distribution of pleasures. It is surely more appropriate to scatter your winter flowering plants in groups among the garden's skeletons rather than assembling them *en masse* in one or two places. We then appreciate more keenly the extraordinary phenomenon of flowers opening in the most inhospitable months and, what is more, their rare and restrained flavours, which are unprepared for competition with other colours, are preserved intact.

Pink, purple and white are the main colours of the winter garden but fortunately there is always plenty of yellow to provide contrast and warmth. *Azara microphylla* is worth risking outside in all but the coldest areas providing it can be given the protection of a south- or west-facing wall. In mild spells during February and March its clusters of tiny orange-yellow flowers will release their strong vanilla fragrance, and it is because of this that we grow it, for the flowers make little impact against their dark evergreen foliage. On a moist soil it will grow to over 15 feet in height. The cream-variegated form, 'Variegata', is very desirable but is slower growing and less hardy.

The winter sweet, *Chimonanthus praecox*, also requires a sunny wall though it prefers a poorer and drier soil to that enjoyed by azara. You need a good deal of patience to grow it, for it can take many years to begin flowering; it should therefore be one of the first plants that you introduce into a new garden. On mature shrubs the naked branches drip with waxy lanterns from December until March; these are such a pale yellow that they appear almost transparent and contain bunches of maroon-red segments within. The scent is one of the most powerful of the season, a warm sweetly spicy perfume which will travel through an open window to scent an entire house. Some of this far-reaching quality is lost in the variety 'Luteus' but the flowers are larger and a stronger lemon colour. You could compensate for the lack of intense colouring in the type by threading some wands of *Jasminum nudiflorum* through its branches and massing some violet *Iris unguicularis* at its feet. Winter sweet is completely hardy and grows to around 8 feet.

It is easy enough to find subjects to plant beneath deciduous trees and shrubs to cheer them up during the winter months but your horticultural knowledge is properly taxed when it comes to finding subjects which will bring interest to their upper parts. The silver seedheads of the autumn-flowering clematis species will still be glistening, of course, and if you are fortunate enough to have mistletoe in your trees their untidy green balls will now be sitting among the branches like rooks' nests. Otherwise there is little available, particularly among plants which actually produce flowers in this season, and it is this scarcity which brings *Clematis cirrhosa balearica* to the fore. If it flowered in the summer we would probably not give it a second glance; now, with no gaudy rivals to distract our attention, its dainty ferny leaves, which have turned maroon with the cold, and its green-white bells, which are flecked crimson inside, invoke our admiration.

It will enjoy the shade cast by its living support during the rest of the year and may well climb to 15 feet. Alternatively it can be confined to the lower branches by spring pruning. I have already suggested partners for it in an earlier chapter but now that I have my mind on winter pleasures let us group green, crimson and white hellebores around the base of the tree and allow some of the clematis's shoots to tumble into them. This clematis is reliably hardy in most parts of Britain but it does need a sheltered spot and protection from the morning sun.

I would be reluctant to offer a place to *Cornus mas* in a small garden in spite of its scented golden blossom in February, its summer fruits and its autumn colour. It is really a shrub for the wild garden where we are less demanding in terms of overall quality of foliage and flower. Instead I would turn to the witch-hazels and plant as many varieties as I could. If you visit Kew in January you will see great thickets of these shrubs in sherbet-sugary schemes, yellow-, orange- and bronze-flowered plants jostling for position, and the air heavy with the sweetest scents infused with incense. To recreate this spectacle acquire the ordinary golden-yellow *Hamamelis mollis* and its magnificent sulphur variety 'Pallida' and plant them beside the coppery-orange *H.* × *intermedia* 'Jelena' and the reddish-brown 'Diane'. The scheme could be backed by evergreens and underplanted with sarcococcas or given a more open setting and outlined against grass and mahogany tree trunks.

Witch-hazels prefer a retentive lime-free soil and dappled shade and in such conditions will produce rich yellow autumn tints. The flowers are twisted and spidery and look exactly like sea-anemones.

No garden can afford to be without the winter jasmine, *J. nudiflorum*. It has such a long flowering period, from November until April, and combines so well with many other winter flowers, providing the brilliant colouring that they lack, that we can be liberal in our distribution of it around our walls. In summer it makes a fine host for slender climbers like eccremocarpus or *Rhodochiton atrosanguineum* (syn. *R. volubile*) whose bright magenta bells are joined to maroon-purple hammers. It does not have to be trained against a wall, of course; many people let it cascade down banks in the company of clematis and honeysuckles, or collapse over tree stumps. There is no end to its uses for it thrives in shade as well as in sun.

The yellow star-shaped flowers have a perfect foil in the fresh green, wiry stems and the absence of foliage is immaterial. Its only fault is that it has no scent, which is why I like to associate it with fragrant shrubs like chimonanthus or lonicera; woven together each corrects the deficiency of the other. Beside dark evergreens it is especially dazzling. I have a stretch over a low group of *Euphorbia robbiae* which is effective against the frozen soil and the adjacent tangle of brown branches.

Mahonias also look well with this jasmine. Following close on the heels of the autumn-flowering varieties is the most famous and deliciously scented species of the whole tribe, *M. japonica*. Its long racemes of yellow bells with their lily-of-the-valley perfume grow out horizontally from the stems and the flowers open from December until March. In cold weather the prickly pinnate foliage often turns crimson and makes a remarkable backdrop for them. The popular hybrid 'Charity' has much coarser leaves, is less fragrant and has only slightly more upright racemes and I would not encourage anyone to plant it.

If the racemes of *M. japonica* are too floppy for you I would turn not to 'Charity' but to *M. bealei* which also has a long flowering season. A mixed planting of mahonias in association with gold and golden-variegated shrubs is a welcoming winter sight and if it was underplanted with something light such as lamiums and euonymus, need not look too gloomy in summer. There is a fine collection of these gaunt and bony shrubs at Borde Hill in Sussex, a skeleton for every cupboard.

Catkins make a significant contribution to the youthful flavour of the garden in January and February, breaking out over the branches before the leaf buds unfurl in spring, and anticipating the warmer weather. *Salix gracilistyla* sprouts some of the finest catkins, which begin grey and turn to yellow, followed by beautifully pale and silky young leaves but it is too large and vigorous for the small garden where space is precious, unless it is cut down annually. Instead turn to the small and dwarf willows like *S. helvetica* and *S. lanata* which offer silvery foliage good enough for later foliage effects (although their catkins do not appear as early as those of *S. gracilistyla*) and to the curious *S. melanostachys* which is reasonably low-growing and has the most bewitching black catkins which bristle with blood-red anthers before turning powdery yellow. Many of the willows that we grow primarily for stem colour also produce attractive catkins, notably the clone of *S. daphnoides* called 'Aglaia' whose long yellow catkins are eye-catching against the floury plum bark.

The flowering stalks of *Stachyrus praecox* look rather like catkins from a distance but in fact they are far more ornamental, like little tassels of cream bells dripping from the mahogany branches. The effect is somehow very oriental and if you grow it between bamboos this evocative quality will be emphasized. The flowers open in late February or early March. The shrub, which thrives in sun and semi-shade, grows to around 10 feet tall and makes little impact for the rest of the year, an ideal candidate therefore for a summer-flowering clematis.

Carpeting the ground beneath the yellow-flowered winter shrubs could be winter aconites, *Eranthis hyemalis*. Their blooms, like bright yellow buttercups framed in an emerald-green ruff, start to appear at the end of January, and are at their peak during February. They prefer a heavy, moist alkaline soil and in such ideal conditions will soon run riot, flooding lawns and woodland with lakes of gold. Elsewhere they may take time to establish themselves but are usually ultimately accommodating. I like to see them around the warm red-brown trunks of cherries and arbutus and the scarlet stems of dogwoods, but they are also splendid with the white bark of birches and brambles in the company of snowdrops. *E. tubergeniana* and 'Guinea Gold' have larger flowers and ruffs flushed with bronze and might be assembled in the choicest positions; they do not seed themselves as furiously as their common cousin.

Unless you grow rhododendrons and camellias you will find it a struggle to furnish any schemes with bright red and orange flowers during the winter months. There are scarlet and flame berries on the pyracanthas and cotoneasters, there is scarlet bark on the willows, dogwoods and maples and there are scarlet and crimson leaves on the bergenias (*B. purpurascens* (*B. delavayi*), and 'Ballawley' are the outstanding ones) and tellimas, but orange and red flowers remain scarce. Often there will be brick-red cowslip flowers on *Pulmonaria rubra* as early as Christmas and blooms on flowering quinces like 'Knap Hill Scarlet', 'Rowallane' and 'Simonii' by February. Sometimes the orange funnels of *Eccremocarpus scaber* persist from autumn until spring, and by early March there ought to be a good number of polyanthus performing. But the timing and extent of these displays depend so much on chance that it is hardly worth giving such plants important roles in colour schemes before the spring.

With such a shortage of warm companions for the yellows of winter we tend to depend heavily on green, not just on evergreen foliage but on green flowers as well. These are supplied by various forms of hellebore, and appear from January onwards. *H. foetidus* is one of our most valuable green foliage plants, its dark-fingered leaves making a striking contrast to the rounded shapes of bergenias and tellimas and the erect rushy growth of *Iris foetidissima*. Its sprays of pale green bells, edged with maroon, are particularly well displayed against this cushion of black-green foliage. It seeds itself into all sorts of unlikely places, often into the driest, sun-scorched cracks far away from the cool shady border where we have thoughtfully sited it. A seedling has just appeared near the front door of my house, next to a silver-variegated euonymus, and is a perfect example of how plants have a habit of improving on the gardener's carefully orchestrated effects by their own devices.

H. corsicus (now properly called *H. lividus corsicus*) is a taller, more substantial species with broad serrated leaves in a greyer almost glaucous shade of green. The flowers are also larger, primrose-green and cup-shaped and presented in dense heads. It makes a very imposing clump, even when out of flower, and is popular with professional garden designers. The ideal setting for it is a landscape of twisted pine trees and great grey boulders but the stone paving of paths and drives has to suffice in most cases and it seems to adjust to living in such reduced circumstances. The true *H. lividus* is not so forgiving and usually sulks unless at least given some protection from our weather. Its leaves are more oval, have pointed tips and are attractively marbled; and there is a pinkish tinge to the flowers and the undersides of the leaves. *H. l.* 'Sternii', which is similar, is more vigorous.

Blue has been elusive throughout the year except for a brief period in spring and remains so in winter. The glaucous foliage of *Euphorbia wulfenii* and *E. myrsinites*, of acaenas, blue grasses and *Hebe* 'Pagei' makes pleasant smoky backdrops for crocuses, snowdrops, and other dwarf bulbs (and for white and deep pink heathers, if you grow them). Another excellent standby is that tireless viola 'Azure Blue' which is seldom without flowers even in the depths of winter; it has large sky-blue flowers with a slightly deeper face.

Anemone blanda causes trickles of clear blue to seep out of the ground as early as February but these do not swell into torrents until the middle of March. The richest coloured daisies are produced by the variety 'Atrocaerulea' and these might be concentrated near the centre of the surge with a few groups of the large-flowered 'White Beauty' on the edge of the scheme to simulate spray. There are some frightful pink and purple forms in circulation which should be avoided at all costs. *A. blanda* proves a willing colonizer on most soils but prefers well-drained, limy conditions; the display in the late Sir Frederick Stern's chalk garden in Sussex was unparalleled. Plants flower as well in half shade as they do in sunlight which means that your rivers may sweep under the pink and white forms of *Prunus subhirtella* before they disappear into the gloomy heart of the shrubbery.

The hepaticas have similar daisy flowers which emerge from the low clumps of purplish-lobed leaves in February and March, and will carry the cool theme into the shady parts of the border. The commonest species is *H. nobilis* and this, like *A. blanda*, comes in a range of colours from pink and mauve to blue and white, so a good form should be sought. One of the most desirable is in fact a hybrid between *H. nobilis* and *H. transsilvanica* and is called *H. × media* 'Ballard's Variety'; its soft powder-blue flowers are superior in every respect to those of its parents and last for several weeks.

The two early squills, *Scilla bifolia* and *S. tubergeniana*, open in February and herald the arrival of their dashing cousin *S. sibirica* a month later. *S. bifolia*'s little wisps of china blue combine well with the creamy yellow forms of *Crocus chrysanthus* or the brighter gold of *C. aureus*, while the blue-white tufts of *S. tubergeniana* are attractive with the clear violet-blue of an *Iris reticulata* such as 'Harmony'. (It is impossible to match exactly the turquoise stripe which runs down each petal.)

From this short list it will be seen that blue is not really one of winter's colours and only begins to arrive in quantity at the very end of the season. It is as if all the trump cards, the acid yellows, blazing scarlets and the brilliant blues, are being held back for that one shattering moment later on when we are shaken out of the sleepy folds of winter and flung abruptly into the carnival of spring. Instead of flaunting itself in gaudy robes, designed to make the observer stand back and gasp, winter adopts a subtler attire and revels in the art of surprise, combining its innocuous colours with weird and intricate shapes or haunting scents, which generally catch us unawares and keep us spellbound. This is nowhere more apparent than among the season's white flowers which have for the most part sacrificed clarity and purity of tone for other qualities.

Abeliophyllum distichum is a small twiggy shrub which remains surprisingly uncommon. The ivory-white star-shaped flowers emerge from their pink buds in February and smother the naked branches (they are carried on the previous year's shoots so shrubs must be hard pruned in early spring to encourage plenty of new growth); the effect is exactly like that of an albino version of forsythia, if you can imagine such a thing. But it is its scent not its colour which gives it a place in the garden, a foreign spicy fragrance that haunts the air and excites the nose. A sunny, sheltered spot will hold it captive, and this is the environment in which the shrub thrives best; certainly the flowers need a solid background to make an impact, whether it be an evergreen screen, a brick wall or a thicket of brown undergrowth.

From one of the rarest of the season's shrubs let us turn to one of the commonest. In its finest male forms *Garrya elliptica* may claim to be the most eerily beautiful of winter's images, the long ghostly grey catkins suspended in their hundreds among the dark, leathery evergreen leaves like a waterfall frozen in mid-flow. I have seen it poised above crimson hellebores, purplish foliage and clumps of fragile snowdrops looking as if at any moment it would come back to life and crash down, scattering these audacious interlopers. Luckily this never happens or we would be reluctant to give it companions, but it does have other faults. Firstly, it insists on clinging on to its catkins long after they have withered and turned black so that in summer it can present a very ugly spectacle. Secondly, it can easily succumb to very cold weather, and was one of the first casualties of the severe 1980–81 winter in many parts of the country. I do not suppose anyone would strike it off their lists of desirable shrubs for these failings, but if wall space is in short supply – and it does need such protection – then you may have to think twice before planting it. It is quite happy in shade, so a north wall is ideal.

The shrubby honeysuckles give us some deliciously sweet scent from December onwards but direct little energy towards the production of handsome flowers. Indeed they may never be detected on *Lonicera fragrantissima* or *L. standishii*, so well buried are they in foliage, unless a sharp frost causes the leaves to fall. Their child *L. × purpusii* is more thoughtful in this respect, being properly deciduous, and displays its tight clusters of creamy tubes with some style; it is equally fragrant. All three varieties grow to 6 feet or more and have rather undistinguished foliage, so positions should be chosen where they can spend the summer unobtrusively. They perform best against a wall, either in sun or in part shade.

The flowers of sarcococcas are also insignificant, puffs of pale yellow stamens tucked between the glossy evergreen leaves. But do not underestimate their power. I have seen grown men grovelling on their hands and knees in Kew Gardens in pursuit of that sticky scent of honey which it exhales. How can such a lowly plant manufacture such a far-reaching perfume? *S. hookeriana digyna* is perhaps the pick of the group for its leaves are long and narrow and its flowers tinged with pink; *S. humilis* has broader leaves and bigger tufts of stamens, and *S. ruscifolia* has shorter leaves so wide that they are almost oval. All are excellent underplanting material for large shrubs, being shade-loving and tolerant of dry conditions, but they might also be used more frequently in place of box, either as a neat, dense edging to a path or as formal evergreen punctuation marks in the border.

If you have ever been to the first Royal Horticultural Society flower show of the year at Vincent Square, you will no doubt have been amazed by the number of named varieties of snowdrop being exhibited on the specialist stands, many of which seem scarcely distinguishable from their companions without the aid of a microscope, and by the cabals of learned plantsmen huddled around them, whispering restricted information about composts and pinpointing remote areas of Bulgaria where particularly unusual strains may be discovered. Either you will have been inspired by the experience, presenting a long order to a nursery and sending off for holiday brochures for Eastern Europe, or you will have been so overawed and taken aback by the complexity of a subject that you had previously thought was so straightforward that you leave the hall quickly and quietly by a side entrance, thankful that your ignorance was not exposed in public and vowing never to attend an early show again.

Gertrude Jekyll counsels us never to be discouraged by 'groping ignorance' for each step in gardening is a step into 'a delightful Unknown' full of pleasures and excitements, and so it is with the bewildering world of snowdrops. I hope, therefore, that if you were in the second category of visitors, you will reconsider, break your oath, and take the first tottering steps forward. I confess that I have not yet found firm ground but am enjoying my education immensely. The first new variety I acquired was the double form of the common snowdrop, *Galanthus nivalis* 'Flore Pleno'. This has sacrificed the simple charm of the single flower by its production of extra segments but gains an old-fashioned bustle-like appearance in the process which makes it a welcome curiosity. It increases speedily and lends itself to naturalizing.

G. elwesii is another obvious snowdrop for the beginner and was the second variety I bought; it is easily grown, is not expensive and is totally different from *G. nivalis*. It opens much earlier than the common snowdrop, in January, and has larger, globular flowers on stems 9 inches tall. The foliage is beautifully broad and grey and intensifies the icy coolness of the bells. Next came the equally tall *G. n.* 'Atkinsii', whose long petalied flowers also appear in January, and the giant 'Sam Arnott', a February performer whose stature puts both the above to shame. Recently I have obtained the small green-leafed *G. ikariae latifolius*.

To snowdrop connoisseurs this will sound a meagre collection deficient in every respect. But it is growing gradually and soon I hope to add the variety 'Straffan' which opens late and apparently produces two flowers from each bulb. I have no desire whatsoever to acquire the autumn-flowering kinds, which make a freakish sight, or those with lime-yellow instead of green markings.

Snowdrops blend attractively with all the other dwarf bulbous plants of winter, including winter aconites, *Iris histrioides* and *I. reticulata*, and crocuses, especially the rampant *C. tomasinianus*. I also like to see them among silver-variegated foliage such as that of arums, pulmonarias, euonymus and *Iris foetidissima* 'Variegata' or backed by the rich crimson leaves of tellimas and bergenias. In your eagerness to pursue rarer varieties do not entirely forget the humble *G. nivalis* whose blankets of white strewn over the grass in every shady corner have sustained you through many a bleak February over the past years. If you desert old friends you will lose that sense of continuity and timelessness which is so essential to the romantic character of a garden.

The Christmas Rose, *Helleborus niger*, is rarely in flower by

Christmas in my garden but there are many forms available and it is all a question of luck. I am more interested in size and quality of bloom than in an early display, and if you are of the same persuasion you should acquire the varieties 'Potter's Wheel' and 'Ladham's Variety'. Gardening journalists command us to preserve clean dry flower-buds by the use of cloches, but these detract so much from the natural winter scene that I always disobey their instructions. The penalty is often mud-splattered petals, for the snow-white cups are held so close to the ground but at least we can enjoy the blooms against their grey-green foliage. I grow my Christmas roses beneath deciduous shrubs in a crisp scheme of silver-spotted pulmonarias and *Galanthus elwesii*, with the odd clump of brick-red *Pulmonaria rubra* to provide contrast.

No winter garden would be complete without the blush-white perpetual-flowering cherry *Prunus subhirtella* 'Autumnalis' or its shell-pink counterpart 'Autumnalis Rosea'. The display begins in November, continues intermittently throughout the winter, and ends with a flourish in early April; and if this were not enough they give us attractively lined trunks and brilliant autumn-leaf colour to boot. There are no finer trees for underplanting with bulbs, from the gentian and frosty blues of scillas and chionodoxas to the glistening whites of snowdrops and the lavenders, mauves and imperial purples of crocuses. Both make spreading open trees, 25 feet or so in height, and make an unforgettable picture when silhouetted against a clear blue sky.

You might also consider growing the white form of the Chinese peach, *P. davidiana* 'Alba', whose pure single flowers appear in January or February. It also makes a medium-sized tree and provides an attractive variation on the cherry blossom theme. Its fiery autumn tints can also be spectacular.

We have already surrounded ourselves with the sweet scents of chimonanthus, lonicera, abeliophyllum, mahonia, hamamelis and sarcococca but our living pot-pourri is by no means complete for winter's pink and purple flowers also breathe bewitching air. Foremost among them are the daphnes. The first to open, in December or January, is the evergreen or deciduous *D. bholua* ('Gurkha' is a good deciduous form) whose reddish-purple and white flowers open in clusters at the top of the erect branches; an evergreen variety called 'Jacqueline Postill' was shown for the first time at the early R H S show a couple of years ago and promises to be a valuable addition to collections. The other species, with the exception of the troublesome *D. blagayana*, begin flowering in February. The golden-variegated form of *D. odora* is hardier and more reliable than the type and forms a lively mound of evergreen foliage at the base of a warm wall. The white stars open from deep reddish-crimson buds and are held in tight bunches like a miniature *Viburnum carlesii*; the flowerheads do not fight with the colour of the leaves, for the gold is confined to a thin strip around the edge. Indeed its name is 'Aureomarginata'.

I do not grow *D. laureola*, another evergreen daphne that grows to around 3 feet in height. It thrives in shade and bears pale yellow-green tubular flowers. Some say that is not as powerfully scented as its cousins but they have clearly never encountered it by night. For early colour effects the finest variety remains the common *D. mezereum* and its white form 'Alba'. The bare upright branches are packed with tiny stars and they stand out well in their shady woodland positions at Wisley, where the rosy-purple forms are associated with deep pink heathers and 'Alba' with *Corylopsis veitchiana*. But the mezereon is quite happy in sunshine as well and can be underplanted with purple and white crocuses or, in the case of 'Alba', with brilliant blue scillas and bright yellow *Narcissus cyclamineus*.

Still more scent comes from the viburnums. The old *V. farreri* (formerly *V. fragrans*) is still planted for sentimental reasons, certainly by me, but has really been superseded by Lord Aberconway's famous hybrid *V. × bodnantense* which has larger flowers, a better shape and an equally delicious fragrance. From this two clones have been selected for their quality of colour, namely 'Dawn', an intense rosy-pink, and 'Deben', a pure white. Both begin flowering in October, before their leaves turn crimson and fall, and continue until March with scarcely a break. A west-facing aspect suits them admirably and if they can be backed by evergreens the display will be noticeably improved. I have seen them partnered with 'evergreen' grey-leaved senecios and phlomis which brightened the scheme considerably.

They could also be underplanted with winter-flowering cyclamen. The season's species par excellence is *C. coum* which performs in January and February. Its magenta-pink flowers are dumpier than those of *C. hederifolium* and its rounded leaves are plain green. There are variants which do have patterned foliage and gentler coloured flowers, going under a variety of names including *C. orbiculatum, ibericum, hiemale* and *atkinsii*, and a superb white form which Margery Fish grew in a trough by itself. The majority are easily pleased, thriving in the same shady well-drained positions as their autumn relatives. They look well with snowdrops and purplish-flowered pulmonarias, if these can be coaxed out of bed in time.

I would love to tempt you with the sweet perfume of *Petasites fragrans* but if, as a consequence of my eulogy, you introduced a plant into your garden, the sense of guilt might weigh heavily on me and, after a short while, my postbag would gradually swell with venomous letters. For the winter heliotrope is a rampant weed, almost impossible to eradicate, which must not be admitted into any tame environment except that of your worst enemy, and then only as a last resort.

The most enchanting package of plants that I have ever received by post came from Helen Ballard's nursery (Old Country, Mathon, near Malvern, Worcestershire). It consisted of a collection of oriental hellebores, all in flower in their box, in a range of colours from white, primrose and lime-green to pink, crimson and plum. None was a named variety: they were all simply selected from the nursery's stock for their individual quality and colour. *H. orientalis* seeds itself freely and with a sound start such as this you soon build up a diverse and interesting population; every seedling is full of promise. Even more surprises are in store for gardeners who add some of the *H. guttatus* forms which are spotted with crimson on the inside of their petals.

The darkest hellebores hold a special fascination for many people, including myself. They have a remarkable bloom on their petals which makes them look almost metallic, and their yellow stamens and green nectaries glow like lamps in a cave. *H. atrorubens* is a deep plum-red species which has proved exceptionally vigorous in my garden, and *H. purpurascens* bears rather small flowers in dark maroon-purple which are as bloomy as grapes. The blackest hellebore I have seen was a form of *H. torquatus* but I never discovered its name; still, I am quite content with *H.p.* 'Ballard's Black' which is marvellously dusky and sinister in its young foliage as well as its flowers.

Oriental hellebores are presented very charmingly and sensitively at the Oxford Botanic Garden. Tucked behind the rock garden and shaded by trees during the summer is a secret border thickly carpeted with them. Even in winter you might overlook it were it not for the wayward scents of sarcococcas and mahonias which draw you towards it (an inspiring way to use scent in the garden); as you turn the corner you are greeted by a wonderful array of subtle colours, arranged as informally as they would be on a wild woodland floor. It is a feature that I covet and long to recreate.

Some of winter's tiniest flowers are so finely sculptured and so delicately fragrant that they have to be grown in raised beds for us to be able to appreicate them properly. A number of crocuses fall into this category and so does the miniature bulbous iris, *I. reticulata*, whose fragrance would not disgrace the name of the greatest French perfumer. The flowers, which are disproportionately large for their 3-inch stems and guarded by several spearlike leaves, are an imperial velvet-purple, illuminated by a blazing orange stripe down the falls. They appear in late February outdoors, but a potful of bulbs in your drawing-room can be enjoyed a month earlier and is a winter delight that every gardener should indulge in; in the warmth of the house the sweet violet perfume can be quite intoxicating. There are many varieties of this iris, nearly all of which are highly desirable, including a violet-blue called 'Harmony', a reddish-purple called 'J. S. Dijt' (I am sure this is not pronounced 'Digit' as I once overheard someone say), a sky-blue called 'Cantab', and a violet-purple called 'Pauline', but none have the strong scent of their parent.

My ignorance of the Dutch language proved an insurmountable obstacle at Chelsea Flower Show some years ago when I tried to get a bulb grower to explain why *I. reticulata* and its forms tended to flower magnificently in their first year after planting and subsequently only manage to send up a pathetic-looking leaf to advertise their presence. The blank look I received was so provoking that I went straight to the RHS library in Vincent Square to do some research. It seems that after flowering bulbs have a tendency to dissolve into a cluster of little bulblets which have to be grown on separately to ensure that they will reach a healthy maturity; they usually take two years to flower. This is a time-consuming process for the busy gardener but I have found that the iris's dreadful deed of giving birth can often be postponed by growing it on very sharply-drained soil and keeping it bone dry in the summer. I should add that *I. reticulata* is generally more accommodating than its named varieties.

The royal blue *I. histrioides* does not have this failing and is a reliable performer. It is similar in shape and size to *I. reticulata* and enjoys the same sunny, well-drained conditions but it flowers much earlier, towards the end of January. A thin channel of clear blue between silver-leaved treasures such as euryops, dwarf artemisias and tanacetums provides an icy scheme for a stone trough beneath a south-facing window.

Apart from the hellebores, the most familiar winter-flowering herbaceous perennial must surely be *Iris unguicularis* (formerly *I. stylosa*). It hales from Algeria and appreciates a hot, dry, starved position at the base of a south-facing wall, but it is totally hardy. The lavender blooms have a splash of white and a streak of orange on the broad falls and nestle in a clump of narrow grassy leaves which is useful as a foliage feature for much of the year. There are rich violet forms called 'Mary Barnard' and 'Ellis's Variety', a pale lilac form called 'Walter Butt' and a clean white called 'Bowles's White'. The type begins to flower in November and does not rest until April. It associates splendidly with all the yellows and creams of winter especially winter sweet and winter jasmine and crocuses like 'E. A. Bowles' and 'Cream Beauty', and of course with the whites and pinks of abeliophyllum and daphnes, and crocuses like 'Blue Pearl' and 'Princess Beatrix'. Its only foible is that it greatly resents disturbance and can take a long time to settle down in a new home; once established, it never needs dividing and the display improves every year.

I have postponed coverage of the crocus family until now because it is the perfect subject with which to end our journey through the frosty months and to return to the warmth of March. Few other plant groups keep us so in tune with the seasonal cycle, for by watching the coming and going of the different species we are led gently in and out of every week from autumn until spring, through landscapes which change from bonfire brown to fleecy white and emerald green. In colour they adhere mainly to the appropriately restrained and cool liveries of their companions, departing occasionally into the realms of butter yellow to challenge the less modest winter and spring performers, and, like many of their peers, they direct much energy towards the manufacture of perfume.

Once the flowers of the colchicums and autumn crocuses have died away, the powerfully scented *C. laevigatus* gets into its stride. Its lilac cups have purple feathering on the outside of their segments (not petals) and are lit up by a yellow throat and an orange style; the variety 'Fontenayi' also has this prominent feathering but is a biscuit colour on the outside. Both require well-drained, sun-baked sites. In January *C. imperati* begins its display. It is a much more reliable outdoor performer than *C. laevigatus* and has a similar combination of colours to 'Fontenayi', a buff exterior striped with purple, a lavender interior and a yellow throat.

In February comes the rich yellow *C. ancyrencis* 'Golden Bunch' whose flowers are flushed bronze-purple and the lavender-blue *C. sieberi atticus* (*C.s.* 'Hubert Edelstein' is a startling form in white and deep magenta with a flame-orange centre, and 'Firefly' is soft mauve); the true *C. sieberi*, from Crete, is similar but less flamboyant.

Also in early February comes *C. tomasinianus* which is one of the finest species for naturalizing. It does not demand a summer baking so it can be strewn casually among the silver trunks of birches and the fallen leaves of last autumn (the romantic gardener is not known for his tidiness), or between the bright stems of dogwoods and willows, where its flowers will make a carpet of lavender. I would want to stain the carpet with some patches of its dark purple variety 'Barr's Purple' or the misnamed 'Ruby Giant' which is really bright violet. Although this crocus will increase furiously on soil, it is not so happy on grass.

Of course it is the various forms of *C. chrysanthus* with which the average gardener will be most familiar. A long edging of their purples and yellows, blues and whites will cheer up any sunny border, and if you bring pots of bulbs indoors you will be able to enjoy their thick honey scents to the full a good month before their flowers open outside. This year my potfuls opened on 18 January. Among the purple and blue varieties I am particularly fond of the silvery-blue 'Blue Pearl' (it has an inky-bronze base, and looks well with clear-white varieties between dwarf grey foliage); the crisp pale lavender 'Princess Beatrix', whose interior is a furnace of orange; and the dashing 'Ladykiller' whose white flowers are smeared with deep purple (it looks stunning near snowdrops and between hepaticas whose foliage is now maroon). Among the yellows and whites the outstanding forms include the creamy honey-yellow 'Cream Beauty' (this combines well with the deeper 'E. A. Bowles' and also benefits from having reddish foliage near by – try tellimas); the golden-yellow 'E. A. Bowles', which has a flush of maroon on its base; the maroon-striped ochre-yellow 'Fusco-tinctus', which is perhaps the strongest scented of all the yellows; the golden-yellow 'Zwanenburg Bronze' whose outer segments are smudged with brown; and the powerfully fragrant, milk-white 'Snowbunting', which can be stirred in among all its cousins.

The giant Dutch crocuses begin to flower in early March and, because of their size, are especially suited to naturalizing in grass. From among the many cultivars of *C. vernus* on the market I would select the lavender-violet 'Queen of the Blues', the mauve-purple 'Remembrance', the dazzling purple 'Paulus Potter', the rich lilac-striped 'Pickwick' and the gleaming white 'Snowstorm'. You can mix these varieties quite freely in sunny, well-drained spots, perhaps providing relief from all the shadowy shades with the occasional golden pool provided by the cultivar 'Large Yellow' or the species *C. aureus*.

We have now come full circle and are poised once more to enter the spring garden, to begin another gardening year. The paradox of this seasonal cycle is that although it is continually repeating itself, its pleasures always seem novel and fresh. Its slow progress and the gradual metamorphosis of one season into another give us time to forget and the endless succession of new delights encourages us to look forward, never back. Last spring is only a distant memory, obscured first by the riotous displays of summer, then screened by autumn's mists and finally smothered by winter's snows. So the flowers that are opening now, in the second part of March, are only half familiar; you may remember their names and their general appearance, but you will have forgotten how silky smooth their petals are to the touch, how intense their hues are when caught by the low-lying sun, how complex and intricate is their structure, and how sharply thrilling is their scent.

The garden too is constantly changing and maturing and never looks the same two years running. Old plants are growing and filling out, young plants are being found new homes, new projects are being undertaken and new schemes attempted. Last year's dreams are becoming this year's realities and the garden is slowly acquiring an unmistakable resemblance to that vision of frothing colours and seething scents which has inspired and sustained you since you first looked out on to your derelict plot.

Gardening is a continuous creative adventure. It requires patience and dedication, sensitive fingers and a strong back but it is the most rewarding and the most accessible of all the arts. A bucket of soil, a sturdy old trowel and a packet of seeds and you can fashion a masterpiece.

Bibliography

It is exceedingly difficult to compile a bibliography for a book such as this. So much has been absorbed subconsciously over the years; the works of Margery Fish, Vita Sackville-West, Gertrude Jekyll, E. A. Bowles, Graham Stuart Thomas, Christopher Lloyd and A. T. Johnson are my constant companions. But the following have been particularly valuable sources of reference:

BEAN, W. G., *Trees and Shrubs Hardy in the British Isles*. London: John Murray, eighth edition, 1970–1980.

BIRREN, F., *Color: A Survey in Words and Pictures*. New York: Citadel Press, 1963.

BROWN, J., *Gardens of a Golden Afternoon*. London: Allen Lane, 1982.

CHEVREUL, M. E., *De la Loi du Contraste Simultané des Couleurs*. Paris, 1839.

CROWE, S., *Garden Design*. Country Life Library, London 1958.

FOSTER, R., *The Garden in Autumn and Winter*. Devon: David & Charles, fifth edition, 1983.

GAGE, JR., *Colour in Turner: Poetry and Truth*. London: Studio Vista, 1969.

HAMPTON, F. A., *The Scent of Flowers and Leaves*. Dulau & Co., London 1925.

HILLIER, *Manual of Trees and Shrubs*. Devon: David & Charles, fifth edition, 1981.

JEKYLL, G., *Colour in the Flower Garden*. Country Life Library, London 1908.

LLOYD, C., *Foliage Plants*. London: Collins, 1973.

MATTHEW, B., *Dwarf Bulbs*. London: Batsford, 1973

———. *The Larger Bulbs*. London: Batsford, 1978.

PAGE, R., *The Education of a Gardener*. London: Collins, 1962.

ROBINSON, W., *The English Flower Garden*. London: John Murray, 1883.

THE ROYAL HORTICULTURAL SOCIETY, *Dictionary of Gardening*. Oxford: Oxford University Press, second edition, 1956.

SANECKI, K., *The Fragrant Garden*. London: Batsford, 1981.

SARGENT, W., *The Enjoyment and Use of Colour*. New York: Charles Scribner's & Sons, 1923.

THOMAS, G. S., *Perennial Garden Plants*. London: Dent, 1976.

WILCOX, M., *Colour Theory for Watercolours*. Colour Mixing, 1982.

UNDERWOOD, D., *Grey and Silver Plants*. London: Collins, 1971.

Index

Plate numbers are in **bold** type